Rethinking the Purpose of Business

Catholic Social Tradition Series

VOLUME TWO

Preface to the Series

In *Tertio millennio adveniente,* Pope John Paul II poses a hard question: "It must be asked how many Christians really know and put into practice the principles of the church's social doctrine." The American Catholic bishops share the pope's concern: "Catholic social teaching is a central and essential element of our faith . . . [and yet] our social heritage is unknown by many Catholics. Sadly, our social doctrine is not shared or taught in a consistent and comprehensive way in too many of our schools." This lack is critical because the "sharing of our social tradition is a defining measure of Catholic education and formation." A United States Catholic Conference task force on social teaching and education noted that within Catholic higher education "there appears to be little consistent attention given to incorporating gospel values and Catholic social teaching into general education courses or into departmental majors."

In response to this problem, the volumes in the Catholic Social Tradition series aspire to impart the best of what this tradition has to offer not only to Catholics but to all who face the social issues of our times. The volumes examine a wide variety of issues and problems within the Catholic social tradition and contemporary society, yet they share several characteristics. They are theologically and philosophically grounded, examining the deep structure of thought in modern culture. They are publicly argued, enhancing dialogue with other religious and nonreligious traditions. They are comprehensively engaged by a wide variety of disciplines such as theology, philosophy, political science, economics, history, law, management, and finance. Finally, they examine how the Catholic social tradition can be integrated on a practical level and embodied in institutions in which people live much of their lives. The Catholic Social Tradition series is about faith in action in daily life, providing ways of thinking and acting to those seeking a more humane world.

Michael J. Naughton
University of St. Thomas

Todd David Whitmore
University of Notre Dame

Rethinking
THE
Purpose
OF
Business

Interdisciplinary Essays
from the Catholic Social Tradition

edited by
S. A. Cortright *&* Michael J. Naughton

University of Notre Dame Press
Notre Dame, Indiana

Manufactured in the United States of America

Library of Congress Cataloging-in-Publication Data
Rethinking the purpose of business : interdisciplinary essays from
    the Catholic social tradition / edited by S. A. Cortright and
    Michael J. Naughton.
        p.   cm. — (Catholic social tradition series)
    Includes bibliographical references and index.
    ISBN 0-268-04008-7 (alk. paper)
    ISBN 0-268-04011-7 (pbk. : alk. paper)
        1. Capitalism—Religious aspects—Catholic Church.   2. Corporations—
    Religious aspects—Catholic Church.   3. Business—Religious aspects—
    Catholic Church.   4. Sociology, Christian (Catholic)   I. Cortright, S. A.
    (Steven A.), 1953– .   II. Naughton, Michael, 1960– .   III. Series.
    BX1795.C35R48 2002
    261.8'5—dc21

2002012609

∞ *This book is printed on acid-free paper.*

To
Monsignor Terrence Murphy,

whose commitment to integrate Catholic social thought
and business made this volume and the conferences
which created the volume possible.

Contents

Foreword

KENNETH E. GOODPASTER

It is a pleasure to welcome the reader of this collection to a provocative exploration of the purpose of business enterprise on the threshold of a new millennium—and to provide something of a context for that exploration.

The second half, and especially the last quarter, of the twentieth century saw serious probing of the morality of free-market capitalism in the context of political democracy. This examination was intensified by concurrent developments: the beginning and the end of the Cold War; the civil rights movement in the United States; the environmental movement; the expansion of women's roles in business; and the phenomenon of business globalization through new technology. Alongside these catalysts for probing the foundations of responsible business behavior, the disciplines of philosophy and theology began to reclaim their normative roots, after a century of preoccupation with meta-questions of a more epistemological nature. "Applied ethics" became a meaningful phrase that was not redundant. Catholic social teaching was not silent during this period, but it became most influential in the world outside of Catholicism with the publication of John Paul II's eloquent *Centesimus annus* in 1991.

Were there any substantive conclusions that emerged from this extended period of social and intellectual searching? I believe that there were at least these three:

1. The proposition that the modern business corporation, if it were to be ethically responsible as a human institutional artifact, needed a form of guidance and leadership that went beyond compliance with the standard external forces of marketplace competition and governmental regulation;[1]

2. The proposition that the decisive factor of production (and therefore wealth) in the twenty-first century would come not from land or manufacturing, but from knowledge and organized information;[2]

3. The proposition that globalization, with its implicit transcendence of national and cultural boundaries, called for an ethical platform rooted not in legal jurisdictions or international conventions, but in a shared human concern for justice and the common good.[3]

The first proposition, that the corporation can and should have a "conscience" and that this conscience needs to be more than market and legal surrogates provide, offers a fundamental and transformative insight. It invites us to supplement our reflections on the consciences of individuals within business and on the morality of the business system itself with reflections on the corporation as a unit of ethical analysis. The challenge that this idea presents to philosophers and theologians—and to business leaders guiding the modern corporation—is hard to overstate. It means understanding with a "new paradigm" not only the role of the corporation within society, but also the roles of boards of directors, managers, and employees within the corporation. The Enron and Arthur Andersen scandals are cases in point.

Sections 1 and 2 of this volume include thoughtful reflections on what the new paradigm *isn't* (pure shareholder wealth enhancement) and on candidates for what it *is* or *should be* (such as stakeholder thinking). We learn quickly that it may be easier to embrace reductions or simplifications of conscience (such as market competition or government regulation) than to differentiate these important imperatives from the imperative of institutionalizing conscience. Easier, but not better.

A move from shareholder thinking to stakeholder thinking may seem to offer the most direct route to corporate conscience, but such a move is no panacea. Indeed, it may be that in the absence of a tradition or a way of life, the cultivation of conscience (personal or institutional) is nearly impossible. The relevance of the Catholic social tradition to this circumstance is both undeniable and problematic: undeniable because it provides a rich context for discerning stakeholder obligations; problematic because it seeks application in a pluralistic, postmodern business community.

The second proposition above, that we are entering the age of the knowledge worker and the knowledge organization, also offers a transformative insight. It invites us to draw upon the Catholic social tradition in support of education that is timely (developing knowledge workers) and widespread (providing opportunities for the poor).

To avoid deepening a "digital divide" between haves and have-nots, the business sector must look for new and creative ways to retrain (if necessary) and enrich the lives of current employees, while seeking to expand employment opportunities to developing regions of the world.[4] Section 3 of this volume includes reflections on the quality of work life in this new work world and on the centrality of human dignity as the touchstone for practical solutions.

The third proposition, that globalization calls for a culture-transcending ethical platform, clearly provides an entry point for a culture-transcending tradition that appeals to the common good and human dignity. Globalization, of course, is also a controversial trend, as evidenced by recent protests aimed at the World Trade Organization in Seattle, Washington, Washington, D.C., Genoa, Italy, and elsewhere. But the controversy itself emphasizes the need for an ethos rooted in human nature rather than either corporate power or national identity.

So we stand on the threshold of this new millennium with a long-term legacy in the Catholic social tradition and a short-term legacy of reflection on the responsibilities of business organizations. We may agree that business leadership is called to a higher standard than either market dynamics or legal requirements have to offer. We acknowledge that the meaning of work and our understanding of management in a knowledge-based economy are essentially incomplete without an embracing account of conscience in human life. Finally, we understand that the challenge represented in the title of this volume, *Rethinking the Purpose of Business,* cannot be met except with a truly global outlook: economic, political, social, and environmental. Let me invite readers to search out their own convictions as the threshold is crossed, while appreciating the provocative essays in the pages that follow.

Notes

1. See Kenneth E. Goodpaster and John B. Matthews, "Can a Corporation Have a Conscience?" *Harvard Business Review* (January–February 1982): 132–41. Also see Kenneth E. Goodpaster, "Conscience and Its Counterfeits in Organizational Life: A New Interpretation of the Naturalistic Fallacy," *Business Ethics Quarterly* (January 2000): 189–201.

2. John Paul II, *Centesimus annus,* 32, in *Catholic Social Thought: The Documentary Heritage,* ed. David J. O'Brien and Thomas A. Shannon (Maryknoll, N.Y.: Orbis Books, 1992). All quotations from papal encyclicals, conciliar documents, and episcopal statements are taken from the O'Brien/Shannon edition unless otherwise noted. The citation number (e.g., 32 in *Centesimus annus*) refers to the section number within the document. "It is important to note that there are specific differences between the trends of modern society and those of the past, even the recent past. Whereas at one time the decisive factor of production was the land, and later capital—understood as a total complex of the instruments of production—today the decisive factor is increasingly man himself, that is, his knowledge, especially his scientific knowledge, his capacity for interrelated and compact organization, as well as his ability to perceive the needs of others and to satisfy them." The spirit of *Centesimus annus* was recently applauded in a *Wall Street Journal* editorial (January 26, 1999): "In his 1991 encyclical *Centesimus annus,* John Paul II celebrated a capitalism that 'recognizes the fundamental and positive role of business, the market, private property and the resulting responsibility for the means of production as well as free human creativity in the economic system.' At a meeting in the Vatican several years later, Nobel prize–winning economist Gary Becker noted with astonishment the congruence between these thoughts and his own. 'I come at it from my end, and you come at it from yours,' he said of the church's social teachings, 'but what surprises me is that we end up in the same place.'"

3. Kenneth E. Goodpaster, "The Caux Round Table Principles: Corporate Moral Reflection in a Global Business Environment," in *Global Codes of Conduct: An Idea Whose Time Has Come,* ed. Oliver F. Williams (Notre Dame, Ind.: University of Notre Dame Press, 2000), 183–95.

4. See Kenneth E. Goodpaster and Thomas E. Holloran, "Anatomy of Corporate Spiritual and Social Awareness: The Case of Medtronic, Inc." (paper presented at the Third International Symposium on Catholic Social Thought and Management Education, Goa, India, January 1999), http://www.stthomas.edu/cathstudies/cst/mgmt/goa/goodpaster.html, accessed July 2002.

Preface

In the introductory chapter of this volume, Jean-Yves Calvez and Michael J. Naughton describe the development of Catholic social teaching regarding the purpose of the business organization. Through encyclical letters, pastoral letters, and conciliar and other official documents, the Catholic Church seeks to provide, in John Paul II's words, "[an] *accurate formulation* of the results of a careful reflection on the complex realities of human existence . . . in the light of faith and the Church's tradition."[1] While these teachings serve as a basic orientation to the good informed by faith, they do not and cannot detail specific answers to economic problems, nor can they provide exhaustive explanations of business firms' complex dimensions or of their complex relations to modern society. The social teachings of the Church seek to clarify and deepen our commitment to the common good by encouraging deliberation over both what we are called to do and how we are called to think. Thus, we may speak of Catholic social *teaching* in service to Catholic *social thought and action,* on the model of deliberate human action in general.

Yet, we also may speak of Catholic social thought and action in service to Catholic social teaching. The reflection on purposes or ends of the business organization through which the mind of the Church takes shape in official, teaching documents owes much to the laity and the clergy's living out "the complex realities of human existence." As Calvez and Naughton (chapter 1) show, for example, the German Catholic laity's declaration, on grounds of natural law, for industrial codetermination (*Mitbestimmung*) at Bochum (1949) was a moving factor in the evolution of Pius XII's teaching on property and labor. Again, *Solidarnosc* was a Polish labor movement before "solidarity" appeared as a leading theme of John Paul II's social encyclicals.

There is, in other words, a dynamic relationship within the Church that reflects the variety of its members' different but complementary roles. While the popes and bishops reserve to themselves the teaching authority of their offices, they nonetheless look to others, and in particular to the laity, to bring social questions and problems to the fore, to examine the social teachings, to build upon them, to develop their significance, and at times to readjust them in light of changing circumstances. In the decree of the Second Vatican Council, *On the Apostolate of the Laity* (*Apostolicam actuositatem*), the laity are exhorted to commit their "intelligent attention and examination" and "competence" to the "renewal of the temporal order," that is, of "the good things of life and prosperity of the family, culture, economic matters, the arts and professions, the laws of the political community, international relations."[2] The social teachings of the popes, bishops, and councils suppose appropriation by a laity whose faith-filled engagement in the concrete, day-to-day complexities of human existence alone can either turn reflection on ultimate ends into practical wisdom concerning intermediate ends and means, or can turn wisdom concerning means into renewing action.

In any human act the controlling end leads in conception, but follows in execution only after a deliberate determination of means. Catholic social teaching becomes Catholic social thought and action only so far as the laity deliberately and reflectively embody its principles in their actions. Again, in any human act deliberation must make an orderly advance to the particulars by which the end can be realized in the here and now. Catholic social teaching becomes Catholic social thought just to the degree that, through an "accurate formulation," a structure of mediate and mediating reflection is erected. Yet again, in any human act the guiding power of the end in view is in part a reflection *of* and a reflection *on* past action. Catholic social teaching becomes Catholic social thought through a continuing conversation: past action speaking to present reflection, present action attending to past reflection.

This volume grows out of the conviction that the conversation which could lead from Catholic social teaching toward the development of robust Catholic social thought on the business organization has faltered for lack of a mediating voice. Popes, bishops, and council have spoken and continue to speak. Businesspeople, unionists, and a variety of organizations have responded as they ought—according to their lights, out of their various and concrete concerns—and they continue to respond. Yet, the Catholic university—the place where (as Rev. Theodore Hesburgh of the University of Notre Dame put it) the Church does her thinking—and, in particular, the business schools which have lately come to prominence within the contemporary Catholic university have been relatively silent on questions which would seem to be peculiarly, concretely theirs:[3] What is the relationship between Catholic social teaching and business theory and practice? Is there an account of the firm which would emerge as an achievement of Catholic social thought? Or would it make no more sense to speak of "Catholic approaches to management" than of "Catholic approaches to mathematics"? If business organizations are the human instruments of human action, can it make any less sense to speak of "Catholic approaches to management" than to speak of "Catholic approaches to human action"?[4]

Why, then, the silence? It might be that the questions above had been closed because of the irrelevance of Catholic social thought for business theory and practice. Yet, there is no developed body of scholarship which makes this affirmation. Again, there may be an a priori concern that such an engagement would impose religious doctrine upon intellectual pursuits that are viewed by many as value-free scientific descriptions of phenomena in the marketplace. For many this vision secures the legitimacy of management education within the academy. Yet, insistence on value-free management education itself reflects a kind of value judgment, and the refusal to engage religious values is a curtailment of free academic inquiry.

In any case, the historical position of the study of business management within Catholic colleges and universities compounded the factors that cultivated the silence. As Catholic business schools began to appear on campuses, their curriculum and research looked no different from their state counterparts. Not only did business education at Catholic universities offer no substantially distinctive characteristics, but as business education began to occupy an expanded role in Catholic and

Christian higher education, its form began to affect the identity of these institutions. Three reasons, in particular, stand out to partially explain the relative non-distinctiveness of business education within the Catholic university.

1. Faculty isolation. As business faculty multiplied at Catholic colleges and universities, many were ignored and isolated by their liberal arts colleagues, who saw them as the administration's solution to the problem of cash flow and themselves as the guardians of emphatically Catholic education. Their view was perhaps best expressed by Mortimer Adler, who wrote, "I hope I step on nobody's toes too hard when I say, as I must say, that therefore it is an absolute misuse of school to include any vocational training at all. School is a place of learning for the sake of learning, not for the sake of earning. It is as simple as that."[5]

2. Focus on technique. Isolated from the liberal arts mission of the university, business faculty concentrated on what they knew best: techniques and skills. Business schools equipped students with a repertoire of financial, marketing, and managerial vehicles for getting from "here" to "there." Little was done in the business program to equip students to reflect on whether the "there" was worth getting to. Liberal arts faculties were largely content to permit their second-class colleagues to pursue training programs, because this freed the liberal arts faculties from any serious encounter with business as a fully human act.

3. Fragmented curriculum. While it was often held that the liberal arts component of the business student's overall education would address the question of the "there," the practical result was an "alongside" education under the implicit motto "isolate, don't integrate." Lack of interaction and integration between liberal and business curricula translated into a kind of wall-eyed view, incapable of a "vision about ways to achieve 'an amalgamation of the two.'"[6] Understandably, students formed the impression that they received two types of education: one to make them more human, and the other to make them more money. Unsurprisingly, they were no clearer than their faculties about how the two fit together.

Too often this has resulted in students leaving a Catholic university with the notion of business as a career, which, as William F. May notes, becomes a "self-driven vehicle through life whereby one enters into the public thoroughfares but moves towards one's own private destination."[7] We realize of course that many business programs, Catholic and non-Catholic, offer business ethics and business and society courses which help business students see their broader responsibilities, but such courses cannot carry the weight of an education marked by the integration offered through Catholic social thought or do justice to the laity's vocation.

What we miss, then, in Christian business schools in general and Catholic business schools in particular is a concrete expression of the heart of their mission as organs of Catholic universities. Graduates of Catholic university business programs have made and will continue to make the personal contributions to the Catholic social tradition that belong to the laity. However, it is often difficult to discern what role their business education plays in those contributions. As indicated above, this is not simply the fault of business schools. Yet, we need not rehearse all the various dimensions of these issues to conclude that without a serious engagement between Catholic social thought and management theory and practice, Catholic business schools cannot fully participate in the mission of Catholic universities.

To begin to address the relationship between Catholic social thought and management theory and practice adequately, one of the first questions to be examined is, What is business? This is a fundamental question both for business theory and for Catholic social thought, a question that cannot be answered unless we understand business's purpose. Until this question has a robust, realistic, and interdisciplinary analysis in light of Catholic social thought, which is precisely what we want to begin to develop in this volume, we will do justice neither to the profound contribution Catholic social thought has for management, nor to the mission and identity of Christian and Catholic universities as it relates to their business programs. Unless a thorough and ongoing examination of human dignity, the subjective dimension of work, the social nature of property, the common good, justice, solidarity, subsidiarity, participation, theological anthropology, and so forth informs its treatment of business organizations, the religiously inspired university will suffer from an acute form of intellectual and moral impoverishment. To the degree that the Catholic and Christian university ignores these relationships, it not only risks the opportunity for intellectual and moral formation of business students, but also contributes to careerism and opportunism in business life by turning itself into an institution that fails to live up to its cultural vocation.

Moreover, disengagement of Catholic business education from Catholic social teaching contributes to an unhealthy uniformity in management education. Lyman W. Porter and Lawrence E. McKibbin, authors of *Management Education and Development: Drift or Thrust into the 21st Century?,* argue that a cookie-cutter mentality exists in many schools of management in the United States, which discourages a diversity of approaches to management education.[8] Porter and McKibbin's argument was taken seriously by the American Assembly of Collegiate Schools of Business when its accreditation standards were reformulated. The new standards are mission-driven and process-oriented. A school of management's mission must be consistent with the mission of the university, and management processes must continually reflect the mission and its accomplishments.

This volume is the result of a multistage process sponsored by the John A. Ryan Institute for Catholic Social Thought of the Center for Catholic Studies, University of St. Thomas, Minnesota. The Institute's purpose is to address the fragmentation of modern life by exploring ways in which faith, as expressed within the broad tradition of Catholic social teaching, can inform management education and practice. In light of the Institute's mission, the organizers laid down two guidelines: (1) the contributors should focus on fundamentals; and (2) the approach to fundamentals should be thoroughly interdisciplinary.

An initial collection of essays resulted from an open call for papers examining the relationship between Catholic social thought and management theory and practice, to be presented at the Second International Symposium on Catholic Social Thought and Management Education, held in Antwerp, Belgium, July 1997. (Papers from the Antwerp Conference may be viewed at http://www.stthomas.edu/cathstudies/cstm/antwerp/, accessed November 2001.) From among the scores of contributors to the Antwerp proceedings, the organizers invited some eighteen authors to present revised versions of their papers at a further, intensive seminar, held at the University of St. Thomas, St. Paul, Minnesota, in August of 1998.

Invitations to the follow-up seminar took into account the diversity of the disciplines represented; the authors' success in bringing fundamental principles of Catholic social teaching—principles concerning the common good, primacy of labor over capital, social nature of property, solidarity, subsidiarity, and so forth—to bear on the question "What is the purpose of the business enterprise?"; and the tendency of each of the selected papers to speak to the others. At the follow-up seminar, invited corporate executives and managers, attorneys, and business educators joined the authors in lively, critical exchanges. On the basis of these discussions, the thirteen papers that form the present volume were selected, and the authors undertook further revisions in consultation with one another and with the editors.

The result merits description as a volume of integrated, interdisciplinary essays. The contributors represent distinct disciplines—law, theology, philosophy, and political science, as well as economics, finance, management, and production engineering—but they write in light of a common set of questions and with attention to a common set of principles.

In light of the growing desire for people to integrate spirituality and work within contemporary culture, we believe that this book fills a critical need for engaging management with the Christian social tradition, and in particular the Catholic social tradition. While it is true that some practitioners and students are not inspired by religious faith, it seems more accurate to argue, as John Langan does, that "for most people in our society their sense of personal roots and their membership in significant groups along with the motivational strength that accompanies such factors are connected with religious bodies rather than with philosophical or ideological systems." With Langan, the contributors and editors draw the conclusion, "It is . . . one of the major limitations of a purely secular approach to business ethics that it leaves out the task of drawing on the motivational power of religious convictions in order to sustain morally correct behavior."[9] The purpose of this volume is to invite faculty, students, and managers to reflect, in light of a rich religious tradition, on means by which to bridge the gap between personal vocation and institutional purpose on the one hand, and managerial theory and practice on the other.

Acknowledgments

We are deeply indebted to the contributors for their collaboration in this work. We wish also to thank by name the consulting participants in the crucial, follow-up symposium, whose critical insights contributed much to the essays' final forms: Michael Ambrosio, Thomas Bausch, Don Briel, Jack Cassidy, Patricio Crichingo, André Delbecq, Paul Dembinski, John Dobson, Edwin Epstein, Jim Larkin, Jean-Loup Dherse, Ray Jones, Ellen O'Connor, Peter John Opio, Stephen Porth, Deborah Savage, Mike Stebbins, Bill Toth, Louis Xavier, and Bob Wahlstedt.

Several institutions provided significant financial support to make this volume possible: the University of St. Thomas's John A. Ryan Institute for Catholic Social Thought of the Center for Catholic Studies, the Aquinas Foundation, the Graduate School of Business and the College of Business Administration at St. John's University, and two donors who wish to remain anonymous.

Special thanks go to Emily Jovanovich, who helped edit this volume.

Notes

1. John Paul II, *Sollicitudo rei socialis,* 41.

2. *Apostolicam actuositatem,* 7, in *Vatican Council II: The Conciliar and Post-Conciliar Documents,* ed. Austin Flannery, O.P. (Collegeville, Minn.: Liturgical Press, 1993).

3. Quoted in Richard McBrien, "What Is a Catholic University?" in *The Challenge and Promise of Catholic University,* ed. Theodore M. Hesburgh, C.S.C. (Notre Dame, Ind.: University of Notre Dame Press, 1994), 156. There are of course notable exceptions to this silence, but that Catholic business schools as a whole have failed to engage Catholic social thought seems an indisputable fact.

4. When Edwin M. Epstein came from the University of California's Haas School of Business to take over as dean of the School of Economics and

Business Administration at Saint Mary's College of California, he thought he would find a robust and dynamic conversation on the relationship between Catholic social thought and management. He was moved to note that while it seemed obvious that Catholic social thought should inform business education at a Catholic university, he has been "struck by the paucity of discussion devoted, in Catholic sources, to business and economics education in Catholic institutions" ("Catholic Social Teaching and Education in Business and Economics," *Saint Mary's College Educational Perspectives* 14 [Fall 1996]: 26).

5. Mortimer Adler, "Leisure, Liberal Arts and Labor," in *Reforming Education,* ed. Geraldine Van Doren (New York: MacMillian, 1988), 105.

6. Michael C. Jordan, "The Tension between Liberal Education and Career Education," in *Papers 1987: Faculty Seminar on the History of the College of St. Thomas* (internal publication at the University of St. Thomas).

7. William F. May, "The Beleaguered Rulers: The Public Obligation of the Professional," *Kennedy Institute of Ethics Journal* 2 (1992): 31. The other most obvious place for this discussion to take place is among businesspeople themselves. The International Christian Union of Business Executives (UNIAPAC), which is the major international organization of Christian business people, has good relations with the hierarchy, yet we have not seen a well-developed discussion between the two on the topic of the purpose of the business organization.

8. Lyman W. Porter and Lawrence E. McKibbin, *Management Education and Development: Drift or Thrust into the 21st Century?* (New York: McGraw-Hill Book Company, 1988). See also Michael J. Naughton and Thomas Bausch, "The Integrity of an Undergraduate Catholic School of Management: Four Integrating Characteristics," *California Management Review* 38 (Summer 1996): 118–40.

9. John Langan, "The Ethics of Business and the Role of Religion" (paper presented at the University of Melbourne, December 1991).

Introduction to Catholic Social Teaching

1

Catholic Social Teaching and the Purpose of the Business Organization

A Developing Tradition

JEAN-YVES CALVEZ
AND MICHAEL J. NAUGHTON

[T]he purpose of the business firm is not simply to make a profit but is to be found in its very existence as a community of persons who in various ways are endeavoring to satisfy their basic needs, and who form a particular group at the service of the whole of society.

—John Paul II, *Centesimus annus*, 35

In 1932 Adolf A. Berle and Gardiner C. Means wrote, in their seminal work *The Modern Corporation and Private Property*, that the corporation "had ceased to be a private business device and had become an institution."[1] What they meant by this statement was that the growth and development of the modern corporation in the twentieth century has made it the dominant way to organize economic life. The concentration of economic power in the modern corporation compares to the concentration of religious power in the medieval Catholic Church or

3

of political power in the nation-state.[2] The corporation cannot be, if it ever could be, understood as only a so-called private enterprise. It has become so pervasive in modern life that a social understanding of the corporation is imperative. The critical questions before us are, What social understanding of the corporation do we have? Does the corporation have the capacity to help people grow?[3]

A year before Berle and Means's classical work, Pope Pius XI, in his encyclical letter *Quadragesimo anno* (1931), began in an explicit way to formulate an answer to these questions. As the leader of the Catholic Church, he realized that as the modern economy develops, and especially as the corporation's role in that economy grows, social understanding of the economy and of the corporate form must be informed by an understanding of the social nature of property, the virtue of justice, the dignity of work, the principles of subsidiarity and solidarity, the common good, and above all by the social and spiritual understanding of the human person; otherwise, the economy and its corporate form of organization fail to create conditions to develop workers within the organization so as to serve people outside it.

In this introductory chapter, we summarize the development of the official Catholic social teachings on one of the most dynamic institutions within the twentieth century: the business organization. Most people, including Catholics, are unaware of this social teaching, and many Christians too often fail to connect faith and business, except in either prophetic critiques or spiritual platitudes. What is missing in the engagement is a serious conversation between the intellectual depth of the Catholic social tradition and the complexities of a business organization.

This engagement of the purpose of business with Catholic social thought is no mere academic exercise. It is critical, especially for the manager or entrepreneur, who not only plays a decisive role in defining, translating, and implementing the purpose of a business, but whose vocation and self-identity as a manager or entrepreneur are at stake.

The problem of recognizing a corporate and common purpose to the business enterprise is present from the first days of the modern social teachings of the Catholic Church.[4] Those first days were indeed the time when the enterprise developed without the name "enterprise." People viewed the corporation as an "anonymous society" (as often stated in Europe), that is, as a society of things (capital, shares) rather than of persons. While there were shareholders, their personal commitment was mitigated by limited liability. The worker was not considered as a member, that is, as a person, of that society; rather, she related to it only from the outside through the labor contract, as one more input or service hired by the anonymous society (see Clark's and Tavis's essays on the economic view of the corporation, chapters 5 and 10).

In the presence of this situation, Pope Leo XIII, in his encyclical letter *Rerum novarum* (1891), did not react by saying that the enterprise is a community of persons with a common good. He did, however, react by not accepting whatever labor contract arose. A wage, for example, is not *just* simply because two parties consent to the bargain. Underlying the contract is a duty that the wage be sufficient for the subsistence of the worker and his family. According to Leo XIII, there is a natural law informed by the nature of the human person governing whatever contract is offered (see Gordley's essay, chapter 4). But Leo XIII does not discuss the context of the enterprise where the contracts are offered.

With Pius XI, at the time of the great modern crisis of the capitalist system, the Great Depression, the question of the nature of the enterprise properly surfaced. In his encyclical letter *Quadragesimo anno* (1931), the pope asked, "Should one not replace the labor hiring contract by a societal (or partnership) contract (a contract among persons forming a society among themselves)?"[5] His first response to this question was negative. He was concerned that a positive answer would encroach upon the rights of owners, who would undergo undue outside influence over their own property. Pius XI was extremely keen on respecting the right of property. He recognized that many social obligations can be put to the charge of the owner; yet property cannot be lost or its owner forfeit property rights because of misuse. Because misuse can be corrected, even punished by the social authorities, the basic property right itself should in any case remain intact.

But Pius XI, after denying the principle that the labor contract should of necessity be replaced by a societal or partnership contract, added immediately: "We however think that it is appropriate to the present conditions of social life to temper somewhat, as much as it is possible, the labor contract by elements coming from the societal [or partnership] contract."[6] Some companies already heading in this direction influenced Pius XI. He realized, through the experience of certain companies, that a deeper relationship could occur within the enterprise through shared ownership and management.[7] Still, Pius XI did not want to make this a strict obligation for all companies; rather, he favored any voluntary initiative in those directions. What Pius XI began to see was that the worker is really not a stranger to the enterprise, or that there really *is* an enterprise made up of persons, not just a society of capital shares. The worker is an agent within the enterprise who in part achieves fulfillment through her work.[8] To reduce a business to merely a legal fiction whereby people are connected by a nexus of contracts so as to be more productive, that is, to reduce a business to a society of things, depersonalizes and alienates members of the firm. This, of course, is a critical issue concerning the nature of a business organization, which will be examined throughout this volume (see in particular Kennedy, chapter 3; Tavis, chapter 10; and Cortright and Pierucci, chapter 7).

In the years preceding World War II, however, not much was made of the hint that was Pius XI's conception of a societal or partnership contract. What dominated much of the discussion after 1931 was corporativism. Whereas the idea of the societal partnership contract focused on the microlevel of the enterprise, corporativism focused on the macrorelationships among labor, employers, and the state within the whole national economy.

There was much more interest in the enterprise as such and in the structure of the enterprise after World War II, at a time when people were eager to make deep and radical social reforms. Reforming the enterprise was one of the main issues. In Germany particularly, under British influence (in the British Occupation Zone), there developed a new system of co-management or codetermination (*Mitbestimmung*) by capital and labor, first in the coal and steel industries and then eventually extended to all the major industries by the German government itself.[9] Already in 1949, a congress of the German Catholics, *Katholikentag* (in Bochum), made a moral doctrinal claim that codetermination in the enterprise was entailed by the natural law itself and therefore absolutely required:

> Catholic workers and employers agree that the right to joint management of all workers in social, personal and economic matters

[codetermination] of common concern is a natural right according to the order laid down by God, and corresponding to the collective responsibility of all. We demand its legal establishment. Following the example given by progressive firms, it should be put into practice everywhere from now on.[10]

Pope Pius XII reacted to this statement, which he considered too extreme. He argued, following his predecessor, Pius XI, for the intrinsic legitimacy of the labor contract. Explaining that all those who work in the enterprise should of course be considered as "subjects" or persons, not as mere "factors" of production, he did not see the need to abandon the system of the labor contract in order to take into account the subjective character of the members of the enterprise.

In particular, Pius XII feared two things concerning codetermination as articulated by the Germans: first, that the new system proposed would deprive the owners of their innate property rights; and second, that by introducing into the administration of the enterprise representatives of the unions who were not necessarily members of the firm, there was a danger of transferring real decision making to "collective anonymous forms."[11]

Throughout the 1950s, however, Pius XII's fears over the eradication of private property did not materialize as a result of the codetermination laws. What worsened at this time was the depersonalization of the worker through the mechanistic production processes of large industries. His attention turned from property to the subject of the corporation—the employee.

While Pius XII never wrote a social encyclical, he would give talks to associations, from beekeepers to bankers, about how the social tradition of the Church could be understood within their particular field of work. In a talk to the International Congress of Catholic Association of Small and Medium-Sized Business, he explained that their vocation calls employers and entrepreneurs to create workplace conditions that allow employees to develop.

The economic and social function to which every man aspires requires that control over the way in which he acts be not completely subjected to the will of another. The head of the undertaking values above all else his power to make his own decisions. He

anticipates, arranges, directs, and takes responsibility for the consequences of his decisions. His natural gifts . . . find employment
in his directing function and become the main means by which his
personality and creative urge are satisfied. *Can he [then] deny to his
subordinates that which he values so much for himself?*[12]

What is of particular interest in this paragraph is that Pius XII articulated for the employer what the principle of subsidiarity means for the
business organization (see McCann, chapter 8; Tavis, chapter 10; and
Fort, chapter 11). While the authority of the owner ought to be protected,[13] no room can exist in such a conception of a business for practices that deny the profound worth of the employees of the enterprise.
Also of particular interest here is to whom Pius XII was talking: owners of small and medium-sized businesses. He believed that large
industries foster, sometimes unavoidably, an impersonal anonymity
between owners and workers. While he insisted, as mentioned above,
that economic responsibility must be legally located with the owners
of capital, he perceived the separation of ownership from control as
an obstacle (although one that could be overcome) to creating a business organization that fosters human development. He believed that
small and medium-sized enterprises could better "connect" labor and
capital through co-ownership and co-management that would create
a real community of work (see Gates, chapter 12, and Murphy and
Pyke, chapter 13).[14]

During the 1950s Pius XII was in many respects weaving a moral
argument for the purpose of the business organization by integrating the right of private property, the proper social use of that property,
and the humanization of the workplace in the face of depersonalization through the technologies of mass production. While his impulse
toward the codetermination movement in Germany was to stress the
right of property in the late 1940s and early 1950s, his addresses to business managers throughout the 1950s made clear that the right of property
did not include uses which promote the dehumanization of the worker.[15]

The controversy after World War II over the nature and purpose of
the enterprise, and Pius XII's successive responses to this controversy,
proved to be a critical phase in the articulation of the Church's understanding of the business enterprise. By incorporating the spiritual and

moral resources of the social tradition—that is, the social nature of property and its private ownership, the role of virtue, the idea of community of persons, and so forth—Pius XII made a significant contribution to the formulation of the Catholic social tradition on the nature and purpose of the enterprise. His final views clearly lead to the idea of a partnership or a community of persons in the enterprise. One can thus speak of a corporate purpose of the enterprise involving all the participants in it. Managerial responsibility, that is a manager's ability to respond, extends not only to capital holders but also to labor holders, whose participation is critical to the business's capacity to be an authentic community of work.

All development in moral teaching requires a period of solidification. In terms of the firm, this period comes about with Pope John XXIII, who succeeded Pius XII in 1958. In his encyclical *Mater et magistra* (1961), John XXIII writes serenely of the enterprise as a community and of its obligation to enable all its members to participate more fully in its activities. This participation cannot be undertaken in an indiscriminate manner and must, of course, take into account the particular input and contribution of each member. Yet, the workplace must represent "in form and substance" a "true community," where workers are treated as human persons and have a chance to take an active role in the organization's operation.[16]

This development on the nature and purpose of the enterprise is formulated at the Second Vatican Council in the document *Gaudium et spes* (1965), in the following terms:

> In economic enterprises it is persons who are joined together, that is, free and independent human beings created to the image of God. Therefore, with attention to the functions of each—owners or employers, management or labor—and without doing harm to the necessary unity of management, the active sharing of all in the administration [in Latin *curatio,* that is, management] and profits of these enterprises in ways to be properly determined is to be promoted.[17]

Building upon *Gaudium et spes,* John Paul II grounds Catholic social teaching on the firm squarely in a theological understanding rooted in the claims of the Book of Genesis. In *Laborem exercens* (1981), he explained that human beings have been given a superior place in the order of creation. Because they have been made in God's image, all people have been given the command, which is both a right and a duty, to subdue the earth. He defines the expression "subdue the earth" as a human activity that discovers all the resources the earth provides so as to use them for people *to develop,* not simply to maximize capital returns or to balance individual interests.[18] It is only through work that people can tap the richness creation has to offer, and it is through organizations that this work is carried out most effectively. Humanity's tremendously accelerated technological advancement, through the organization of various occupations, provides, for John Paul II, "a historical confirmation of man's dominion over nature."[19] This dominion does not constitute a license for individual exploitation, but just the opposite. The enhanced potential offered by business organizations can be a "means for the practice of work which realises the human person."[20]

Business as the major form of economic organization is consequently the major mechanism to achieve dominion. Yet, to properly understand dominion, a business must conceive itself responsible for the use of an inheritance or gift. For John Paul II, people who make up a business enter into a twofold inheritance: (1) what is given by the Creator in terms of natural resources, and (2) what is given by others in terms of what has been already developed on the basis of those natural resources.[21] Each human generation is indebted both to the Creator and to its predecessors for the means and the opportunity to share in the goods of creation. Moreover, since the Creator's gift is given for the use of all in pursuit of their development, this twofold inheritance—the gift of creation and the productive instruments already forged from it—has, in the formula of *Gaudium et spes,* "a universal destination" (69). The destination is "universal" in that the human inheritance should benefit all present humanity and in that it should be developed and transmitted to future generations. On this theological foundation of creation as gift, John Paul II builds his understanding of property, especially corporate property. Consequently, any idea of an absolute right to property and capital, expressed through formulas of shareholder wealth maximization, or any idea of a corporate body as merely a nexus of competing interests is rejected, because it denies the significance of this human vocation to work and impedes persons' development in and from their work. Nevertheless, this principle of universal destination "does not delegitimize private property; instead it broadens the understanding and management of private property to embrace its indispensable social function, to the advantage of the common good and in particular the good of society's weakest members."[22]

For John Paul II, persons' development within the business organization depends upon whether the business is a community of work (see Kennedy, chapter 3). To understand the importance of what John Paul II means by a community of work, it is helpful to distinguish it from what Robert Bellah and others call a "life-style enclave."[23] In a lifestyle enclave, a group of people come together to have their interests served. As a life-style enclave, a business consists in each member serving his particular interests, using others to get his "due"; each member's concern for others is determined by their effect on his interests or "stake" (see Cortright and Pierucci, chapter 7). In contrast, a community of work unites its members in the pursuit of common goals, shared goods through which each develops. In a talk to Italian managers and workers, John Paul II explained that the social teaching of the Church makes

> clear that *the sole criterion of profit is insufficient,* especially when it is raised to the level of an absolute; . . . Indeed, a business firm is not merely an instrument at the service of the well-being of its management; rather, it is itself a common good of both management and labor, at the service of the common good of society."[24]

Speaking to Peruvian businesspeople, John Paul II reminded them that the social teaching of the Church implores them to see "their enterprises as a social function. They must not conceive them only as instruments of production and profit, but also as a community of persons."[25] Philip J. Chmielewski puts it well when he writes that since "work must complete itself in the service of persons," a community of work is only authentic when it serves those outside it, which is the basis of developing those within it.[26]

One may of course raise obvious questions: Do John Paul II and those before him expect too much from business organizations? Is this not merely theological idealism that has no bearing on the globalization of corporations? These are legitimate questions. Yet John Paul II, as well as the whole tradition behind him, raises the critical question that must be at the fore of any business: Can managers and employees *develop* in the corporate form of organization in which they find themselves?[27] John Paul II's idea of business as a community of work does not suppose a disembodied community disconnected from the economic pressures of profit, risk, competition, and productivity. Rather, he sees that only through a community of work can these economic values be properly ordered within a business so that they serve to develop people and society. Because of the nature of a business, profit and productivity are necessary and critical dimensions; but unless a community develops within a business to provide a proper ordering of these economic dimensions, the possibility of the business becoming a place where people can develop evaporates. For example, in his encyclical letter *Centesimus annus* (1991), John Paul II states that "Profit is a regulator of the life of a business, but it is not the only one."[28] Profits, like any instrumental good, must be at the service not just of individual agents, such as shareholders or employees, but of the common good; otherwise, profits corrupt the agent who pursues them (see Alford and Naughton, chapter 2).

John Paul II praises the modern business economy for its positive aspects. He sees that the business organization gives people a chance to develop in the economic sphere, just as people develop in the political, cultural, and religious spheres. The role of business in the modern economy demands the person's best qualities: the capacity to investigate and to know, the capacity for solidarity in the organization, and the capacity to work toward the satisfaction of the needs of fellow employees.

Unfortunately, however, not enough businesses reach their full potential for developing people, and instead of developing people, they alienate them. John Paul II describes this alienation in business as ensuring "maximum returns and profits with no concern whether the worker, through his own labor, grows or diminishes as a person."[29] This alienation in part stems from persons' refusal to transcend themselves by instrumentalizing everything, including their own relationships, within the firm. For example, managers treat employees well not because they are created in the image of God, but because it will

maximize shareholder wealth. This pervasive logic of instrumentaliza-
tion within corporations today obstructs the habits of mind and heart
by which persons authentically give themselves to God and others.[30]
John Paul II crystallizes this social and theological insight by explaining that

> The concept of alienation needs to be led back to the Christian
> vision of reality, by recognizing in alienation a reversal of means and
> ends. When man does not recognize in himself and in others the
> value and grandeur of the human person, he effectively deprives
> himself of the possibility of benefiting from his humanity and of
> entering into that relationship of solidarity and communion with
> others for which God created him.[31]

This brief survey of the official Catholic social teaching concludes
that the enterprise is a community of persons, even if each of the persons
participating in the community has a specific contribution to offer, jus-
tifying a specific reward and treatment. If the enterprise is in this sense
a community, then the ideas of coresponsibility, co-management, and co-
ownership come strongly to the fore again and are decisive. These critical
organizational issues will be discussed in detail in the last two chapters
of this volume (see Gates, chapter 12, and Murphy and Pyke, chapter 13).
This view of the enterprise also challenges the prevailing shareholder and
stakeholder views of the corporation, which will be addressed throughout sections 1 and 2.

Finally, it is important here not to overstate the case. What should
not be missed through this discussion of the nature and purpose of
the business organization within official Catholic social teachings is that
while the popes and bishops raise the importance of business, they never
absolutize its value. As Murphy and Pyke explain in the last chapter of
the volume, work is more than an instrumental good, but it is not the
highest good in human life. While people develop through work, they
cannot fully develop as human beings only through work. Unless they
participate in other communities, such as family, church, and civic and
cultural associations, their full humanity will always be stunted. All members of the enterprise have social obligations beyond the enterprise itself, which has been suggested many times throughout the Catholic social tradition.[32]

Notes

1. Adolf A. Berle, Jr., and Gardiner C. Means, *The Modern Corporation and Private Property* (1932; reprint, New Brunswick, N.J.: Transaction Publishers, 1991), li.

2. Ibid., 309.

3. Regarding the corporation as the new human institution on the stage of human history, Berle and Means stated, "we have to consider the effect on property, the effect on workers, and the effect upon individuals who consume or use the goods and services which corporation produces or renders" (ibid., liii).

4. See Amata Miller's helpful summary s.v. "Corporations" in *The New Dictionary of Catholic Social Thought,* ed. Judith A. Dwyer (Collegeville, Minn.: Liturgical Press, 1994), 242–44, and Philip J. Chmielewski's entry s.v. "Co-partnership," 237–41. See also Jean-Yves Calvez and Jacques Perrin, *The Church and Social Justice* (Chicago: Regnery, 1961), 285–301.

5. Pius XI, *Quadragesimo anno,* 65. As Robert G. Kennedy notes, in Latin the phrase is *per societatis contractum,* so in one sense the word "societal" rather than "partnership" should be preferred. However, the word "societal" may have a meaning in English that it might not normally have in Latin (or in French, for that matter, where *société commerciale* may mean a partnership). We hear "societal" and think about something to do with the civil society; here "societal" should be thought of as "association."

6. Ibid.

7. See Oswald von Nell-Breuning, *Reorganization of Social Economy* (New York: Bruce Publishing Co., 1936), 164–65.

8. For a good description of Oswald von Nell-Breuning's thought, see Philip J. Chmielewski, *Bettering Our Condition* (New York: Peter Lang, 1992), chapter 4; he states, "A crucial, positive dimension to the need for work which is often emphasized by Nell-Breuning is encapsulated in the scholastic axiom that every agent achieves its fullness in its own action (*omne agens agendo perficitur*)" (177).

9. Manfred Spieker, "Labor, Property and Co-determination: Guidelines of the Christian Social Teaching and Experiences in Germany" (http://www.stthomas.edu/cathstudies/cstm/antwerp/p25.htm, November 2001); Chmielewski, *Bettering Our Condition,* 191–202; Robert Kühne, *Codetermination in Business: Workers' Representatives in the Boardroom* (New York: Praeger, 1980); and E. A. Kurth, "Codetermination in West Germany," *Review of Social Economy* 23 (March 1965): 54–69.

10. Jeremiah Newman, *Co-responsibility in Industry: Social Justice in Labour-Management Relations* (Cork: Cork University Press, 1954), 3. One of

the primary purposes of this *Katholikentag* was to discuss the postwar reconstruction of West Germany's socioeconomic life. The authors of the codetermination resolution perceived it as an application of Pius XI's idea of modifying the wage contract into a contract of partnership. However, nine months later, Pius XII entered the debate. He condemned the right of "economic" participation or codetermination as contrary to Pius XI's partnership contract. (He did not include social and personal participation in his condemnation.) It is interesting to note that Oswald von Nell-Breuning, who was the principle author of *Quadragesimo anno,* supported the codetermination laws. Furthermore, he insisted that the right of private property supersedes the right of workers to economic determination. For Pius XII, the nature of the wage contract did not establish a natural right to economic participation. He explained that as long as the wage contract respects the personal and social nature of the person, "there is nothing in the private-law relationship as governed by the simple wage-contract" to violate the dignity of the worker (Pius XII, talk on June 3, 1950, "Address to the Catholic International Congresses for Social Study," *Catholic Mind* [1950]: 507–10). The primacy of the person can be achieved on the basis of a wage contract, making it unnecessary for the wage contract to be modified by a partnership contract. See Oswald von Nell-Breuning, S.J., "The Formation of Private Property in the Hands of Workers," in *The Social Market Economy: Theory and Ethics of the Economic Order,* ed. Peter Koslowski (Berlin: Springer, 1998), 312ff.; Kurth, "Codetermination in West Germany," 54–69; Gerald J. Rooney, "The Right of Workers to Share in Ownership, Management, and Profits," *Catholic Theological Society of America Proceedings* 18 (1963): 131–49; and John A. Ryan, *A Better Economic Order* (New York: Harper and Brothers Publishers, 1935), chapter 7. The debate over the question of the purpose of the enterprise became quite intense in the late 1940s and early 1950s in the context of West Germany's 1951 codetermination laws.

11. In a series of statements through the years 1949 and 1950, Pius XII insisted on those points. He also had occasion to recall his predecessor Pius XI's suggestion about the advisability of tempering the labor contract by elements taken from the societal contract, but he did so in order to explain that this suggestion was of a subordinate and secondary nature in Pius XI's views. Pius XI's main concern was, said his successor, corporativism among the professions. The suggestion of a modification of the labor contract by societal elements was a side remark. See Pius XII, "Address to the Ninth International Congress of the International Union of Catholic Employers," *Catholic Mind* (1949): 446–48; "Address to the Italian Catholic Association of Employers," *Catholic Mind* (1952): 569–72; and "Address to the Catholic Association of

Jean-Yves Calvez and Michael J. Naughton

Small and Medium-Sized Businesses," *The Pope Speaks* (1957): 405–09. For commentaries on these addresses, see Richard L. Camp, "Corporate Reorganization or Comanagement?" *The American Ecclesiastical Review* (May 1971): 319–32, and Raymond Miller, "Papal Pronouncements on the Entrepreneur," *The Review of Social Economy* (March 1950): 35–43.

12. Pius XII, "Address to the Catholic Association of Small and Medium-Sized Businesses" (italics added).

13. The question of authority is critical to understanding the nature of a business organization. An interpretation of authority in light of the principle of subsidiarity would occasion a helpful analysis. Chmielewski points out that "It is important to recognize that free, working persons do not object to their dependence in the work situation but, rather, reject a dependence which is shaped by an authority foreign to the intelligence and responsibility of the workers. Since such an authority would treat people not as subjects but, rather, as objects, it presents itself as alien to them. In the case where the working person is treated only as an object, then the exercise of authority, since the personal participation of the workers does not inform it, runs the danger of affecting them as arbitrary or capricious choice. The workers perceive such a distant authority as exploitative" (*Bettering Our Condition,* 180).

14. See James V. Schall, S.J., "Catholicism, Business and Human Priorities," *The Judeo-Christian Vision and the Modern Corporation,* ed. Oliver Williams and John Houck (Notre Dame, Ind.: University of Notre Dame Press, 1982), 122. Pius XII anticipates E.F. Schumacher's call in *Small Is Beautiful* for smaller plant sizes. See "Small is Beautiful Now in Manufacturing," *Business Week,* October 22, 1984, 152–56.

15. In a talk to businesspeople, Pius XII argues that "In principle a right as such of co-management (co-determination) does not belong to the worker, but it is not forbidden for employers to make it possible for workers to participate in management in a certain form and to a certain extent, nor is the State prevented from giving the worker power to make his voice heard in the management of certain enterprises where the extraordinarily great accumulation of power in the hands of anonymous capital could, if left to itself, do manifest harm to the community" (Pius XII, To the Italian Social Week, 1952).

16. John XXIII, *Mater et magistra,* 65. See Oswald von Nell-Breuning, S.J., "Some Reflections on *Mater et Magistra,*" *Review of Social Economy* (Fall 1962): 104–5; see also Michael J. Naughton, *The Good Stewards: Practical Applications of the Papal Social Vision of Work* (Lanham, Md.: University Press of America, 1992), chapter 3.

17. Second Vatican Council, *Gaudium et spes,* 68.

18. John Paul II, *Laborem exercens,* 4.2. In an address to labor leaders, he states: "The world of work . . . is the world of all the men and all the women

who, through their efforts, are trying to respond to the call to dominate the earth for the benefit of all. The solidarity of the world of work will therefore be a solidarity that broadens horizons to include not only the interests of individuals and particular groups but the common good of society as a whole, whether nationally, internationally or worldwide. It will be a solidarity for work, manifesting itself in the struggle for justice and for the truth of social life." This material was delivered as an address on June 15, 1982, in Geneva, Switzerland, to the International Labor Organization. The translation was taken from *L'Osservatore Romano,* June 28, 1982, pp. 10–12, 20; see also Robert G. Kennedy, Gary Atkinson, and Michael Naughton, *The Dignity of Work* (Lanham, Md.: University Press of America, 1994), 199.

19. John Paul II, *Laborem exercens,* 5.4; see also 10.3. John Paul II, however, warns that technology can become humanity's enemy, "taking away all personal satisfaction and the incentive to creativity and responsibility" (5.4) when the objective aspect of work dominates the subjective aspect.

20. Quoted from Kevin P. Doran, *Solidarity: A Synthesis of Personalism and Communalism in the Thought of Karol Wojtyla/Pope John Paul II* (New York: Peter Lange, 1996), 210.

21. John Paul II, *Laborem exercens,* 13.

22. John Paul II, World Day of Peace Message, January 2000, http://www.vatican.va/holy_father/john_paul_ii/messages/peace/documents/hf_jp-ii_mes_08121999_xxxiii-world-day-for-peace_en.html, accessed November 2001.

23. Robert Bellah et al., *Habits of the Heart* (Berkeley and Los Angeles: University of California Press, 1985), 72.

24. He goes on to say, "Anyone who collaborates, at any level, possesses the rights that correspond to his role in the common enterprise, as well as the respective obligations. In particular, he enjoys those rights and duties which proceed from his dignity as a man or a woman called, indeed obliged, to live a life that is truly human in all its dimensions: affective, cultural, social, spiritual, religious. This, once again, is a consequence not merely of legal impositions, valid though they may be, but of the obligations of conscience, both human and Christian (as quoted in Kennedy et al., *The Dignity of Work,* 128). This material was delivered as an address on April 17, 1988, in Verona, Italy, to managers and workers. The translation was taken from *L'Osservatore Romano,* May 2, 1988, pp. 7–8 (emphasis added). See also Chmielewski, *Bettering Our Condition,* 188.

25. This material was delivered as a homily on February 4, 1985, in Trujillo, Peru, to Peruvian workers and businesspeople. The translation was taken from *L'Osservatore Romano,* April 22, 1985, pp. 6–7 (as quoted in Kennedy et al., *The Dignity of Work,* 108). Critical to the culture of business as a

community of work are the intentions of its individual members. Business literature tends to reduce the importance of the firm's culture to results, to the bottom line, and to meeting goals. It tends to disregard the intentions that enabled people to achieve results and instead focuses on the means of achievement. John Paul II, however, argues that the intentions of all people involved are significant: "[I]n spite of the fundamental importance of the means, it is your attitudes which you must first of all examine in the light of faith, in order to change whatever needs to be changed, in accordance with the demands of that same faith." What faith elucidates for the Christian is that business can be a place where people may grow and develop through the work they do. John Paul II sees that the "ideal of the human and humanizing community must enlighten the concrete reality of business in the midst of a society that is open and pluralistic, by offering a more open and responsible creative force through which effective and rational production of services and goods can be achieved." He goes on to say, "Nonetheless, one cannot but lament the fact that there are a number of employers—in different areas of business— who do not respond to the gifts they have received and who appear to ignore their responsibility towards those who work in the company and towards the whole of society. Some seem to forget that they should indeed be the organizers of wealth, but always people who have the common good as their goal; they should not be carried away by the sole desire for what is useful to themselves alone. Always remember that solidarity and subsidiarity are sure guides for the Christian development of business and society. Business is not only a productive activity, but it is also intended to be a means in which the human person finds fulfillment through work. Always remember that the worker has no capital but himself, and that for him, in the right understanding of business as ordered for the common good, work has priority." This material was delivered as an address on May 15, 1988, in Lima, Peru, to Peruvian leaders of business and culture (as quoted in Kennedy et al., *The Dignity of Work*, 54). To businesspeople in Rome he stated: "You must seek to act with the best professional skill in order to develop the best relations among all the personnel of your businesses, with those who use your products or services, with the various social agents or authorities responsible for the common good, all of this without ever losing sight of the primary objective, which is the construction of a just society in which the whole ensemble of people can achieve true social balance. I also note that business constitutes one of the intermediary bodies called to allow those who participate in its activity not only to earn a living for themselves and their family, but allow to develop a large part of their capacities." This material was delivered as an address on March 9, 1991, in Rome, to members of International Christian Union of Business Directors. The translation was taken from *The Pope Speaks,* (September–October 1991): 78.

26. Chmielewski, *Bettering Our Condition,* 188.

27. For John Paul II, the confirming experience to this theological understanding of work and the business organization is the reality that we change and hopefully develop through our work, what he calls the subjective dimension of work. Because we bring our whole selves to work, both body and soul, the business organization cannot be confined to only financial transactions and self-interest calculations precisely because it is so difficult for people to develop within such a business. See John Paul II, *Laborem exercens,* 24.

28. John Paul II, *Centesimus annus,* 35.

29. Ibid., 41.

30. Ibid.

31. Ibid.

32. See John Paul II, *Dies domini (On Keeping the Lord's Day),* http://www.cin.org/jp2/diesdomi.html, accessed November 2001.

Section I

Engaging the Shareholder Model of the Firm

Introduction

To highlight the extremely competitive nature of business, a story is often told of two hikers who are awakened by a hungry tiger in their camp. As the first hiker rushes for his running shoes, the second informs him that he will have little chance to outrun the tiger. The response stings: "I don't have to outrun the tiger; all I have to do is outrun *you*."

From within an environment which suggests that raw survival is the prime imperative, the first hiker's response may seem quite rational. Adopting the style of management theorists, we might say that his behavior represents an opportunistic strategy for survival. Still, an environment is not the whole world of action, and to affirm that some behavior responds to the constraints of a given environment is not the last word on its practical rationality. Human action, after all, is distinguished by the capacity not merely to respond to, but to manage, environments; rational decision making supposes the critical evaluation of ends or goals as well as of means.

The story of the hikers and the tiger suggests the sort of business environment supposed by the economic-financial theory, or shareholder model, of the firm. The shareholder model defines the firm as an enterprise whose purpose—reason for being, *ratio*—is to maximize wealth for its shareholders. One of the model's best-known defenders, Milton Friedman, writes:

> there is one and only one social responsibility of business—to use its resources and engage in activity designed to increase its profits

so long as it stays within the rules of the game, which is to say, engages in open and free competition, without deception or fraud. . . . the very foundation of our free society [is] to make as much money for . . . stockholders as possible.[1]

Friedman has been highly critical of those theories of the firm, so-called stakeholder theories, which include among the firm's controlling purposes the fulfillment of social responsibilities that either equal or supersede the responsibility of maximizing shareholder returns. He does not, of course, argue that corporations ought to ignore the quality of their relationships with employees, surrounding communities, and customers. He argues, rather, that a firm should regulate those relationships according to their calculable effects on the controlling end—maximizing shareholder wealth.

Neoclassical economics, together with its applied "arm," finance, have dominated contemporary discussion of the theory of the firm, propagating Friedman's view. The neoclassical account supposes economic agents whose decision making is ordered to maximal satisfaction of their preferences: customers demand maximal satisfaction of their consumption preferences, seeking goods and services that offer the greatest utility at the lowest price; workers seek maximum wages for the least effort; investors (with allied managers) seek to maximize returns on assets at the least possible risk.

Given the competitive environment shaped by utility maximizers, the neoclassical account proposes, the firm's dedication to increasing shareholder value follows deductively: because the shareholding owners of the firm are, inherently, wealth maximizers, capital holders must construct and run the firm in a way that guarantees maximum returns— most accurately measured by share price—so as not to lose out to other maximizers.

Although contested in various circles, the shareholder model dominates the thinking in most university finance and economics departments and exercises increasing influence over publicly traded companies throughout the globalizing market. At the same time, the fundamental assumptions by which this theory of the firm at once supposes a business environment and tailors itself to that environment are rarely examined. Typically, the shareholder model's sense of what is practically rational in the conduct of business is tacitly conceded; its picture of a constraining "business environment" is taken for a worldview.

The essays in this section take issue with the proposition that the conventional shareholder model offers a comprehensive view of the firm's purposes "in the round," or suggests an adequate account of what makes for practical rationality in the conduct of business. It seems fair to say that they have in common the view that the shareholder model achieves an acute description of certain dimensions of business activity at the cost of systematically neglecting others, and that attention to the neglected dimensions is necessary if we are to consider the purposes of the firm synoptically, "in the round."

Again, it seems fair to say that the contributors agree that the economic-financial theory tends to flatten unduly our view of the firm under the cumulating weight of at least three, ultimately philosophical, assumptions (though perhaps no contributor would express them exactly as below):

1. as a positive or descriptive inquiry, concerned with the means to strictly limited ends, shareholder theory can afford to ignore the ethical-normative context of business activity (that is, the theory assumes that economic activity can be adequately described other than as ethical activity);
2. economic agents do not act (at least, economically) for common ends or common goods (in other words, community is not a term of economic analysis);
3. economic benefits are by definition quantifiable (that is, economic rationality is inherently calculative and instrumental).

Finally, it seems fair to say that each contributor finds, in the tradition of Catholic social teaching, some corrective(s) for the deficiencies each highlights in the shareholder model. Here, however, agreement (and qualified agreement at that) ends. For Charles Clark, the shareholder model is a destructive fiction, while Catholic social teaching offers principles to guide the construction of an authentic alternative. In contrast, Peter Koslowski argues that elevation of the shareholder value principle to the sole criterion of corporate success represents a one-dimensional response to economic dislocations following the globalization of capital markets. Catholic social teaching can offer only a limited corrective, by showing that the firm's ownership need not subject the good of the firm *tout court,* productive excellence, to the ownership's narrower end, increased shareholder value.

Again, Robert Kennedy suggests that the leaven of Catholic social teaching must be worked into the corporate dough by "a kind of evangelization and conversion that will be painful for everyone involved." James Gordley, on the other hand, thinks that the leaven is already there—though we may benefit from explicit attention to its working—since orderly economic activity depends on the cardinal virtues from which Catholic social teaching begins. Similarly, Michael Naughton and Helen Alford suggest that close attention to how firms actually cohere and succeed shows that architectonic principles of Catholic social teaching are tacitly at work in every organization. By explicating the latter as elements of what they call the "common good model," Naughton and Alford seek to show that the sorts of grim trade-offs which are thought to constrain management are not inescapable features of ordinary business activity, but are largely symptoms of the shareholder theory's inherent tendency to substitute financial technique for synoptic judgment.

Robert Kennedy's sober assessment of the task facing those who wish to develop a body of Catholic social thought on the firm and its purposes may be invoked to summarize the implications of this section. The project, he cautions, "will require some very serious intellectual work and aggressive demonstrations that the principles of the Catholic social tradition really are practical." No contributor to this section would disagree with Kennedy's reliance on the future tense.

Note

1. Milton Friedman, *Capitalism and Freedom* (Chicago: University of Chicago Press, 1962), 133.

2

Beyond the Shareholder Model of the Firm

Working toward
the Common Good of a Business

HELEN ALFORD, O.P.,

AND MICHAEL J. NAUGHTON

"The time has come," Pope John Paul II proclaimed in his New Year's Message (2000), "for a *new and deeper reflection on the nature of the economy and its purposes.*"[1] Given the centrality of the corporation in today's economy, a good place to start such an examination is with an analysis of the nature of the corporation and its purposes. Within the Catholic social tradition this involves thinking about the "common good," both at the level of the firm (by asking what is the common good of its members and other "stakeholders") and at the level of society as a whole (by asking how the firm contributes to the wider common good of the society of which it is a part). While business schools and the media avoid terms like "common good" when referring to the purpose or mission of a business, in practice the business organization must face the issues raised by such terms even if they do not appear in the firm's mission statement. Therefore, such terminology is useful for business managers and can give people a better hold on what a business is really doing than if they consider the firm merely as a "money-making machine." A purely financial description of the firm is appealing in that it is quantifiable and allows the creation of both simple decision-making rules and complex mathematical analyses of the financial structure of the business, but this description is inevitably abstract and disconnected from the real world of business, compared to one which recognizes the fact that the members of a business build their own common good and may contribute to the wider common good.

An explicit discussion of the common good of the firm can help people grasp the complexities of real business life, which are too often submerged in financial formulas. As a result, business activity can be more effective and robust since it will be built on a clearer understanding of the purpose of business. In particular, asking the question "What is the purpose of the business organization?" from within the tradition of the common good helps us recognize why a firm's defining and overall purpose cannot merely be "maximization of shareholder wealth" and why we must go beyond the shareholder model of the firm to understand the purpose of the firm. As recent studies have shown, the wider society on which business institutions rely for support increasingly distrusts businesspeople and their actions. Businesses need to consider how they contribute to the common good not only because it is better for society as a whole if they do so, but also because if they do not, they are storing up a whirlwind for themselves in the future.[2]

Our primary purpose, relying on ideas we have developed elsewhere, is to examine the "shareholder model" as it pertains to the purpose of business and, in the light of this model's weaknesses, examine how the useful insights of finance can be incorporated into a realistic concept of business based on the idea of the common good.[3] As a first step, we will discuss in some detail agency theory, which provides the wider philosophical basis for the shareholder model, and then indicate how the principle of the common good can be coupled with the technical refinement of finance to provide a richer theory of the firm.

A secondary purpose of this essay is to bring into the mainstream of discussion the principle of the common good as it relates to the theory of the firm. The acceptance of a model of business based on the common good tradition moves people out of the universe of the liberal tradition that has dominated the question of the purpose of an organization since the Enlightenment. Instead, we move into a much older theological and philosophical tradition, which, as far as business thinking is concerned, has been a largely untapped resource.[4]

An initial problem may seem to block this retrieval of the common good tradition for business practice: in the past, thinking about the common good has been carried on largely in terms of the political community. We would be the first to agree that a business is not a political community and thus is not fully responsible *for* "the common good." At the same time, we contend that a business does have its own common good and is also responsible *to* the common good of the wider human community. Obviously, some adjustment of the idea is needed if it is to be applied to an economic rather than a political community. We argue not only that this adjustment is possible, but also that it is imperative in the light of the growing importance of business in our increasingly interdependent world and the increasing backlash against business, most graphically represented by the "No Global" protesters. Speaking in terms of the common good allows us to deal directly with the connection between the goals and "goods" of the firm and those of the wider society.

The Shareholder Model of the Firm

A theory of the firm explains its reason for being. The most influential and authoritative theory of the firm has emerged from the discipline of finance, and is usually referred to as the shareholder model. This theory of the firm operates on the premise that stock price maximization should be the primary goal of corporate managers. While firms will have other goals, wealth maximization for shareholders should be the ultimate purpose that orders all the other goals of a firm.[5] Here we want to stop and ask: why should maximizing shareholder wealth be considered *the* purpose of the firm, with all other goals of the business relegated to second place? This question is rarely addressed in any systematic way in financial textbooks (see Tavis, chapter 10). In order to understand more fully this claim made by the shareholder model, we examine the normative presuppositions of agency theory, where the relationship between shareholders, managers, and the firm is defined.

The discipline of finance envisions the firm not in terms of the production of particular kinds of goods or services or its contribution to the wider society, but rather as "a conglomerate of assets and liabilities" that are used to maximize shareholder wealth. Tarascio explains that

> the firm not only produces specific outputs with specific inputs, it continually searches for the optimal structure of assets and liabilities which will secure it the largest long-run profits. Assets are only held because they potentially generate cash flows. Real assets (durable capital goods) are not purchased because they provide a specific product. Nor are they maintained because they produce a particular kind of output. Real assets, in this sense, are no different from financial assets; they are bought because their owners expect that they will yield an income stream.[6]

This notion of the purpose of a firm as the maximization of cash flows on assets is based on a contractual view of exchange. As Jensen and Meckling in their seminal article on the topic explain, "contractual relations are the essence of the firm," and "most organizations are simply *legal fictions which serve as a nexus for a set of contracting relationships among individuals*."[7] This is why they argue that it is "seriously misleading" to personalize the firm by attributing "social responsibilities" to it, since the organization is a legal fiction that mediates the "complex process in which the conflicting objectives of individuals . . . are brought into equilibrium within a framework of contractual relations."[8]

Agency theory, then, describes social relationships in terms of contracts between principals and agents. The agent acts on behalf of the principal, just as a doctor acts on behalf of the patient, a lawyer for her client, a union leader for his worker, and a manager for her shareholder. Jensen and Meckling see the "agency relationship as a contract under which one or more persons (the principal[s]) engage another person (the agent) to perform some service on their behalf which involves delegating some decision-making authority to the agent."[9] According to agency theory, shareholders have "entrusted" their wealth to a manager who acts as a fiduciary or trustee for the shareholders in the matter of maximizing their wealth.

The means for maximizing shareholder wealth is the firm. The firm is thus an instrument of its shareholders. Although ownership and use of wealth are separated between principals and agents, respectively, the trustee or fiduciary relationship between them is meant to ensure that the money is used in the interests of the owners. The goal of the managers ought to be the same as that of the shareholders. Shareholders, who own the firm, elect managers to operate the firm in the property interests of those same shareholders. In most public companies, property interests are reduced to wealth maximization because the large number of owners makes it nearly impossible to determine any shared interests beyond the common denominator of material gain. Those in business are simply managing an investor's savings in a way that maximizes returns (see Koslowski, chapter 6, on the spillover effect of financial logic in business).[10]

However, this fiduciary relationship can be weakened by the multiplicity of shareholders, none of whom have sufficient ownership of the firm's assets to make them a threat to the agents (managers) using these assets. Where this is the case, "there is good reason to believe that the agent will not always act in the best interests of the principal."[11] If managers begin to act toward goals other than maximizing wealth for the owners, then this is known in agency theory as "moral hazard." Agents are also self-interested actors and may not keep their obligations if it is not in their self-interest to do so. For example, a manager may not "decide to work as strenuously to maximize shareholder wealth, because less of this wealth will go to him or her, or may take a higher salary or consume more perquisites, because part of these costs will now fall on the outside stockholders."[12] The potential (even likely) conflict between principals' self-interest and agents' self-interest thus raises the problem for the principal of spending time and resources on verifying that the agent is acting on his behalf.

In treating this problem in agency theory, Eisenhardt develops two principles with regard to controlling agent self-interest:

1. When the contract between the principal and agent is outcome based, the agent is more likely to behave in the interests of the principal.
2. When the principal has information to verify agent behavior, the agent is more likely to behave in the interests of the principal.[13]

Thus, in order to ensure that agents do not follow their own self-interest, the owners must either give the agents incentives so that promoting the self-interest of the owners simultaneously promotes the self-interest of the agents, or they must pay for access to information ensuring that managers are not shirking in their duty to promote the self-interest of the principals.[14]

Executive compensation is one obvious area where conflict of interest can occur between shareholder and executive. To get around this problem, stock options for executives can be developed on the basis of increased shareholder price, so that the interests of shareholder and executive are closely aligned and linked. Shareholders as principals also rely on various governance mechanisms, such as boards of directors, government regulations, audits, and so forth, to keep agents "honest" through limiting the influence that their self-interest can have on their decisions. Through these governance mechanisms, principals are informed "about what the agent is actually doing," and thus the principals "are likely to curb agent opportunism because the agent will realize that he or she cannot deceive the principal."[15] Using the two methods in conjunction can be most cost-effective. According to agency theory, when neither outcome-based pay nor information systems are in place, high salaries, lucrative severance packages, and so forth tend to find their way into executive pay contracts, since they benefit executives but not shareholders.[16]

Technique vs. Social Philosophy

The shareholder model of the firm, based as it is on agency theory, assumes a constrained account of human nature. We have touched on this point already with the observation that agency theory presupposes narrowly self-interested, wealth-maximizing behavior on the part of principals and agents alike. Here, finance has borrowed heavily from classical liberal economic theory and its seedbed of philosophical liberalism. The discipline of finance regards individuals related by chosen roles (agents and principals), rather than persons sharing goals, communities, and cultures, as the central unit of analysis. On this basis, the shareholder model of the firm regards a pact between managers and shareholders to maximize shareholder value as the paradigm of business relationships: contracts backed by sanctions (legal or otherwise).

Proponents of the shareholder model of the firm hold that the discipline of finance consists in discovering and describing all the courses of action necessary to maintain any firm's long-term economic viability (cash flow, cost of capital, risk-to-return, etc.) so as to maximize shareholder wealth. Here, finance qualifies as a theory because it seeks a complete view of this question; it takes responsibility for working on and developing *all* possible means to the given end of shareholder wealth maximization. Since it strives to work out exhaustively all possible means for achieving narrowly—that is, precisely defined—shareholder objectives, finance must treat human beings and "human factors"—the skills of managers, the loyalty of customers, the efficiency of suppliers, no less than the labor of employees—as "organizational resources" to this end. This limited and mathematically quantifiable view of human nature allows the development of financial techniques. Put another way, financial thinking is deliberately *constrained* thinking. It is the discipline of thinking *as if* "good" could only mean "good for earnings" or "good for net profit" or "maximization of share price," so as to achieve the most exact and detailed view of how earnings or profits can be increased by all possible means, i.e., maximally. So-called "pure financial logic" does not *allow* wider knowledge of relationships among various goods to interfere with and complicate the exercise. This deliberate withdrawal from "thinking in the round" is the essence of technique and is necessary for the creation and development of a technical discipline.

Insofar as finance consists of a set of techniques or is considered a technical discipline, it is an essential component in the successful operation of a business. However, the deliberately constrained nature of its assumptions about the human person and what counts as the purpose and good of the business necessarily makes it unable to give a full and complete account of the nature and purpose of the business. Nevertheless, through the shareholder model, financial theorists, using agency theory, aim to do just that—define the overall purpose or "good" of the business organization. In doing so, finance has stepped beyond the realm in which it is competent (that of technique). It tries to set itself up as a *social philosophy* using agency theory as its philosophical basis (which is itself based on the wider philosophical tradition of liberalism). It no longer merely articulates techniques or aims to describe what effects will follow if certain financial measures are adopted; it goes much further than this, by prescribing what a business ought to be. That prescription is, necessarily, philosophically loaded.[17] As a social philosophy, finance proposes an understanding of private property (see Cortright and Pierucci, chapter 7), and a theory of what motivates people to act (see Kennedy, chapter 3, and Clark, chapter 5), two issues we examine in more detail at the end of this chapter.

While maintaining adequate return on capital employed is a crucial management issue for any firm, describing the whole purpose of the business as that of providing maximal return on capital radically impoverishes the idea of what a business is when compared to the reality of business life. According to Peter Drucker, shareholder return "is not the purpose of, but a limiting factor on, business enterprise and business activity."[18] Financial considerations involve no more than one function of the firm, and the whole work of the firm can hardly be reduced to one of its functions. Moreover, according to Drucker, the purpose of business must be found not in business, but in society, since the enterprise is an organ of society. Here Drucker begins to move us toward a common good model of the firm. His distinction between a function and the purpose of business points to a relationship that the shareholder model of the firm has reversed (see Koslowski, chapter 6).

For Drucker, the description of a firm's purpose according to the shareholder model fails the empirical test—that is, he thinks that many managers do not act according to this theory. Furthermore, Drucker maintains that it would be very dangerous to try to get managers to act according to the shareholder model. He argues that maximization of shareholder wealth "is a major cause of the misunderstanding of the nature of profit in our society and of the deep-seated hostility to profit which are among the most dangerous diseases of an industrial society."[19]

Drucker's insight points us toward understanding the importance of a richer model of the nature and purpose of the business based on the principle of the common good. The inadequacy of the shareholder model as a social philosophy is so obvious to most people in society that when managers and shareholders continue to uphold it, they threaten to undermine the very basis of business itself, namely, the acceptance on the part of the community of the positive contribution of the business sector to the good of society as a whole. If that acceptance is lost, and is instead replaced by a "deep-seated hostility to profit," then business leaders and their shareholders will have undermined the very institutions they claimed to be promoting.

The Common Good Model of the Firm

Our critique of agency theory is not designed to lead us to reject outright the discipline of finance. Finance is a critical function in any organization, and any realistic theory of the firm must incorporate it as part of its model. There is much to be gained, for example, from the emphasis in finance on important economic dimensions of the firm, such as: (1) shareholders ought to receive fair returns; (2) financial techniques can control costs so customers can pay lower prices; (3) governance mechanisms ought to be developed to reduce shirking; (4) efficiency must be achieved in economic exchanges; and so forth (see Koslowski's essay on the situation in Russia, chapter 6). However, when financial theorists find in these dimensions the whole account of the firm and thereby reduce all relationships to financial exchanges, they distort our understanding of the operation of a business. They have turned finance from being a source of essential and necessary techniques for managing the economic dimensions of the firm into a global philosophy of the firm that prescribes maximizing shareholder wealth as its normative basis. The discipline or function of finance now decrees how the firm *ought* to operate.[20] What we argue below is that a realistic theory of the firm must account for a richer notion of relationships than finance theory can provide. We call this theory the common good model of the firm.

At the heart of the common good model lies a distinction between two kinds of goods, "foundational" or instrumental goods (e.g., profits) and "excellent" or inherent goods (e.g., human development and community). Agency theory makes foundational goods supreme in its understanding of the firm. From the common good perspective, then, agency theory provides a deficient theory of the firm as a whole, even if its insights at the foundational level remain important. On the other hand, if these important but limited insights can be properly resituated within the common good model, then we can begin to create an effective model of the purpose of the firm, one that can make use of the effective financial management techniques that form part of the fruits of agency theory.

The distinction between foundational and excellent goods is based on a simple observation: some things we need and want in order to obtain other things, and some things we need and want just for themselves, even if they have no other "use" or value for us.[21] Foundational goods are of the first type, and excellent goods are of the second.[22] Many material and practical goods whose use involves their consumption, occupation, or exchange—money, profits, technology, real estate, capital equipment—fall into the category of foundational goods. They are as necessary to the firm's functioning as are air, food, and water to human functioning: without the latter goods, we die; without the former, the firm "dies." Since our need for foundational goods is all too urgent, concern for gaining them can sometimes crowd out our concern for the excellent goods. This is irrational, however, since we only need foundational goods *in order to obtain the excellent goods.* Money is a classic case in point: to want it for its own sake is irrational, for to do so is to make an end out of a means. Nevertheless, without enough money to live decently, the kind of goods and ends we hope for and pursue for their own sake are difficult if not impossible to achieve.

What we mean by excellent or inherent goods are those internal qualities which develop between human persons and within communities, such as friendship, personal cultivation, and moral self-possession. These goods in the workplace are often described in terms of virtues such as justice, prudence, courage, solidarity, and patience, that is, internal qualities that foster the growth of people and contribute to a community of persons. The reason why articulating the purpose of the firm in terms of these goods is so important is that all human work necessarily involves the promotion or distortion of the excellent goods of human development. When we work, we are not only creating added value and other forms of objective output that can be measured, financially or otherwise, but we are also at the same time forming ourselves as human persons. John Paul II calls this the subjective dimension of work.[23] We are developing new capacities, reinforcing those we have, helping others to develop their abilities and talents, and serving the wider community through the products and services we provide. Many of us have experienced the difference between organizations where these goods are actively valued and promoted and those where every excellent good is sacrificed to the profit motive. The excellent goods mark the "humanity" of an organization.

What we call excellent goods may, indeed, serve some further purpose in our lives,[24] but we nevertheless regard them as worthwhile in themselves even without this assumption. Similarly, we can talk of an "ennobling" of foundational goods when they are incorporated into our pursuit of excellent ends. Working may become, and ought to become, an exercise in developing human excellence: important foundational goods like profits, capital, technology, and production processes ought to be used to promote craftsmanship and skill development, powerful and fruitful relationships, a spirit of service to the community, a community of work, and so on. Just as four walls and a roof may be elevated to a work of fine art, and become nourishment for the spirit as well as shelter for the body, so too the work of an organization may become a source of nourishment for the spirit as well as a source of income for supplying our physical needs.

An analogy may help illustrate the difference between foundational and excellent goods. Thomas Aquinas argues that there are three basic human inclinations: (1) toward self-preservation; (2) toward the passing on and nurturing of life; and (3) toward living with others (social living) and toward knowledge and love of God. The last of these inclinations is based on the first two. If we do not take care of ourselves and, at least at the level of the human group, maintain openness to new human life, our social and spiritual inclinations have no foundation upon which they can flourish. However, if all we do is only aimed at self-preservation and procreation, we are operating out of a radically truncated view of the meaning of human life. Our desires for self-preservation and for procreation need to be ordered to our social and spiritual inclinations if we are to develop a *fully* human life.

Similarly, if a business does not create sufficient foundational goods, such as profit, there is no point trying to create a workplace where human development is valued, since the business has no hope of survival and is therefore ultimately irrelevant. At the same time, if a business organization is only concerned about profits, it is operating out of a radically truncated view of the purpose of the organization. The description of an organization simply in terms of foundational goods is insufficient and deficient. The firm is a community of persons who spend many hours working together and who are part of a wider community of customers, suppliers, and local residents, not to mention their own families. The firm is a site where excellent goods such as solidarity should be pursued, because human beings work within the firm and no human being should be reduced to a mechanism for producing money (a foundational good).

To repeat, profitability and efficiency are worthy goals because their realization is foundational to the development of the business as a whole. Nevertheless, the pursuit of foundational goods alone does not constitute a meaningful purpose for the firm. Foundational goods account neither for the ultimate motivation for our work as human beings, nor for the first principles of the business organizations in which we do our work, precisely because such foundational goods are not big enough to provide meaning to the human spirit.

The distinction between foundational and excellent goods gives us the basis for a working definition of the organizational common good: *the promotion of all the goods necessary for integral human development in the organization, in such a way as to respect the proper ordering of those goods.*

Given the distinction between foundational and excellent goods, we can take our critique of the shareholder model further by pinpointing two difficulties for which agency theory cannot account, but which in practice must be part of any theory of the firm: an understanding of property that is based on the principle of the universal destination of goods, and an understanding of the particular way people need to develop in work, that is, the idea of developing in virtue. What we begin to see very clearly in this discussion is that the shareholder model and the agency theory that informs it present a distinct set of values that, as we have argued, are in conflict with a view of the world that seeks moral and spiritual integration. As Charles Clark writes (chapter 5), every theory or model has a vision about what gets understood and measured and what gets ignored. The shareholder model holds up foundational goods as the purpose of the firm and either ignores or instrumentalizes excellent goods. As a result it operates under value-laden notions of property and persons.

Property: According to agency theory, the relationship of an owner to her stock in a public corporation is based on what Adolf A. Berle and Gardiner C. Means call the "traditional logic of property."[25] The financial relationship between the firm and its employees (wages), suppliers (payments), customers (affordable products), government (taxes), and so forth, is founded on the basis of generating shareholder wealth. A company's ability to raise capital today depends upon its cash-generating ability in the future. This cash-generating ability determines capital investment, which in turn determines shareholder wealth.[26]

Risk and return are the exclusive categories in terms of which property is evaluated. Managers, for example, are not responsible to customers or employees in the same sense that they are responsible to shareholders. They may respect employees or customers as one of their goals, not because of their dignity as human persons, but rather because respecting employees and customers generates greater return and less risk for shareholder wealth than not respecting them.[27]

By contrast, the common good model orders foundational goods such as property to the higher, more excellent goods precisely because goods, like capital, have a "universal destination," that is, ultimately they exist to serve the human race in general. Property and capital are meant to serve more than just the pecuniary interests of shareholders; systems of private property are justified insofar as they serve the wider common good. The basic value assumptions of agency theory mean that there is no way to express this underlying vision of the universal destination of goods within the shareholder model of the firm. The common good model, instead, works on the premise that all foundational goods, including goods we own as property, ought to be used in such a way that they promote the excellent goods, otherwise we have turned them into ends in themselves. Systems of ownership and private property exist so as to promote the universal destination of foundational goods, and these in turn should be used to promote the excellent goods of human development.

When Thomas Aquinas, for example, considers the distribution of economic goods, he frames the question in a way that respects the presumption that goods as such are a gift from God for the common benefit. He asks, *Is it ever licit to hold private property in the goods of the earth?*, thus acknowledging that, in the overall scheme of things, the earth is a gift for the benefit of all.[28] Thomas thinks that if human beings were not sinful, we would not need systems of private ownership; we would use the goods of the earth well without needing the incentives provided by private ownership. Instead, since we do in fact sin and misuse the goods of the earth, we need systems of private property in order to promote the universal destination of goods. He vindicates the right to private property by arguing that it leads to greater care for the goods of the earth, that it helps promote the creation of goods through the incentive to make more of what one owns, and that it tends to create peace in society. Thus, for Thomas, and for Catholic social thought, the right to property implies a duty to use that property to meet the common need and to promote the common good.[29]

Unfortunately, this social understanding of property faces an uphill battle with the current ownership patterns of publicly traded companies. Public companies are usually concerned with only one element of the relationship between shareholder and company: share price. This leads to a *disconnection* in the relationship between property holders, labor, and the communities in which the property exists.[30] This is why Jeff Gates's essay (chapter 12) on ownership is so important. The proposals he describes for financing techniques designed to encourage widespread ownership distribution, such as ESOPs (Employee Stock Ownership Plans), CSOPs (Customer Stock Ownership Plans), RESOPs (Related Enterprise Share Ownership Plans), and other stock ownership plans, are creative mechanisms toward operationalizing a theory of the firm that is consistent with the principle of the universal destination of material goods. These plans are not without their own problems and limitations, but if managed well, they can *reconnect* capital to the communities that generate it, and create the conditions for richer property relationships than those where the only value is financial.

One of the reasons why employee and community ownership has long been embraced as a preferred capital structure in the Catholic social tradition (see *Laborem exercens* 14, *Gaudium et spes* 71, *Mater magistra* 77, and *Quadragesimo anno* 65) is precisely because employee and community ownership increases the possibility for the common good model of the firm to become realized. Where ownership is personalized and localized, firms are more likely to be places where it is easier to promote the common good and, consequently, easier to promote human development.

Virtue: If we treat foundational goods as if they were excellent, we usually end up treating the excellent goods as foundational to the creation of more foundational goods. This inversion of goods, along with the inversion of the proper ordering of human intentions and action, frustrates the promotion of virtue, which is the development in the human person of the habit of correctly choosing and ordering means and ends. When such inversion takes place, we become the servants of the foundational goods. In other words, the pursuit of the excellent goods is frustrated. By raising shareholder wealth to the status of the chief good, the shareholder model in effect erects a "tyranny of foundational goods," inhibiting managers from considering more excellent goods except in instrumental terms. This reversal is a corruption of the traditional understanding of virtue. Ironically, Gordley argues in this volume that it is precisely this tried-and-tested understanding of virtue that is the only logical basis for profit seeking (chapter 4).[31] Instead, inverting means and ends creates a vicious (as opposed to "virtuous") and distorted environment at work, preventing the genuine growth of working people through their work.

Organizations actively trying to apply the shareholder model of the firm create an organizational culture where every action is instrumentalized toward financial gain. Managers may want to treat their employees justly, but they are only allowed to do so if it maximizes shareholder wealth. Since treating people justly is a good thing in itself (an excellent good) and loses its meaning and sense if it is *only* done as a means of maximizing a foundational good like shareholder wealth, the managers involved are left with a direct conflict of ends. This conflict is very likely, if nothing else, to compromise their integrity.[32]

Within the common good model of the firm, managers and employees are expected to create conditions within the firm that foster a holistic notion of human development. Managers, in particular, are called to the complex activity of explicitly and intentionally ordering a wide variety of goods in the course of managing the business. Through this explicit ordering of goods, the character of a manager is formed and he grows in virtue. Peter Drucker articulates the importance of integrity and virtue in management in this way:

> One can learn certain skills in managing people, for instance, the skill to lead a conference or to conduct an interview. One can set down practices that are conducive to development—in the structure of the relationship between manager and subordinate, in a promotion system, in the rewards and incentives of an organization. But when all is said and done, developing men still requires a basic quality in the manager which cannot be created by supplying skills or by emphasizing the importance of the task. *It requires integrity of character.* [33]

By integrity Drucker refers to consistency and unity of purpose in a person. This integrity cannot be achieved through techniques alone or through an inversion of ends and means. A person of integrity has the ability to integrate his intentions or purposes and his actions with a consistent vision or understanding of himself. Similarly, integrity in an organization means that its members are able to maintain and develop organizational conditions or structures that allow them, and those with whom they work, to become and to remain true to themselves.

Conclusion

In this essay, we have shown that agency theory, which is the normative basis of the shareholder model of the firm, promotes an instrumental rationality that inverts the relationship between foundational and excellent goods, thereby distorting our understanding of the universal destination of goods and the possibility for people to grow in virtue at work. The result is that shareholders can, and have, privatized the social benefits that should arise from their capital and that managers can, and have, lost their integrity as professionals. Our business economy, no matter the amount of profit generated, will always be moving in the direction of moral bankruptcy (and the resulting weakening of the social fabric upon which wealth generation relies) if relationships within business are regarded only as exchanges of material interests and if the purpose of the firm is regarded only as that of producing foundational goods.

The strength of the shareholder model lies in its emphasis on the foundational goods, just as its deficiency lies in its sole emphasis on those goods. That it remains the practical wisdom of most corporate organizations, demonstrates how crucial it is to accord financial and other instrumental goods *foundational* importance. As a foundational good, profit is a necessary means and serves, as John Paul II points out, as a "regulator" of organizational policy.[34] For all that, it remains a means in relation to the excellent ends of business activity.[35]

Notes

1. John Paul II, "A Message of His Holiness Pope John Paul II for the Celebration of the World Day of Peace," sec. 15, 1 January 2000 (author's emphasis), http://www.vatican.va/holy_father/john_paul_ii/messages/peace/documents/hf_jp-ii_mes_08121999_xxxiii-world-day-for-peace_en.html, accessed January 2001.

2. Robert Keen in a recent discussion paper writes: "Every study over the last decade, on both sides of the Atlantic, attests that corporate management remains persistently at the bottom of the league in any comparison of public perceptions of 'trustworthiness' among the professions. A Business Week–Harris Poll study in the United States in 1989 clearly denoted a strong public opinion that, in its quest for greater profits, business will not always be averse to harming the environment, endangering public health, selling inferior products and even putting workers' safety at risk. . . . Ten years on this perception has deteriorated further. A Leeds University study suggests that UK society is riddled with a mistrust of business, not believing that it cares about the community, the environment or even about customers as individuals. . . . A MORI/Financial Times poll reveals that business now attracts the lowest approval rating since records began. Asked 'Do you agree that the profits of large British companies make things better for everyone?' only 25% 'do' compared with 52% who 'do not.' This result is exactly the opposite of that recorded in the first such poll carried out in 1970. . . ." (See Robert Keen, "Knowing What the Right Thing Is," Discussion Paper 1 in the series *Ethics,*

Helen Alford, O. P., and Michael J. Naughton

Excellence and Leadership (Cambridge: Von Hugel Institute, St. Edmund's College, 2000), 2. The studies Keen cites to make these points are T. Lloyd, *The Nice Company* (London: Bloomsbury Publishing, 1990), 4; Leeds University, "Life at the End of the Twentieth Century" (cited in the *Times*, 5 September 1998); MORI/Financial Times Study (cited in the *Financial Times*, Weekend Money Section, 27 February 1999, 2) .

3. We have addressed these questions in our book *Managing as if Faith Mattered* (Notre Dame, Ind.: University of Notre Dame Press, 2001), which is the first volume in this series on the Catholic social tradition.

4. The reader may find this engagement between Catholic social thought and organizational purpose a rather odd or misguided attempt at mixing oil and water. Modern accounts of organizational purpose, some may argue, should not take religious traditions seriously because they are sectarian and because religious thought, unlike economics or philosophy, is a private rather than a public discipline. These are important objections. We live in a pluralistic culture. If we take this seriously, we should consider all relevant voices in a discussion over the purpose of the organization, whether they are religious or secular. Within a public debate, religious sources stand or fall on their own merits and should not be excluded on the basis of whether one accepts or rejects the particular tradition. For example, one would not avoid reading Karl Marx or Frederick Taylor simply because one is not a Marxist or Taylorist. The Catholic social tradition, with its communal orientation, provides an understanding of organizational purpose that is a serious alternative to that of classical or revised liberalism, and on that basis alone deserves consideration. (See José Casanova, *Public Religions in the Modern World* (Chicago: University of Chicago Press, 1994). See also David Hollenbach, *Catholicism and Liberalism* (Cambridge: University of Cambridge Press, 1994), 143, on the debate between Alasdair MacIntyre, who argues that we should bring the fullness of our traditions to bear on public argument, and John Rawls, who argues for a "method of avoidance."

5. For a typical textbook explanation of the shareholder model, see Eugene F. Brigham and Louis C. Gapenski, eds., *Financial Management: Theory and Practice*, 6th ed. (New York: Dryden Press, 1991), 14–15.

6. Vincent J. Tarascio, "Towards a Unified Theory of the Firm: An Historical Approach," *Atlantic Economic Journal* (September 1993): 10.

7. Michael C. Jensen and William H. Meckling, "Theory of the Firm: Managerial Behavior, Agency Costs and Ownership Structure," *Journal of Financial Economics* 3 (1976): 310 (emphasis in original).

8. Ibid. "In this sense the 'behavior' of the firm is like the behavior of a market; i.e., the outcome of a complex equilibrium process" (ibid., 311). See

Koslowski's discussion on spillover effect (chapter 6) and Tavis on agency theory (chapter 10).

9. Jensen and Meckling, "Theory of the Firm," 308. For a critique of this view of the firm see David W. Lutz, "Christian Social Thought and Corporate Governance, in *Religion and Public Life,* ed. Robert G. Kennedy et al. (Lanham, Md.: University Press of America, 2001), 121–40.

10. Within agency theory, there is a debate over whether the principal owns the firm as distinguished from owning the capital of the firm. See Benjamin M. Oviatt, "Agency and Transaction Cost Percentages on the Manager-Shareholder Relationship: Incentives for Congruent Interests," *Academy of Management Review* 13, no. 2 (1988): 214–25.

11. Jensen and Meckling, "Theory of the Firm," 308.

12. Brigham and Gapenski, *Financial Management,* 19.

13. Kathleen M. Eisenhardt, "Agency Theory: An Assessment and Review," *Academy of Management Review* 14, no. 1 (1989): 60.

14. For an extensive discussion on monitoring and policing shirking, see Armen A. Alchian and Harold Demsetz, "Production, Information Costs, and Economic Organization," *American Economic Review* (December 1972): 777–95.

15. Eisenhardt, "Agency Theory," 60.

16. Ibid., 64.

17. Dobson argues that "agency theory has led finance away from a conception of itself as strictly a descriptive and technical discipline. Agency theory, as the name implies, focuses on the 'agent,' a human being. Thus, finance is increasingly recognizing itself as a 'social' science in which human behavior and motivation are central." See John Dobson, *Finance Ethics* (Lanham, Md.: Rowman Littlefield Publishers, 1997), 90.

18. Peter F. Drucker, *Management* (New York: Harper and Row, 1974), 60.

19. Ibid. See also note 2 above on studies showing in what a bad light business is regarded by the general public.

20. Charles Perrow, *Complex Organizations: A Critical Essay* (New York: Random House, 1986), 222.

21. For a more extensive analysis of this distinction see chapter 2 of *Managing as if Faith Mattered.* This chapter explores a second level of analysis where we distinguish between "private," "individual," or "particular," and "public" or "common" goods. In concept, a common good is a human perfection or fulfillment achieved by a community, such that the community's members share it all together—i.e., as a community—and achieve it singly, in their persons. A common good, then, is *neither* a mere summing or balancing together of private and particular goods *nor* is it a good of the whole as opposed

to the goods of its members. On the basis of these comparisons, we offer a qualified critique of the *stakeholder model,* which understands the firm as a "balancer" (by means of negotiation) of the interests of its stakeholders. The stakeholder model, in its well-known forms, brings under management's purview the "interests" (as we understand them, the private and particular ends/ goods) of the members of various groups connected to the firm.

22. In other works, we have made the distinction between "foundational" and "excellent," using terms such as "instrumental" versus "inherent," or "extrinsic" versus "intrinsic," respectively. We choose the terms "foundational" and "excellent" because they convey the correct impression that both types of good are important in their own right.

23. John Paul II, *Laborem exercens,* 6.

24. Some writers would call such goods "mixed"; that is, they are (in our terms) both excellent (desirable in themselves) and foundational to the attainment of other goods.

25. Adolf A. Berle and Gardiner C. Means, *The Modern Corporation and Private Property,* rev. ed. (New York: Harcourt, Brace and World, 1967), 293–308. For a more extended analysis of Berle and Means see S. A. Cortright, Ernest Pierucci, and Michael Naughton, "A Social Property Ethic for the Corporation in Light of Catholic Social Thought," *Logos* (Fall 1999): 138–54.

26. Alfred Rappaport, *Creating Shareholder Value* (New York: The Free Press, 1986), 22.

27. We are grateful to David Lutz for this insight.

28. See *Summa Theologiae* II-II, q. 66, a. 2.

29. For more on Thomas's understanding of property and its relationship to corporate ownership see our book *Managing As If Faith Mattered,* chapter 6.

30. It is interesting that agency theory rests much of its descriptive power on the separation of ownership and management. If firms, for example, are employee-owned, the need for agency theory in terms of its ability to describe shirking, monitoring, contracts, and other items lessens, since managers and employees are now the principals and there are few agency costs (see Jensen and Meckling, "Theory of the Firm," 330).

31. For a different view on this inversion as it relates to governance and industrial relations see Koslowski, chapter 6.

32. Alchian and Demsetz, for example, explain that the "relationship of each team member to the *owner* of the firm . . . is simply a 'quid pro quo' contract. Each makes a purchase and a sale." Armen A. Alchian and Harold Demsetz, "Production, Information Costs, and Economic Organization," *American Economic Review* (December 1972): 783. It is interesting to note

that people who advocate a neoclassical agency theory will compare the firm to a game of poker, other games, and to policing (see Jensen and Meckling, "Theory of the Firm," 334 n. 39).

33. Peter Drucker, *The Practice of Management* (New York: Harper and Row Publishers, 1982), 348 (authors' emphasis).

34. See John Paul II, *Centesimus annus,* 35.

35. See John XXIII, *Mater et magistra,* 83; John Paul II, *Centesimus annus,* 41.2. Maximizing shareholder wealth is a relatively clear, precise, and measurable end. Contributing to full human development, as the purpose of the organization, will always generate more questions than answers for managers. Yet, if managers see themselves as professionals and not as mere technicians, such ambiguity is inescapable. Human decision making, even in corporations, cannot be reduced to one simple formula. See William F. May, "The Beleaguered Rulers: The Public Obligation of the Professional," *Kennedy Institute of Ethics Journal* 2 (1992): 28.

3

The Virtue of Solidarity and the Purpose of the Firm

ROBERT G. KENNEDY

One of the first things you hear upon entering a business school is references to something called the "real world." This "real world" consists of concrete, contingent things, current business practices, rules of the market, black-letter laws, and statistics. It dictates what you can and can't do. Some students enter business school infatuated with this world. They want to live in it and don't want to change it in any fundamental way. It smacks of certainty and promise and appeals to those who pride themselves on having their feet planted squarely on the ground. Neither immoral nor amoral, the real world does not preclude morality—it just has a hard time making it fit in. . . . You can't teach ethics to business students without first forcing them to confront their childlike faith in things like the rules of the market.

— Joanne Ciulla (1991)[1]

The great problems affecting culture today originate in the desire to separate public and private life from a true scale of values. No economic or political model will fully serve the common good if it is not based on the fundamental values which correspond to the truth about the human person. . . . Systems which raise economic concerns to the level of being the sole determining factor in society are destined, through their own internal dynamism, to turn against the human person.

— Pope John Paul II[2]

Those of us in the academy are often reminded by others that, whatever else it is, the workplace we inhabit is "not the real world." The real world is the world of business, or politics and law, or healthcare, or social work, or some other activity that comes into contact with and struggles to overcome the problems of life. By contrast, a college or university is an artificial environment, a place to discuss ideals not realities, a place where mistakes are only practice and do not really count.

Those of us who work professionally in ethics receive a double dose of this reminder. After all, ethicists are thought to dream about how things ought to be, about how things would be if the world were a better place. It is commonly supposed that we think about rules to impose on others who are compelled to grapple with the hard realities of life. We encourage naive students to altruism and pass judgment on those outside the academy who fail to embody our ideals. Nevertheless, the real world is still hard, competitive, unforgiving, and demanding, and all the musings of ethicists (and theologians) cannot change its aspect.

Of course, the situation is not improved at all for those of us who are concerned about ethics within the context of a faith tradition. The general problem that we face is how Catholic social thought can be integrated successfully with sound business practice. Or, to put it a bit differently, does the Catholic social tradition have anything to offer the practical disciplines of management and business administration?

To that question, at least two approaches may be taken. The first is what we might call the *economic paradigm,* on which the shareholder model is based. This paradigm has its roots both in the individualistic philosophies of the past few centuries and in the heavily quantified economic theories of the twentieth century. The question of what a firm is and should be has received a great deal of attention within this context (to say nothing of the Nobel prize that Ronald Coase won in 1991 for his contribution to the discussion). As within any school of thought, there is considerable disagreement among adherents to this point of view about the specifics of the nature and purpose of the firm,

but there is a great deal of consensus about the principles that underlie the discussion. These principles are also widely influential in shaping the conceptual framework within which most managers practice
their trade.

The other approach, of course, comes via the Catholic social tradition, which has had rather little to say about the character of intermediate associations such as business firms, but which possesses a depth
and breadth that may permit us to draw some solid conclusions (see
Calvez and Naughton, chapter 1, on Catholic social teaching and the
firm). The purpose of this chapter is to explore these two models in an
effort to understand more clearly what makes a firm genuinely good
and whether the virtue of solidarity, so fundamental to Catholic social
thinking, has any relevance for the management of the good firm.

We might make a good beginning by considering what conclusions are available to us as possible outcomes of our investigation. We
might, for instance, end our investigation by concluding that the fundamental assumptions of the economic paradigm are true, and that we
need to rethink the Catholic social tradition wherever its principles are
in conflict with this paradigm. This is the conclusion preferred by most
economists, by many business people, and by anyone who insists upon
a sharp distinction between the world of theories and principles and
the real world. It is also the conclusion of a handful of ethicists and
management scholars who see ethics (and the Catholic social tradition
by implication) as an instrument offering a competitive advantage to
organizations that commit to it.

A second possibility is that the axioms of the economic paradigm
are true, but that their practical implications may be "adjusted" a bit
by our tradition so as to achieve a marginally more just outcome or
slightly more respect for human dignity. On this view, the vision of the
Catholic social tradition is an unrealizable ideal, but its presence in the
marketplace of ideas might soften the harsh realities of the economy,
just as, say, the tradition of just war theory may restrain here and there
the worst excesses of military enthusiasm. Many Christians, even those
who are proponents of the Catholic social tradition, are inclined to this
view. Some of these believe that the economic paradigm may be true
enough, but only because the world, and so also the business system, is
a corrupt and fallen place in need of conversion and reform. Therefore

to conduct oneself in a morally worthy way in this world it is necessary to abandon self-interest (which is merely selfishness under another name) and to embrace sacrifice: of income, of career ambitions, and of whatever other rewards might accompany "success" in business. Other Christians think that the real world has a bad reputation it does not deserve, that business is not so corrupt after all, and that modest adjustments to business practice under the influence of the Catholic social tradition really are achievable.

The third possibility is that the economic paradigm is founded upon several false but seductive propositions. In this case, assuming the Catholic social tradition is grounded in the truth, the falsity of the economic paradigm must be exposed and the greater practical utility of our tradition must be explained and demonstrated. This is, I believe, the posture of the popes of the last century or so, including John Paul II. Even so, it is not an inviting conclusion. If true, it calls for a kind of evangelization and conversion that will be painful for everyone involved, and that will require some very serious intellectual work and aggressive demonstrations that the principles of the Catholic social tradition really are practical. We may be inclined to accept this third possibility as the true conclusion, but if it is we should be strongly cautioned against underestimating the difficulty of carrying through the project it implies.

Principles of the Economic Paradigm

The tension between the economic paradigm and the Catholic social paradigm is quite real. Its roots, however, lie not so much in different descriptions of the way in which business is conducted as in philosophical differences; that is, in different conceptions of the human person and of what it means for a person to be practically rational. These differences can be reduced to three basic convictions, two of which we will consider now and a third to which we will return later.

The first conviction in the economic paradigm is that human beings are, by nature, solitary individuals. That is to say, human communities are instruments for the satisfaction of the needs and desires of the individuals who constitute them. If there were a successful way of providing for individual satisfactions without communities, so much the better, because social life inevitably imposes constraints on the pursuit of individual happiness. Implicit in this conviction is a view of the common good for a society that maintains that the best society would be one in which such a balance of liberties and protections exists as to provide the greatest practical opportunities for seeking individual satisfactions. Proponents of this view are philosophical descendants, consciously or otherwise, of such early modern philosophers as Thomas Hobbes and John Locke.

The second conviction is that human happiness consists principally in possessing and experiencing. In other words, the happiest person would be one who had the largest quantity of desirable possessions coupled with an indefinite series of the most pleasurable experiences. Of course, this description seems quite familiar, especially for Americans, for whom the pursuit of things and pleasures has come to be the stuff of the American dream. But then, considering the number of people who wish to emigrate to America (or at least the America they imagine), the dream clearly knows no national boundaries.

At minimum, two things follow from this conviction about the nature of happiness. First, since property is so crucial to individual fulfillment, a good society is one in which individual rights to property are strenuously protected. Not only are property rights extensive (most "things" may be individually owned), but they may be almost unqualified. What qualifications exist are defended on the basis of expediency. (For example, someone might say that, although taxes to support welfare benefits are a seizure of an individual's property, it may be necessary to do this to prevent destructive class conflict, thereby protecting what remains of that person's property.) Ownership is effectively separated from responsibility.

A second implication is that the important aspects of work, especially in the context of employment, are almost entirely objective. That is, we address work adequately as a human phenomenon if we focus our attention on the external (to the worker) effects of the work and on the external rewards it brings. Work is good to the extent that it is useful to others and to the extent that it brings valuable possessions or experiences to the worker. We might even say that from the perspective of the worker, the only bad work is work that is poorly compensated. If we pay someone enough, the most isolated, tedious, dangerous, unpleasant job becomes a good job.

Principles of the Catholic Social Tradition

The Catholic social tradition also has something to say about the nature of the human person and human happiness, but its convictions are quite different.

This tradition denies that human persons are radically solitary and insists instead that we are naturally social. Communities are not expedient artifacts that serve as more or less imperfect instruments for promoting human happiness; they are integral elements of that happiness. Not only is human satisfaction impossible outside of a community, but we might even say that a human person permanently detached from a community can never be fully human. Indeed, in the ordinary course of events, individuals come to be in the context of the community created by a husband and wife, are educated within the community that is the city, and live their lives within a web of relationships. When someone is involuntarily detached from his community (as a refugee, for example), we are urgently concerned to find a community into which to reinsert him. If this fails, he is in danger of becoming, practically speaking, a nonperson.

The Catholic social tradition insists, then, that it is a serious mistake to assume that communities are merely instrumental in human life; they are in fact integral to and inseparable from human fulfillment. Indeed, social collaboration (one of whose highest forms is friendship) is a basic human good. Some associations or communities may certainly be no more than instruments at times, and some people may tend to instrumentalize every community to which they belong with the intention of achieving their own fulfillment, but the importance of community in human life is much greater than this alone. One consequence of this position is that the proper definition of the common good for a society is not simply a matter of liberties and protections, but is instead the complete set of conditions necessary for every member of the community to flourish *as a member of the community.*

The character of human flourishing is the substance of the second conviction. While things and experiences may be instruments or even elements of human fulfillment, human happiness most properly involves acting and being. In other words, genuine human fulfillment consists in being a certain sort of person and in being capable of acting in certain ways. The economic paradigm sees happiness as something that someone has (that is, as something external, like a possession, or something passive, like an experience), while the Catholic tradition insists that happiness is a dynamism or activity (that is, something internal, like one's character, or active, like one's performance or the personal relationships in which one participates).

While the American dream may sometimes be represented in terms of possessions and experiences, it is nevertheless the case that a common and pitiable character in American popular culture is the man who is rich in possessions and poor in relationships. (A. P. Kirby in Frank Capra's *You Can't Take It with You* and Henry Potter in his *It's a Wonderful Life* are classic examples.) The American myth is a portrait of the rugged individual; the American reality is neighbors spontaneously pitching in to help one another in times of trouble. We do not really believe in self-reliance as much as we believe in mutual support. Indeed, we count it as a national strength that, in spite of a multitude of differences, Americans find ways to collaborate with fierce commitment when it is necessary to do so. We argue so passionately about our common life because we think it is so important, not because we would rather be left alone.

This second conviction, that human flourishing is a matter of "being" rather than "having," affects the character of property rights. There is no particular reason why the right of individuals to own certain kinds of property cannot be as extensive as under the economic paradigm. The conditions attached to property rights, however, are much more significant. The tradition acknowledges that all of creation is the work of a benevolent God, and therefore must insist that anything that might be the object of a property right—from land to tools to knowledge—is potentially intended for the good of the entire human community. As Pope John Paul II has put it: "Private property . . . is under a 'social mortgage.'"[3] Furthermore, since property is instrumental for, but not constitutive of, genuine human flourishing, it is possible for an individual to have more than he needs. Even if he has earned his possessions through honest work, others in real need may have a legitimate claim on his surplus. Here, though, the explanation for the claim is not expediency but rather a moral obligation, in justice, to address the real needs of others.

Once again, in various ways, our actual cultural practices belie the economic paradigm. We are quite prepared, for instance, to spend great sums of public money to save the life of someone in peril, as evidenced by the investment that any community of size makes in emergency equipment and personnel. And consider that a significant portion of the cost of our military comes from our determination to protect the lives of soldiers and sailors, making equipment of all sorts more expensive, requiring more extensive training, and so on. (The Japanese, for example, were astonished at the willingness of the American military to risk and sacrifice equipment for the sake of personnel. The Japanese, as a matter of policy, would never risk a submarine to rescue a single downed pilot, while the Americans regarded rescue operations as a routine task for their submarines.)

Finally, the Catholic social tradition attributes to human work a richness unknown under the economic paradigm. While acknowledging the importance of the objective or external dimension of work, the tradition calls special attention to the subjective dimension of work. This dimension concerns the effect that the work done has upon the worker. There is a rich literature on this topic, and I can only scratch the surface here. The key concept, however, may be (again, in John Paul II's words) that all work is ultimately *for* the person; the person is not *for* work. No work, in other words, however richly compensated, is sufficiently important to justify the dehumanization of the worker. Furthermore, while employment must surely be fairly compensated, the best work is not necessarily the work with the best pay. It is the work that most completely draws out the potential of the worker and develops him as a human person, a point brought out in more detail in Murphy and Pyke's essay on job design (chapter 13).

The Catholic paradigm results in a more expansive view of the functions and purposes of a business firm than that which results from the economic paradigm. A firm exists to create wealth and to satisfy customers, but this is not all. Since work on this view contributes to what a person becomes, not merely to what he has, and since participation in friendships and communities is good in itself, the business firm has a richer set of functions and a broader set of goals. Additional criteria must be invoked to judge whether a certain firm functions well or badly. These criteria include an evaluation of the work itself, of the character of the firm as a community, and of the contribution the firm makes to the common good of the society.

Clearly these two paradigms—the economic paradigm and the Catholic paradigm—are in sharp contrast to one another. This contrast is also evident in what is recognized as rational behavior within each paradigm.

Under the economic paradigm, rational behavior is essentially utility-maximizing or wealth-maximizing behavior. One participates in relationships and in communities in order to acquire the possessions and experiences that are understood to constitute satisfaction and happiness. The thoroughly rational person here is careful to calculate how this relationship will be useful or that one pleasant. Strictly speaking, promises and other commitments are rationally and ethically binding only to the extent that they can be expected to be useful or pleasant. It would be irrational to be faithful or honest in any given situation if the result, in however long a term, would be neither useful nor pleasant. What saves most of us from being thoroughly rapacious and untrustworthy, according to this paradigm, are both formal constraints (laws, for example) and the recognition that (as the game theorists tell us) fidelity and honesty are more likely over the long run to increase utility and pleasure. Hence we have a sketch of what passes for sound business practice: don't lie, cheat, or steal, except perhaps in those circumstances in which you may clearly get away with it.

Rationality in the Catholic social tradition takes on a different character. Since human fulfillment consists in being and acting, practical rationality requires that a person seek to develop a certain character (that is, to become virtuous), which in turn both depends upon and results in acting well. It is rational to be faithful and honest, not only because this is likely to maximize utility or pleasure (and the tradition would not deny this), but principally because these are components of acting well and developing more fully as a person. To put it another way, the person who lies habitually, or who is honest only because he is constrained by the prospect of punishment, is an underdeveloped person and fails to achieve happiness to the extent that he *is* underdeveloped.

Furthermore, since human persons are understood to be essentially social, practical rationality requires behavior that supports the common good of the various communities of which they are members. Acting so as to diminish the set of conditions that support human flourishing in a community, or so as to decrease the likelihood of an association's reaching its common goal, would be irrational. A more mature, more fully developed person would be committed to acting in such a way as to achieve or sustain the common good of any community of which he was a member. Such a person, in the language of the Catholic social tradition, would possess the virtue of solidarity.

The Purpose of the Firm

A business firm, like any human institution, is an artifact, something that people make deliberately. The purpose of any artifact, including a business firm, is to bring some human good into being, either directly (as in a work of art) or indirectly (as in a tool). One artifact may be better than another in several different ways. It may be better because it brings about a good more fully, or because it brings about a better good. If it is a tool, it is superior if it brings about its proper good more efficiently, or with more certainty, or if it is useful for producing more than one good effectively.

These criteria can also be applied in combination. For example, the page of a medieval manuscript might be a good artifact if it communicates clearly; that is, if it is legible, properly spelled, and so forth. It may, however, be an excellent artifact if, in addition to its textual function, it is also illuminated and therefore a work of art. We often apply aesthetic criteria to very functional artifacts, concluding that a tool that performs its function well becomes better if it is also elegant and aesthetically pleasing. And we criticize the maker or the designer for missing an opportunity by constructing functional but ugly artifacts.

By the same token, a human association is an artifact that deserves to be judged on a combination of criteria. Some associations, such as friendships, bring about a human good directly, the good of participation in community. Others are instrumental by design, which means that they are intentionally directed to some goal outside themselves, but like the best tools, they are superior when they bring about other goods as well.

According to the economic paradigm, a business firm is strictly instrumental. That is, the proper activities of a business firm are entirely directed to goods that are external to the firm itself (even those internal activities that are necessary to maintain the firm in a "healthy" state are ultimately directed to the achievement of these external goods). Further, the purposes for forming or participating in a firm are also instrumental. A firm is established to create wealth for the shareholders, who will use that wealth for their individual purposes, and it produces goods and services that customers will once again use for their own satisfaction. Nor is participation in the firm's proper activities by employees understood to be intrinsically valuable. Since, on the economic paradigm, work is purely instrumental, so also is the activity of employees as members of the firm.

A good firm will be one that succeeds in efficiently producing goods and services that customers are willing to pay for, and so creates a significant amount of wealth for shareholders. The fair and respectful treatment of employees is not a good in itself, but an appropriate means of accomplishing the ultimate (though still instrumental) goal of wealth creation. Incompetent managers may make the firm a less effective instrument for this goal, but they do not destroy by their incompetence a good intrinsic to the firm. Indeed, it would not be too much to say that on this model it is no part of the firm's purpose to attend to other, non-instrumental human goods, except perhaps to the extent that such goods (beauty, community, skillful performance, knowledge), when realized, help to attract and retain employees whose labor will benefit the shareholders (see Naughton and Alford's essay which develops this critique, chapter 2).

By contrast, the Catholic social tradition proposes a richer conception of the firm, one which sees in the formation of such an association the real possibility of bringing about much more than the instrumental good of wealth.[4] The creation of wealth is a good thing, but not in and of itself. It is good only if we can give a satisfactory answer to the question of what it is to be used for, a point well developed in Gordley's essay (chapter 4). The creation of wealth for the purpose of prosecuting an unjust war is simply not good, nor is the creation of wealth that requires the destruction of other human goods along the way.

The Catholic social tradition, in my judgment, applauds the creation of wealth when it is likely to be used well and when the process of its creation brings about other human goods to the extent possible. A business firm, then, realizes its potential not simply when it conforms to the criteria of efficiency and effectiveness (though it certainly must do this), but when it also becomes a real human community and contributes to the genuine development of the persons who participate in its activities. A good firm on the Catholic model is not one that rejects the criteria of the economic paradigm; it is rather one that meets these criteria and more. *The problem is not that we expect too much of firms, but rather that we are prepared to settle for too little.* An example of how a firm can be more than we have come to expect can be found in the concept of solidarity.

Business and the Virtue of Solidarity

Solidarity has entered the common language of the Catholic social tradition over the past fifteen years partly because of the emphasis placed upon it by Pope John Paul II. In particular, he has frequently insisted that business needs to be characterized by solidarity, by a firm commitment to the common good and a determination to consider the impacts of its decisions on others, especially employees and the poor.[5]

But is the principle of solidarity, which calls businesspeople to be mindful of the impacts of their decisions on others and to make courses of action that benefit others a priority in their decision making, consistent with sound business practice? John Paul II emphatically believes that it is, and it will repay us to consider briefly why he thinks this is so.

The object of the virtue of solidarity is the just society, characterized first by right relationships among all of its members, and second by fairness in the distribution of resources, knowledge, opportunities, cultural participation, and anything else that may be needed for human flourishing. (Note that fairness here *does not* necessarily mean equality, nor does it mean that differences in distribution cannot result from laziness or bad choices in general. It *does* mean that differences in distribution will not be the result of selfishness, dishonesty, and abuses of power.) Given the reality of personal sin, a just society is not the ordinary human condition. It is rather something that must be laboriously built and continuously sustained; hence the need for solidarity.

In speaking to business leaders and intellectuals in Santa Cruz, Bolivia, John Paul II explained:

> The just society to which we all aspire is constructed day by day through the collaboration of all its members, fulfilling in this way the loving vocation with which God entrusted human beings when creating them. To construct a city, we might say, is to construct humanity; that is, taking the complete and integral human being as the measure and goal of all social activity, we create the necessary conditions so that each and every member of the human community can realize his full potential.[6]

Business cannot be insensitive to this project because, among other things, one of the characteristics of modern life is extensive interdependence. Few communities of any kind can exist successfully in isolation now; few, no matter how large or small, can truly be self-sufficient. This is not a regrettable situation, and I have no doubt that in John Paul II's mind it is part of the unfolding of the divine plan. Nevertheless, it does require that each of us, especially those with decision-making responsibilities, recognize this interdependence and act accordingly. Business, too, is caught up in this interdependence, both internally and with respect to the larger community. As John Paul II pointed out to managers and workers in Verona, Italy,

> The first characteristic of a modern firm and of its social function, in [the] context of great complexity, is without doubt that of interdependence. Each of its components is equally necessary, and it is useless to speculate about the primacy of one or another of them. However, there is a similar interdependence between society and the world of industry and services; society has need of what is provided by the activities of production, and these latter, in turn, have need both of the outlet offered by society in terms of its purchasing capacity and of the resources it provides in the form of potential workers, investments, and technology. We are all aware that that interdependence is no longer contained within the boundaries of a society or nation, but extends to continental and intercontinental dimensions.[7]

The result is that the problems of the community as a whole (including the global community) are also, in some instances, the problems of businesses as well. More precisely, there are kinds of problems—unemployment, unfulfilled needs for goods and services, needs for investment opportunities and resources, and so on—that business may naturally address, if it chooses to do so. To be sure, businesses legitimately aim to make a profit, but that is not their only purpose. They have an appropriate contribution to make to the society, and they must not shut themselves off from that society.

This is not to say, however, that businesses have a generalized duty to use their resources to address whatever problems happen to be significant in the communities in which they operate (a standard conception of corporate social responsibility theorists, but one that I do not find emphasized in John Paul II). This is a point further developed by Fort in his essay on intermediate institutions (chapter 11). Rather, businesses have a duty to conduct their operations by choosing courses of action that deliberately support not only the common good of the businesses itself, but the common good of the society as well. To business leaders in Rome, John Paul II explained that

> Even if a business is an economic entity, even if it is one of the things that are essential for an area's prosperity, it cannot be reduced to that alone. Inasmuch as it is a community of persons, it is basically a human structure whose activity and economic and technological involvement must be inspired by and oriented to the ethical and moral values of justice and social solidarity."[8]

In a similar vein, he stated in Lima, Peru, that

> One cannot but lament the fact that there are a number of employers—in different areas of business—who do not respond to the gifts they have received and who appear to ignore their responsibility towards those who work in the company and towards the whole of society. Some seem to forget that they should indeed be the organizers of wealth, but always people who have the common good as their goal; they should not be carried away by the sole desire for what is useful to themselves alone.[9]

The businessperson that John Paul II has in mind—whether entrepreneur or manager—has a set of functions, both internal and external to the business, and a set of duties that accompany those functions. Among these functions are the organization of work, the creation and production of goods and services that truly contribute to human fulfillment, the creation of wealth, and, in general, the humanization of economic activity. The related duties require that the activities of the business are properly oriented toward the good of others, and the businessperson's firm commitment to fulfill these duties is the virtue of solidarity.

The Utility of the Catholic Social Tradition

Now what about this application of the concept of solidarity is inconsistent with sound business practice? Solidarity does not require businesspeople to sacrifice their own welfare for the sake of others, though it may sometimes require them to choose courses of action that will not produce the greatest possible economic reward (at least in the short term). It may also require them to make moral evaluations of the goods and services the business produces, and to choose not to produce those that tend to undermine the good of the persons they are intended to serve. And it may require them to ensure that the workplaces they manage are truly characterized by fairness and a concern for the development of the worker in addition to efficiency in production. But is this not consistent with many of the best examples of management practice? Why do we think that a tension exists between sound business practice and Catholic social thought?

The reason, I think, brings us back to the beginning of this essay and the conflict I explored between the economic paradigm and the Catholic paradigm. On a philosophical level this conflict is quite genuine; the basic assumptions of the two paradigms are indeed contrary propositions. However, if we press the economic paradigm a bit further, we may often find that its defenders are somewhat reluctant to say that human persons *are* naturally solitary, or that their genuine fulfillment *does* lie in possessions and experiences. Instead, they may say that observations of human behavior suggest very strongly that people *behave* as if these propositions were true, and that the paradigm simply aims to describe and predict behaviors.

Perhaps this is so. In a sinful world, we often do act selfishly, and we often do pursue goals that appear good for us but probably are not. This is nothing new. If the economic paradigm said nothing more than this, we could easily reconcile it with the Catholic paradigm by noting that people often make choices that are inconsistent with authentic human flourishing, and that these choices often constitute a pattern (see, for example, John Paul II's comments about "structures of sin").[10] Nevertheless, better choices are possible, and the best choices—as well as the best business practices—are based on a sound understanding of the reality about human beings, not merely their frequent behavior patterns.

In this regard, the Catholic paradigm is richer and stronger in its explanatory power. It can account for the behaviors observed by the economists, but the economists have limited ability to account for behaviors that fall outside their paradigm. The reality is that while people often do seek individual satisfaction, they also flee from loneliness; and while they often do seek to accumulate possessions, at times of crisis they often abandon their possessions before they abandon their friends.

The economic paradigm is powerful in the context of business partly because it systematically ignores many of its harmful consequences (for example, unstable employment, inequitable distributions of wealth, wasteful and harmful products and processes, dehumanized workplaces, and so on). The criteria of business success that it proposes take no account of these consequences unless they provoke a response that affects one of the criteria. It is not an accident that one of the most popular authors in the United States is Scott Adams, the cartoonist who created *Dilbert*. Adams holds up a mirror to corporate America and ruthlessly exposes the pain, waste, and frustration generated by a soulless application of the economic paradigm. Tens of millions of American employees understand all too clearly what Adams is depicting.

There is more to life than profit, market share, and other narrowly defined measures of economic success. Even so, the third basic conviction of the economic paradigm, to which I alluded at the beginning of the chapter, discourages us from embracing this larger vision and attempting to reconcile the paradigm with Catholic social thought. This is the conviction that most of the regularities identified by economics and related disciplines are immutable laws (for example, Ricardo's iron law of wages) to which business practice is subject. The Catholic tradition disagrees. Pope John Paul II has often lamented the fact that the "laws" of economics are not sufficiently placed at the service of humanity but instead are too frequently used to dominate people.

The conviction of the Catholic tradition is that we can choose differently. The "laws" of economics can be amended to place them at the service of human flourishing and the common good, and more human considerations can be introduced as part of the definition of genuine success in business. What is required is a more comprehensive vision of the proper function of business in society, clearer practical guidelines about how management professionals can give life and breath to that function, and a firm commitment to move forward. In short, what is needed is informed solidarity.

Notes

1. Joanne Ciulla, "Business Ethics as Moral Imagination," in *Business Ethics: The State of the Art,* ed. R Edward Freeman (New York: Oxford University Press, 1991), 213 ff.

2. John Paul II, *Dignity of Work,* ed. Robert Kennedy, Gary Atkinson, and Michael Naughton (Lanham, Md.: University Press of America, 1995), 50.

3. John Paul II, *Sollicitudo rei socialis,* 42.

4. As an aside, it is worth observing that the Church has long held a mixed judgment about wealth. On the one hand, it is crucially necessary for many of the Church's missions, but on the other, it is suspect for its ability to distract and to tempt men to evil. This mixed judgment also extends to the business firm, partly because any institution whose stated purpose is the accumulation of wealth aims at a questionable goal, but also because it seems to neglect other human goods.

5. John Paul II, *Sollicitudo rei socialis,* 38–40.

6. John Paul II, *The Dignity of Work,* 45.

7. Ibid., 126.

8. Ibid., 81–82.

9. Ibid., 54.

10. John Paul II, *Sollicitudo rei socialis,* 36.

4

Virtue and the Ethics of Profit Seeking

JAMES GORDLEY

Economists presuppose that a firm maximizes its profits. Lawyers say that its managers are under a fiduciary duty to do so. Should a firm always do so? What if the managers could increase their profits by marketing junk or worse, by downgrading jobs, or by firing employees who are unlikely to find other work?

Proponents of the shareholder model of corporate responsibility say that managers should simply try to make a profit within the limits the law allows. To many people that model seems ethically untenable. The alternative they usually offer is a stakeholder model in which managers have responsibilities not only to owners but also to customers, suppliers, employees, the local community, and anyone else their decisions might affect. S. A. Cortright and Ernest S. Pierucci claim that this model is the only alternative to a shareholder model that "liberalism" can offer (chapter 7). The trouble with it, as contributors in section 2 of this volume explain in more detail, is that it does not indicate how to weigh the conflicting claims of these groups. It does not explain why the management's responsibility to make a profit for shareholders seems basically different from its other responsibilities. Moreover, these essays point out that the ethical foundation of the stakeholder model is not clear, particularly if we imagine each of these groups to be out for itself.

To answer such questions as these, we must ask why a firm should pursue profit at all. In thinking about that question, all of us are influenced by economists' descriptions of how the economy works. One account is given in almost every basic textbook on economics. An advanced book on fundamental economic principles—for example, Paul Samuelson's *Foundations of Economic Analysis*[1]—is a mathematically sophisticated version of it. This account starts with self-seeking agents: consumers who maximize the satisfaction of their preferences within the limits of their resources, and firms that maximize their profits. It then explains how, through self-seeking, preferences are satisfied to the maximum extent possible given the initial stock of resources, the initial distribution of them, and the technological possibilities for using resources to satisfy preferences. When preferences are satisfied to the maximum extent possible given these constraints, economists say that the economic system is "efficient."

Some economists draw normative conclusions from this account. They think that efficiency is normatively valuable—that it is an objective that we ought to strive for. From the standpoint of a traditional moralist, that position sounds odd. It sounds like saying that selfishness is a good thing. And yet, it would be odd if this position were totally wrongheaded. Most of the time we want the economy to be efficient, and we seek the economists' guidance as to how it can be more so. We have to ask, then, why and when efficiency is normatively valuable. If we answer that question, we may be able to see why and when a firm should try to make a profit.

To answer it we need conceptual tools that economics itself does not provide. In particular, the moral philosophy of Aristotle and St. Thomas Aquinas provides the tools we need, above all, the concept of virtue as Aristotle and Thomas understood it. The goals of efficiency, wealth maximization, and therefore profit maximization are normatively valuable only on the assumption that people are actually practicing the virtues that Aristotle and Thomas describe but which the economists never mention. Ethical problems arise for the managers of firms whenever that assumption no longer holds.

Aristotle and Thomas: The Virtues and Economic Life

For Aristotle and Thomas, virtues are acquired abilities to live the kind of life that is right for a human being, a life that most fully realizes his human potential. Living this sort of life constitutes human goodness and happiness. The four key human virtues, for Aristotle and Thomas, are prudence, justice, courage, and temperance.

Through prudence, a person recognizes what actions are appropriate or inappropriate for living such a life.[2] For Aristotle and Thomas, the sorts of behavior that economists describe as preference satisfaction and profit seeking were both exercises of this virtue. When a person decides how to spend his money, he exercises the virtue of *prudentia œconomica* which is usually translated as "economic prudence" or "household management."[3] When he seeks a profit, he exercises a different judgmental ability, which Thomas calls *pecuniativa*.[4] For Aristotle and Thomas, spending money and making profits are good, like all other human activities, to the extent that they contribute to one's ultimate end. The point of spending money is to acquire things that contribute.[5] The point of making money is that one then has it to spend, although Thomas mentioned two other good reasons for seeking a profit: to have enough money to help the poor, and to help one's country by providing it with things it might lack.[6] In seeking these ends, one would realize one's own end as well, because a person is a social animal who realizes his end by helping others toward their own.

The basic claim that Aristotle and Thomas are making accords with most people's common sense: that good judgment is required to spend money or to make it, and that good judgment is not something we are born with, or that we always exercise, or that we all have to the same degree. Whether or not we use words such as "virtue" or "prudence," we all assume that this position is correct when we encourage our children, our subordinates, or ourselves to exercise better judgment or to guard against bad judgment.

We can now see that efficiency or wealth maximization is normatively valuable only if we assume, not only that there is such a thing as prudence or good judgment in spending or making money, but that people are actually exercising it. Economists must implicitly assume people are exercising good judgment in making money even for their descriptive models of the economy to work. Prices and output respond to supply and demand only because of the decisions of a firm's managers. If these decisions were random, prices and output would not respond in the way the economic models predict. According to Peter Lynch, entire markets can behave imprudently: "The pattern is always the same. Frantic investors pay ridiculous prices in order to get in on a spurious opportunity, and sooner or later, the prices come crashing down."[7] Thus, even on the descriptive level, economic models work only to the extent people actually exercise the judgmental ability that Thomas called *pecuniativa*.

On a normative level, whether efficiency or wealth maximization is valuable depends on whether it is a good thing for people to satisfy their preferences. There are two basic ways one can answer that question. One way is to admit that it all depends on whether the preferences in question are normatively good. If we take that approach, we will say, along with Aristotle and Thomas, that preferences may be good or bad, and that people have a capacity to tell which are which. We will conclude that preference satisfaction is good only if people exercise that capacity, or, to put it another way, only if they practice the virtue that Aristotle and Thomas called *prudentia œconomica*.

Alternatively, one can claim that preference satisfaction is somehow normatively good in and of itself, whatever the preferences may be. That is a much stronger claim than Aristotle or Thomas made. They merely said that satisfying one's preferences is sometimes good, not that it always is. Such a claim is also at odds with common sense. We often think hard before we satisfy a preference, and sometimes regret having done so. Nevertheless, economists who treat efficiency or wealth maximization as normatively valuable have traditionally taken this second approach.

In the nineteenth century, many economists were avowed utilitarians. They believed that each set of choices a consumer might make gave him a certain quantity of pleasure or satisfaction, and that the consumer tried to maximize this quantity much as a firm tries to maximize its profit. These economists equated goodness, in a normative sense, with the maximization of this quantity. If that position were correct, it would be morally irrelevant whether we took pleasure in the pursuit of knowledge and the appreciation of beauty or in the most degraded or vapid activities one can imagine; and the only objection to taking pleasure in another's pain would be not to the pleasure, but to the cost at which it is obtained. There is no need to rehearse the arguments against classical utilitarianism. Let us simply note that it contradicts our deepest intuitions about how we should live.

Today, most economists claim to have abandoned utilitarianism. As Paul Samuelson noted fifty years ago,

> many writers have ceased to believe in the existence of any introspective magnitude or quantity of a cardinal, numerical kind. With this skepticism has come the recognition that a cardinal measure of utility is in any case unnecessary; that only an ordinal preference, involving "more" or "less" but not "how much," is required for the analysis of a consumer's behavior.[8]

Thus, according to Samuelson, to build a descriptive model, economists merely need to assume that a consumer can rank his choices. Confronted with a choice between A or B, the consumer can say which he prefers or whether he is indifferent. There is no need to assume that in doing so, the consumer is maximizing some quantity called "pleasure" or "satisfaction."

Along with this change came another in the normative claims economists made about the ideal state of society. The old-style utilitarian economists thought it possible, in principle, to compare one person's satisfaction with another person's or even to add them together. The ideal could be defined, for example, as the greatest possible sum total of human satisfaction. For economists who think one can only speak about an individual's rank order preferences, comparing the extent of one person's satisfaction with that of another is not possible. Nevertheless, some of them claim that one can still say that a normative improvement is made if one person can be made better off, in terms of his own preferences, without making anyone else worse off. Such an improvement is efficient in the strictest sense of the term: it is "Pareto efficient."

To claim that efficiency is normatively good, one must still explain why it is good that a person can satisfy a preference. If the answer is that satisfying it is a pleasure, and that pleasure is good, whatever the pleasure may be, then we are back to the utilitarianism that most econo-mists have rejected. Instead, some economists define a preference opera-tionally as whatever an individual chooses: he prefers A to B if he chooses A when he could have chosen B. "Thus," as Samuelson observes, "the consumer's market behavior is explained in terms of preferences, which are in turn defined only by behavior. The result can very easily be cir-cular."[9] It is not only circular but very odd to say that whatever the in-dividual chooses is good simply because he has chosen it. Not even Jean-Paul Sartre would say a thing like that. Yet some economists take it for granted. We can escape the circle only by saying that preference satis-faction is good to the extent that the preferences in question are good. But then we are talking about *prudentia œconomica* whether we use that term or not. And we will have to conclude that wealth maximization or efficiency is valuable just to the extent that people practice this virtue when they spend money.

We can reach a similar conclusion about the virtues of courage and temperance more quickly. For Aristotle and Thomas, these virtues are concerned with the way we respond to things that we fear and that we desire. It is quite possible, they thought, for a person to understand the right course of action and still to act wrongly because it entails pain or danger or the sacrifice of pleasure. The virtues of courage and temper-ance enable one to do the right thing anyway.[10]

Common sense tells us that it is indeed possible for us to choose a course of action even when we know that it is worse for us. We overeat because it is pleasurable or smoke because it is painful to stop. In these instances, it is hard to see how satisfying our preferences could be nor-matively good, since we do so against our own better judgment.

For many economists, however, any choice *ipso facto* satisfies a pref-erence, and preference satisfaction is *ipso facto* good. I have put the fol-lowing case to five prominent economists, one of whom won the Nobel prize. As a man's yacht is sinking in the Caribbean, he radios his posi-tion to the Coast Guard. Their ships have been crippled by a storm, but they know exactly how long it will take to repair them, and they say that they can reach him in six days. He gets into a rubber life raft with a six-pack of beer, which is all that he has on board to drink. He knows, let us suppose, that if he drinks one can each day he will be picked up on the sixth day alive. If he drinks them at a faster rate he will die. He drinks four cans the first day, two the second, and is found on the sixth day dead. Is this result efficient? Four of the five economists said that it was. The fifth—the Nobel prize winner—said that it couldn't happen.

We turn next to the virtue of justice. Aristotle and Thomas distinguished distributive and commutative justice. Distributive justice, Aristotle said, "is manifested in distributions of honor or money or the other things that fall to be divided among those who have a share in the constitution."[11] It follows a "geometric proportion": each citizen receives in proportion to merit. Corrective or commutative justice "plays a rectifying part in transactions between man and man."[12] It follows an "arithmetic proportion": it preserves the share of each party to a transaction so that neither gains at the other's expense.

The concept of distributive justice allows one to address a basic normative question about our economic system: why, when different people want the same goods, do the goods go to whoever will pay the most for them? If Tom will pay sixty-five dollars for something, and Harry will only pay sixty dollars, why should Tom get it?

For Aristotle and Thomas, the point of distributive justice is to get people the resources that they need to achieve their ends as human beings to the fullest extent possible. Nevertheless, they identified two different and conflicting principles by which this goal might be realized. One principle is that every person should ideally have the same amount. The other is that those who have a superior capacity should ideally have more resources. They note that the first of these principles will be favored in a democracy, the second in an aristocracy. They hint that there is some truth in both of them.[13]

They also make it clear that these principles are ideals. They do not propose that a democracy confiscate the wealth of rich people, even rich people of distinctly limited moral capacity, and divide it up equally. Indeed, Aristotle warns against doing so.[14] We can see why he thought so if we consider his objections—with which Thomas concurred—to Plato's proposal to abolish private property. Do that, Aristotle said, and there will be endless quarrels, and people will have no incentive to work and to take care of property.[15] Thus the principles that ideally govern how purchasing power is distributed must be compromised in practice to give people an incentive to work, to care for property, and—as scholars in the Thomistic tradition were to note[16]—to take risks.

This theory does not tell us what institutions we need to secure distributive justice. It does tell us what principles are at stake and why they sometimes must be compromised. I think it answers to our common-sense ideas of why, if Tom outbids Harry, it is fair that he obtains something that they both want. One possibility is that they started with equal purchasing power but Harry chose to spend his a different way. Another less democratic explanation would be that Tom ought to have more purchasing power because he has a greater capacity to pursue goals that are genuinely worthwhile. Another would be that Tom acquired more purchasing power because he worked hard, managed property effectively, or successfully took risks. I think most people accept our economic system because they see that often, though not always, the distribution of purchasing power reflects these considerations.

In contrast, modern economists admit that they do not have any theory at all about why one distribution of resources might be better than another. In the nineteenth century, economists who were wedded to utilitarianism theorized that the best distribution of resources is one that maximizes the total amount of pleasure or satisfaction experienced by all individuals. That theory never worked well on a common-sense level. If it were true, the most degraded pleasures of a few people, if sufficiently intense, would trump the pursuit by many people of the genuinely worthwhile.

In any event, as already mentioned, most economists no longer believe that, even in theory, one can sum up the amounts of satisfaction that consumers receive. As a result, they lack a normative explanation of why, if Tom will pay sixty-five dollars for something and Harry will only pay sixty, Tom gets it instead of Harry.

As mentioned already, some say that normative improvement is made whenever one person can be made better off, in terms of his own preferences, without making anyone else worse off. Such an improvement is, again, Pareto efficient. Suppose Ann has something she does not want for which Tom will pay sixty-five dollars and Harry only sixty. If Harry were to get it, it would still be possible to move to a state in which he and Tom will both be better off: he could resell to Bob. A further improvement is not possible if only Tom ends up with the object.

As this example illustrates, one problem with this argument is that one person, merely by having the preferences he does, may make another person worse off by driving up the price of something they both want.[17] If Ann sells directly to Tom, Harry will be worse off than if Bob hadn't wanted the object at all, since then he could have bought it for sixty dollars.

Another problem is that, like the economists' definition of preferences, this argument is circular. We are seeking a reason why it is normatively better that goods go to whoever will pay the most for them. Supposedly, the answer is that unless they are sold to that person, it will be possible for a further transaction to make everyone better off and no one worse off. That transaction is possible, however, only if the rule of law is in force that a person can sell what he owns to whoever will pay most for it. To make a normative claim, one must assume not only that this rule is in force but that it should be. But that is, in effect, to assume that goods should go to whoever will pay the most for them—which was the conclusion to be proven.

To illustrate, suppose we are in a society in which nearly everything is owned by a small group who live in decadence while the rest go hungry. Suppose Tom is one of the rich and will pay Ann sixty-five dollars for a side of beef for which Harry, who is starving, cannot pay more than one dollar. Why would it be an "improvement" for Tom to have it? Many people might think it a definite improvement if someone like Robin Hood stole the meat and gave it to Harry. If Bob then offered to buy it back for up to sixty-five dollars, many people might think it a still further improvement if someone stole the sixty-five dollars from Bob as well. These "improvements," of course, can only be made by violating the rule that Ann, who owns the beef, is free to sell it to Tom if he offers to pay more than anyone else. If we assume that rule will be followed, then, even if Harry owned the beef, both Harry and Tom will prefer for Tom to acquire it at a price that Harry will accept. But to conclude that it is normatively better for Tom to end up with the beef, we need to assume not only that this rule will be followed but that, normatively, it should be. That is to assume the conclusion: that people who are willing to pay the most for things ought to have them.

Moreover, the proposition assumed is far from obvious. Thomas thought that since the ultimate purpose of external things is to serve human needs, a starving person had the right to take what he needed to live without the owner's permission.[18] In time of war or famine, most governments ration goods rather than leave their allocation to the market. An economist might object that war, famine, and the extremely unjust society just described are aberrational cases. But that concedes the point. Whether a situation counts as aberrational depends upon one's theory of distributive justice.

Consequently, we can draw the same conclusion about distributive justice as we did about prudence, courage, and temperance: efficiency and wealth maximization are good only to the extent that a society actually practices virtues that the economists never mention. Only to the extent that purchasing power is justly distributed is it better to allocate goods to those who will pay the most for them.

We can now turn to commutative justice. While distributive justice ensures that each citizen has a fair share of resources, commutative justice preserves the share that belongs to each. Aristotle and Thomas identify two kinds of commutative justice that correspond roughly with what a modern lawyer would call torts and contracts. In the case of involuntary commutative justice (or tort), one person takes or destroys another's resources against his will. Commutative justice then requires that he pay the amount necessary to restore the other person's share of resources. In the case of voluntary commutative justice (or contract), people voluntarily exchange resources. Commutative justice requires that they do so at a price that keeps the shares of the two parties equal.[19]

Elsewhere I have argued that one cannot make sense of modern contract or tort law unless one conceives of them as Aristotle and Thomas did: as institutions that secure, for each citizen, his preexisting share of resources.[20] Here a more basic claim is in order. Justice cannot be regarded as preference satisfaction. Quite the contrary, a just person is one who will not satisfy his preferences when he can only do so by behaving unjustly toward someone else. The economists speak about preference satisfaction, not about justice. Yet, to the extent that people behave unjustly, even the economists' descriptive models will not work.

Imagine a society in which people regarded the rules of contract and tort as mere instruments to enable them to satisfy their preferences, and broke these rules whenever they could get by with it. To use the economists' terminology, imagine that everyone played by the rules to just the extent that the marginal benefit of doing so exactly equaled the marginal cost. If the supply of some commodity increased, a board of directors might lower prices, but only after seriously discussing whether to dynamite a competitor's plant instead. If supply decreased, consumers might pay higher prices, but only after deciding it was inadvisable to loot the stores. It would take a bold economist to predict the effect of changes in supply or demand. He might as well try to predict which wolf pack will end up with the last scrap of meat in a severe winter. Here again, then, the economists' models give results that are normatively acceptable—and in this case, that are descriptively accurate—only on the assumption that people practice virtues of which economists never speak. On that assumption, however, their conclusions do have normative significance. I am not as pessimistic about economics as Kennedy and Clark seem to be in their essays (chapters 3 and 5).

The Ethics of Profit Seeking

We can now see why, normatively, it is good for the managers of a firm to try to maximize its profits. As long as they and other people actually practice the virtues just described, their pursuit of profit will make others normatively better off. Conversely, when people do not practice these virtues, managers may maximize profits without making others normatively better off, and so without performing the tasks for which the firm exists and which entitle it to a profit.

The most obvious case is the one just mentioned in which the managers themselves commit gross violations of commutative justice, for example, by dynamiting a competitor's plant. Suppose, however, that other people in the society are deficient in prudence, courage, temperance, or justice. To the extent that they are, by pursuing profit, managers are no longer making other people better off.

If we suppose, for example, that everyone always acts with good judgment about how to make money, then the managers of a firm could simply seek profit without fear that they are taking advantage of those with whom they contract. Suppose the managers want to have an office building built and can see that the builder has foolishly offered them too low a price. For example, he may have ignored a clause in the contract that places the risk of bad subsoil conditions on him when subsoil conditions are known to be bad. He may have forgotten to include the cost of wiring or plumbing in his bid when the cost is substantial. It may be obvious that he underestimated his other costs. Should the managers take advantage of these mistakes? I do not think so. Not if the justification for making a profit is that other people will be made better off.

A still more sympathetic case is that of imprudent employees. If employees always acted with prudence, managers could make the highest profit by offering job security and medical and retirement benefits. Employees would sacrifice some current income to avoid jobs that deprive them of personal development, time that they need elsewhere, and control over their own work in the ways that Murphy and Pyke note in their essay (chapter 13). Their contracts would be in practice what the economists are always assuming them to be in theory: the best deal for both parties. Employers will concede these benefits because employees will give up in pay at least what they cost; and employees will make that sacrifice because what they gain is worth more to them than what they give up. If employees are imprudent, however, they might make contracts that are not best for them. In the extreme case, employers might know that those who accept certain terms of employment when they are young regret having done so when they are old.

This is a trickier problem than that of the builder who makes an obvious mistake. The employer may not be taking financial advantage of the situation, and he cannot solve the problem by simply calling it to the other party's attention. Moreover, if he offers less current pay and more long-term benefits, his employees may go with competitors who do not do so. But that is merely to say that there is an underlying ethical problem here that defies easy solution. It doesn't make the problem go away. By hypothesis, the solution that maximizes profits is not in the employees' best long-run interest. Consequently, the manager will have to recognize that while making a profit is still a legitimate objective, it cannot be the sole objective if the very reason the firm is entitled to profits is that it betters the lives of others. Moreover, one can say, as an absolute rule, that managers should not exploit the imprudence of their employees to increase profits. They would do so, for example, if they took advantage of imprudent preferences for ready cash to lure employees away from more prudent contracts with other employers.

The same is true if the firm's customers lack prudence in deciding what to buy or courage or temperance in sticking by their decisions. When people practice these virtues, firms maximize profits simply by providing people with what is good for them. But suppose customers lack the prudence to buy quality products instead of tasteless junk. Suppose they lack the temperance to wait to buy rather than run themselves into debt, or to buy more food and less alcohol. Suppose they lack the courage to break an addictive habit such as smoking. At that point, maximizing profits no longer coincides with promoting the best interests of others. Consequently, there is an ethical problem which, as before, has no easy solution. Certainly, there is no point in making a high-quality product if no one appreciates it. Nor should one refuse to sell alcohol or to extend credit because some people might abuse it. Maybe the same goes for tobacco. But one can at least recognize, in deciding what to sell and how to promote it, that pursuing profit can no longer be the sole objective if the very justification for profit is the contribution that the firm makes to others' well-being. Moreover, as before, one can say as an absolute rule that managers should not increase profits by actions that simply exploit the weaknesses of others. They should not market a product that cannot improve the lives of those who buy it. They should not promote a product by appealing to people's folly, intemperance, or irrational fear. There is no such thing as an ethical pornographer or an ethical advertisement that appeals to our worst side.

Again, to the extent that the system of distributive justice in a society is imperfect, the managers of a firm can no longer assume that whatever maximizes profits is morally acceptable. When people grow up in homes and with schools that teach them to be productive, when there are job opportunities for everyone, and when costs of changing jobs are low, then a firm can hire and fire employees without much fear that it will make the distribution of resources less fair. It isn't the same, however, when a segment of the population does not have the social or educational background to compete effectively for jobs. It isn't the same when people cannot find other employment because of their age, their lack of knowledge, or the depressed state of a region. Then, as

Koslowski and Tavis point out in their essays (chapters 6 and 10), one cannot assume that the interests of others are best served by the employment practices that most reduce the firm's costs. That does not mean that managers should spend the investors' money curing social problems that their firm itself did not create, as Kennedy and Fort note in their essays (chapters 3 and 11). It does mean that if they merely pursue profit, the net effect of their actions may be to make other people worse off. Managers should ask how their firm might be positioned to help with the underlying problem: for example, by training or retraining people. They might weigh the benefits the firm will reap by laying people off, which may be marginal, against the impact on people's lives, which may be severe. Moreover, as before, one can say as an absolute rule that managers should not deliberately place people in a weak position in order to exploit it. Murphy and Pyke (chapter 13) think that one factor that led to routinized, humdrum factory jobs is that unskilled people are easier to control. If so, managers who downgraded the skill level in order to control workers might be maximizing profit, but not by improving the lives of others.

Although neither Aristotle nor Thomas contemplated the modern corporation, we have been proposing what one might call an Aristotelian or Thomistic model of corporate responsibility. It has an ethical foundation that both the shareholder and the stakeholder models lack: it is founded not on what each group wants for itself, but on what is normatively good for that group and for others. Unlike the stakeholder model, it explains why the duty of managers to seek a profit is different from their other obligations. Managers who do so will be behaving exactly as they should, provided that they and others are practicing virtues never mentioned by the economists.

Ethical problems arise as soon as we recognize that people do not always practice these virtues. These problems often cannot be resolved by clear rules. They require good judgment and a sensitivity to the individual situation. For that reason, one cannot get the right results, as some proponents of the shareholder model suggest, if the government merely enacts the right regulations and firms maximize profits while obeying the law. Nevertheless, these problems are more discrete than those identified by the stakeholder model. They arise when people are not acting in their own best interests or when their options have been limited in a way that violates distributive justice. Although the question of what a manager should do must be left to his good judgment, he is not told that he can ever act without balancing the interests of everyone affected.

Notes

1. Paul Anthony Samuelson, *Foundations of Economic Analysis* (New York: Atheneum, 1976).

2. Aristotle, *Nicomachean Ethics* VI.v, trans. W.D. Ross, in *The Basic Works of Aristotle,* ed. R. McKeon (New York: Random House, 1941), 935; Thomas Aquinas, *Summa theologiae* II-II q. 47, a. 2 (Madrid: La Editorial Catolica, 1963).

3. Aristotle, *Politics,* trans. B. Jowett, in *The Basic Works of Aristotle,* ed. R. McKeon (New York: Random House, 1941), I.viii; Thomas Aquinas, *Summa theologiae* II-II q. 50, a. 3.

4. Thomas Aquinas, *Sententia libri politicorum* I.vi 1256a 10–19, in *Opera omnia XLVIII* (Rome: Thomas Aquinas Foundation, 1971).

5. Aristotle, *Nicomachean Ethics* I.v; *Summa theologiae* I-II q. 2, a. 1; II-II q. 66, a. 1.

6. Thomas Aquinas, *Summa theologiae* II-II q. 77, a. 4.

7. Peter Lynch and John Rothchild, *Learn to Earn: A Beginner's Guide to the Basics of Investing* (New York: John Wiley and Sons, 1995), 31.

8. Samuelson, *Foundations,* 91.

9. Ibid., 91.

10. Aristotle, *Nicomachean Ethics* III.ix 1117a 30–34; III.x 1117a 24–25; Thomas Aquinas, *Summa theologiae* II-II q. 123, a. 3; q. 141, a. 3.

11. Aristotle, *Nicomachean Ethics* V.ii 1130b; Thomas Aquinas, *Summa theologiae* II-II q. 61, aa. 1–2.

12. Aristotle, *Nicomachean Ethics* V.ii 1130b; Thomas Aquinas, *Summa theologiae;* II-II q. 61, a. 2.

13. Aristotle, *Nicomachean Ethics* V.iv 1131b–1132b; Thomas Aquinas, *Summa theologiae* II-II q. 61, a. 2.

14. Aristotle, *Politics* V.ix 1310a, 1113.

15. Aristotle, *Politics* II.iv 1263a–1263b; Thomas Aquinas, *Summa theologiae* II-II q. 66, a. 2.

16. See, e.g., Domenicus Soto, lib. 6, *De iustitia et iure libri decem* lib. 6, q. 2, a. 3 (Salamanca: Andreas a Portonariis, 1556); Ludovicus Molina, *De iustitia et iure tractatus* disps. 348, 366 (Venice: Sessas, 1613).

James Gordley

17. As noted by Michael J. Trebilcock, *The Limits of Freedom of Contract* (Cambridge: Harvard University Press, 1995), 58.

18. Thomas Aquinas, *Summa theologiae* II-II q. 66, a. 7.

19. Aristotle, *Nicomachean Ethics* V.ii 1131a, 1–10; Thomas Aquinas, *Summa theologiae* II-II q. 61, a. 3.

20. James Gordley, "Contract and Delict: Toward a Unified Law of Obligations," *Edinburgh Law Review* 1 (1997): 345; "Tort Law in the Aristotelian Tradition," in *Philosophical Foundations of Tort Law: A Collection of Essays,* ed. D. Owen (Oxford: Clarendon Press, 1995), 131; "Enforcing Promises," *California Law Review* 83 (1995): 547; "Equality in Exchange," *California Law Review* 69 (1981): 1587.

Competing Visions

Equity and Efficiency in the Firm

CHARLES M.A. CLARK

The purpose of this chapter (and this book) is to examine what insights Catholic social thought might have for our understanding of the place of the firm in a modern capitalist economy. In the previous chapters we have seen that many of the fundamental assumptions upon which the conventional understanding of a capitalist economy rests—the nature of the person, the purpose of business activity, the role of ethics in business (to name just a few)—are brought into question by the Catholic social tradition and more generally by the principles of Christianity. These chapters suggest that our understanding of the role of business in our society and of its potential for promoting the common good would be improved if we adopted the more holistic and realistic understanding of human activity that is developed in the Catholic social tradition. In this chapter we will directly address what, as I argue, is the heart of the conventional wisdom on the economy and economic activity that dominates contemporary analysis of economic society. By examining the concepts of efficiency and equity in the neoclassical theory of the firm, I hope to highlight the root cause of the divergence between a Christian perspective on the economy and the perspective of the reigning economic orthodoxy, neoclassical economic theory.[1] Only by getting to the root of the differences can we start to develop a truly Christian understanding of the place of business in society, and then, it is hoped, construct business institutions, relations, and ethical standards that ensure the dignity of all persons and promote the common good.

The proposition that insights from Catholic social thought can improve our understanding of a modern economy is highly contentious. Even Catholic business practitioners and scholars are often leery of the Church's teachings on social and economic issues. This attitude stems from many factors, not the least of which is the judgment that the Church's attitudes haven't adjusted to the realities of the modern economy. Yet the position of this chapter is that the modern economy suffers by ignoring the two-thousand-year-old message of the Church, especially the core values of this message, and that unless these core values inform business practice, in any economic situation or environment, the economy will not best serve the needs of the people. In fact, what we frequently find in our economic life is that the economy forces people to serve it, which is contrary to the demands of social justice. Catholic social thought does not offer a fully developed alternative economic theory (or management, marketing, or accounting theory either), nor does it seek to replace economic theory (or the business disciplines) with theology. What it does seek to do is to use the yardstick of social justice as the true measure of how our economic and social institutions and practices foster human dignity.

In this chapter we see how Catholic social thought contradicts some of the core ideas of neoclassical economic theory. Economists will, no doubt, protest that their "science" is being unfairly judged, that all they do is objectively observe the economic activities of individuals and seek to explain this activity in an unbiased manner. However, a strong case can be made (and has been made by many economists, the two most prominent being Thorstein Veblen and Gunnar Myrdal) that neoclassical economic theory falls far short of being an objective and scientific understanding and explanation of the facts economists seek to explain. Closer to the truth is the view that neoclassical economic theory asserts a set of values, and that upon these values a body of doctrines has been developed to support and defend the social and economic order these values suggest. Orthodox economic theory has become, in many ways, a "competing Gospel," to use Robert Simons's term, in that it offers "a way of proclaiming a life which holds out a promise of well-being and is supposedly 'good news.'"[2] This is seen most clearly in developments in the former socialist countries and all over the third world. The gospel of free-market capitalism is being preached and spread with a vigor that would generate the envy of previous generations of missionaries. The fact that this free-market ideology is wreaking havoc everywhere it is being spread, and that it is not remotely practiced in the countries from which the apostles of laissez-faire come, seems to be beside the point.

I would argue that the limitations of orthodox economic theory's ability to explain and to guide toward improving our economic system stem from a crisis of values in economic theory, that the problems we face in our economic system stem from the values upon which neoclassical economic theory is constructed. These values are contrary to the true nature of the person and of the just society, and the theories which have been built upon them have become a barrier to a better understanding of our economic system and to a construction of a more just and humane economic system. The challenge of Catholic social thought to our understanding of the role and place of business in modern capitalism goes to the heart of how we explain, legitimate, and understand the economy, because it goes to the underlying values upon which both our economy and our understanding of the economy are based. It provides a more solid, realistic foundation upon which to build an understanding of the economy and the place of business in our society. In this chapter I hope to show how Catholic social thought challenges our understanding of two of the foundational concepts upon which contemporary economic theory is based, efficiency and equity, and thus forces us to rethink how we define and formulate them as goals within a business. The end result of this exercise is that we will need to look toward more than just market outcomes to define what is efficient and equitable, since social, political, and spiritual considerations must be given their due when we decide what is an efficient outcome and what is equitable.

The argument is in four sections. In the first section we will look at the preeminence of values and value judgments in the theoretical understanding of social phenomena, what Joseph Schumpeter called the role of the "vision."[3] Here we will see how differing "visions" lead to differing explanations of reality. In the second section we will look at the conceptions of efficiency and equity contained in the neoclassical theory of the firm, paying particular attention to the role of values and value judgments in their constitution. We hope to show in this section how the underlying values, as exposed in the concepts of efficiency and equity, shape our understanding of the firm. In the third section we will introduce the vision of Catholic social thought as an alternative to the vision underlying neoclassical economic theory, and from this develop an alternative conception of efficiency and equity. In the final section we will argue that this competing vision calls us to rethink many commonly accepted premises and conclusions of the theory of the firm and the role of the firm in promoting the common good.

The Role of Vision and Value Judgments

Economists like to believe that their discipline, at least at the theoretical level, is a positive science, that it contains no value judgments. Whenever values or value judgments are admitted, economics becomes normative economics, and here we typically find discussions of specific policy goals. But almost all economists would contend that in terms of economic theory itself, values play no role, that like the natural sciences, economic theory considers only the facts as we find them in nature. This positive-normative distinction in economics has never stood up to philosophical scrutiny, for, as Gunnar Myrdal has convincingly argued, every aspect of economic theory is normative, that is, reflects values and value judgments.[4] From the outset, economists make value judgments as they decide what to investigate and what to exclude from their analyses. When we examine the "hard core" of economic theory, we find that the theorists' vision, their philosophical preconceptions, greatly determine and shape the development of their theoretical structures. Conceptions of what society is, what human nature entails, and, indeed, of the real and ideal order of society are all part of the body of preconceptions theorists bring to their efforts, and are often accepted without critical reflection on their role in shaping a vision of the economy.

The perspective adopted by the observer (theorist) is crucial, for it guides both the classification and the theoretical handling of phenomena. Yet, this perspective is rarely held up for scrutiny. It is most often a preconception, accepted on faith and requiring neither justification nor confirmation from either facts or experience. In one sense, this omission is perfectly understandable: theorists can hardly take a full and objective account of themselves—their own life experience, their own socialization—as one of many phenomena requiring investigation. Nevertheless, every observer and every theorist should never lose sight of the fact that vision is not and cannot be value neutral; that the hard core of any vision reflects numerous value judgments; and that, therefore, value judgments deeply influence every aspect of the analytical effort. The theorist's vision goes to shape his judgment of what is relevant fact and what is mere background noise, of how observations are to be classified, of what the final term in the analysis (that is, the basis of theories' acceptability and unacceptability) is, and—most important—of what is the underlying ideal or value with which to compare the real and actual outcomes. Thus, theoretical vision influences what gets understood, how it is to be understood, and, finally, what evaluative assessment will be made of what is observed.

In economics, as with all social sciences, it is impossible to completely separate the real from the ideal, since our view of each is shaped by the other. Indeed, the ideal plays a particularly important role in how economists understand the real (or observed), as is seen in the prominence given to the concepts (ideals) of general equilibrium, perfect competition, and consumer sovereignty. These concepts, which are never observed, serve as the ideal types by which observed economic phenomena are both understood and evaluated. They are both yardsticks to measure reality *and* goals of economic policy (a reality to be achieved). All microeconomics is understood through the lenses of these concepts, and each is an expression of an economic vision, not the objective conclusion of unbiased empirical investigations.[5]

All science, especially social science, is indebted to implicit value judgments. The vision and value judgments that shape economic theory play a key role in our understanding of the theory of the firm, and it is here that Catholic social thought can make important contributions toward a deeper and richer understanding of the place of the corporation in modern life and, more important, can help to shape the corporation into an institution which better promotes the dignity of the individual and the common good.

Orthodox Theory of the Firm

The neoclassical theory of the firm starts, as does all neoclassical economic theory, with a particular vision of society and human nature, both grounded in the marginal utility theory of value, a theory which leads to the conclusion that the ultimate good in society is the consumption of utility achieved through market exchange. As Marc Tool has noted, "in the classical and much of the neoclassical tradition in economics, the maximal satisfaction of wants, notably consumer wants, has been and remains the basic criterion of judgment between good and bad, proper and improper, and desirable and undesirable."[6] Following Jeremy Bentham, economists have based their understanding of human nature on utilitarianism, where the search for utility (pleasure) and the avoidance of disutility (pain) are the twin determinants of how humans will act, as well as the ethical criteria that determine how they should behave. These dual aspects of the utilitarian moral philosophy and psychology are clearly stated by Bentham himself:

> Nature has placed mankind under the governance of two sovereign masters, pain and pleasure. It is for them alone to point out what we ought to do, as well as to determine what we shall do. On the one hand the standard of right and wrong, on the other the chain of cause and effects, are fastened to their throne. They govern us in all we do, in all we say, in all we think: every effort we make to throw off our subjection, will serve but to demonstrate and confirm it. . . . The principle of utility recognizes this subjection, and assumes it for the foundation of our system, the object of which is to rear the fabric of felicity by the hands of reason and law. Systems which attempt to question it, deal in sounds instead of sense, in caprice instead of reason, in darkness instead of light.[7]

Although modern economists have abandoned much of the rhetoric of utilitarianism, they have never abandoned the substance of this outdated philosophy and completely discredited psychology (see Gordley, chapter 4, for further discussion on this point). Neoclassical economic theory is based on the premise that the search for utility is the driving force in human nature, and thus all explanations need to be reducible to this term.[8] This is the reason that just about any question in neoclassical economics is eventually reducible to a cost-benefit analysis. With utility through exchange as the underlying value at its foundation, neoclassical economic theory developed a hard core of tenets that can be summed up as follows: methodological individualism is the only approach to understanding human activity; human nature is essentially hedonistic; and conflicting claims and desires of individuals are brought into harmony through the process of competition in the market

The theory of the firm in neoclassical economics is merely an extension and expression of the vision and associated value judgments that form the hard core of neoclassical economic theory. It is not an empirical treatment of real firms. Conclusions drawn from this theory must be seen in this light, and challenges to these conclusions posed by Catholic social thought should not be dismissed merely because they are at variance with "economic science."

The Neoclassical Theory of the Firm

The neoclassical conceptions of efficiency and equity are embedded in the theory of the firm, for it is in the firm that efficiency and equity are generated. In reality, both concepts are also first embedded in the theory of exchange, yet this theory is so divorced from any real economy that it fails to adequately address the issues of efficiency and equity.[9] Accordingly, we will look at the three attempts by neoclassical economic theory to explain why firms exist: firms are markets; firms are mental fictions; and firms exist because of transaction costs. All three are based on neoclassical theory's individualistic and mechanical conception of society, its hedonistic conception of human nature, and its assumption of a tendency toward general equilibrium—elements of the neoclassical vision.

The neoclassical conception of society gives methodological individualism as the accepted approach to the analysis of economic phenomena. All satisfactory explanations must transpire at the level of individual actions and motives. Society is reduced to a collection of individuals and is thus seen as a mental fiction. The hedonistic conception of human nature, derived from utilitarianism, gives neoclassical theorists the final term in their analysis of individual actions: utility, the measure of what *is* and what *ought* to be. The existence of a society made up of self-interested individuals has long presented a problem to philosophers, for, as Thomas Hobbes long ago pointed out, individuals who pursue only their own self interest, without outside control (that is, state intervention), naturally enter into a "war of all against all." Economists contend that Adam Smith's conception of the "Invisible Hand," the coordinating role of the market, solves this problem. This is the idea of a tendency toward a general equilibrium.

Into this "ideal" world inhabited solely by purely self-interested individuals who act under the discipline of the market in pursuit of satisfactions—that is, utilities—neoclassical theorists place the firm. Yet, by placing the firm in this context, the very existence of firms becomes problematic. Firms *remove* economic activity from the marketplace; thus, their existence must challenge the ideal that markets always produce optimal outcomes. In fact, this problem is significant, since most economic activity takes place inside firms and thus outside markets. One way that neoclassical economic theory gets around this problem is by treating the internal dynamics of the firm as another market-exchange environment. As Geoff Hodgson has demonstrated, neoclassical economists

> argue that there is no vital distinction between ordinary market exchange and the organization and allocation of resources within the firm. They deny that there is any essential difference between the exchange of everyday commodities in the market and the employment contract within the firm: "Telling an employee to type this letter rather than to file that document is like my telling a grocer to sell me this brand of tuna rather than that brand of bread."[10]

In a seminal article, Alchian and Demsetz hammer home this point:

[the firm] has no power of fiat, no authority, no disciplinary action any different in the slightest degree from ordinary market contracting between any two people. . . . To speak of managing, directing, or assigning workers to various tasks is a deceptive way of noting that the employer continually is involved in renegotiation of contracts on terms that must be acceptable to both parties.

I suspect that most neoclassical economists would hold that Alchian and Demsetz's position is a bit extreme, and that the firm is essentially different from the market. Nevertheless, Alchian and Demsetz's argument is consistent with neoclassical economic theory, and in fact most of the understanding of the firm within the neoclassical tradition does treat the internal relations of a firm essentially as market exchanges.[11]

The second approach to the theory of the firm is to claim that the theory of the perfectly competitive firm is a mere mental fiction, designed not to explain how firms act but to explain how price changes come about. As Fritz Machlup has written:

The model of the firm in that theory (perfect competition) is not . . . designed to serve to explain and predict the behaviour of real firms; instead, it is designed to explain and predict changes in observed prices . . . as effects of particular changes in conditions (wage rates, interest rates, import duties, excise taxes, technology, etc.). In this causal connection the firm is only a theoretical link, a mental construct helping to explain how one gets from the cause to the effect.[12]

Machlup's is not a satisfactory explanation of the role of the theory of the firm for two obvious reasons. First, economists *should* understand the real behavior of firms, and not just the hypothetical behavior necessary for neoclassical price theory. The firm, especially the large corporation, is the most significant institution in a modern capitalist economy and thus requires understanding. Second, the perfect competition model of the firm is not used merely as a mental fiction, as Machlup suggests, because it *is* the ideal according to which all firms are evaluated, and it is an important part of the basis for the faith in a free-market economy and in much of our economic policy.[13]

The third approach to the theory of the firm argues that firms are distinct from markets, and they exist because of transaction costs. This approach, first developed by R. H. Coase, argues that firms exist to take some economic activities out of the marketplace for reasons of efficiency. Coase's reasoning is fairly straightforward. The process of producing a final good or service includes numerous (sometimes hundreds) of steps. If each step in the production process were subject to market transaction, then the production process would be longer and more costly. Imagine an assembly line in which each intermediate worker had to buy the output of the worker before and sell the unfinished product to the next worker on the line. Removing these steps from the market allows cost and time to be minimized. It also allows for planning and a reduction in uncertainty.[14]

This transaction approach provides for a more satisfactory explanation of the reason firms exist, but it does so at a cost to neoclassical economic theory, for it is a significant move away from the vision of neoclassical free markets. It also abandons the notions of efficiency and equity (so far, at least, as they are determined within the firm), for markets no longer determine these. This result follows since, according to neoclassical economic theory, efficiency and equity are defined as market outcomes, and since, even if they are idealized market outcomes, the market process is the key to their moral legitimacy. Apart from the market process, outcomes are determined by institutional structure and the relative power of economic agents. This is a far cry from the world envisioned by neoclassical theory.

Equity and Efficiency

The ideal through which neoclassical economic theory attempts to understand equity and efficiency in the firm is the model of perfect competition.[15] This model is based on a set of assumptions which enable the theory to reach determinate results but which, for the most part, are contradicted by observation and reason: (1) a large number of buyers and sellers so that no firms, or small groups of firms, can influence prices (that is, all are price takers); (2) no significant economies of scale (this keeps firms small); (3) perfect mobility of firms among industries and perfect mobility of factors of production (land, labor, and capital) among firms; (4) homogenous products (that is, absence of brand loyalties or product differentiation); and (5) perfect knowledge (so that only market-clearing prices will prevail). From these assumptions, economists arrive at the long-run equilibrium of perfect competition: over the long run, marginal costs equal marginal revenue which equals average costs. At this point, and only at this point, each firm is producing the most goods and services at the least sustainable cost, that is, producing the maximum amount of consumable utility while earning an average rate of return.

The equilibrium of perfect competition results in maximum market consumption of utility,[16] for market forces continually act to keep prices at the lowest sustainable levels, ensuring the greatest possible consumption of utility (measured as the consumer surplus). Thus, the theory of perfect competition *is* economists' argument that markets are efficient, and it comes down to the demonstration that the maximum amount of utility is being produced and consumed. However, only utility that is obtained through consumption in a marketplace is considered by the theory. Any satisfaction or pleasure that is obtained outside the market (such as a home-cooked meal, parents raising their own children, walking in the woods) is excluded. Furthermore, under the theory, all consumption in the market is good by definition (no one would freely consume something that did not yield greater utility than the disutility which is its cost), even if what is consumed is the dose of heroin on which the drug abuser overdoses.

Neoclassical economists address the question of equity with the marginal productivity theory of distribution. This theory argues, in the words of its originator, John Bates Clark, that "the distribution of the income of society is controlled by a natural law, and that this law, if it worked without friction, would give every agent of production the amount of wealth which that agent creates."[17] This theory holds that profit-seeking firms will hire factors of production (land, labor, and capital) in the quantities that will yield the firm the maximum profits. The firm will substitute each factor for the other to reach this point, and—in equilibrium—each factor's marginal cost will equal its marginal revenue product (value created). Thus, each factor will get what it contributes, at the margin, to output; each will be rewarded based on its worth (that is, the consumable utility it creates). The marginal productivity theory is another example of how a theory explains and justifies at the same time.

The loopholes in this theory are many, but two especially demand mention. First, no one has yet been able actually to measure the marginal contribution of a factor of production, owing partly to the fact that perfect substitution (or anything close to it) does not exist between the factors of production (no one hires more workers without also hiring more machines [capital] for them to work on and hiring more land [inputs] for them to work with). Second, no explanation is offered as to why some people have land and capital to sell or rent, while others have only their labor to sell (see Gates, chapter 12, on the consequences of this problem). Neoclassical economic theory does not and cannot bring in the question of initial endowments, for the obvious reason that most endowments are not market determined.

To a large extent, the neoclassical theory of the firm is developed to show the welfare-enhancing effects of free markets, and it is thus one of the foundations of the argument for laissez-faire policies over government intervention and planning. Here the case is made that free markets maximize efficiency and promote equity, under the condition that firms act so as to maximize their profits. Thus the theory provides the moral justification for the argument that the firm's only responsibility is to maximize its profits, since in so doing it best promotes society's interests.

The weakness in the neoclassical theory of the firm stems from its unrealistic assumptions. In order for the theory to demonstrate the idea that social efficiency and equity are promoted best when firms maximize shareholder value (profits), neoclassical economics have to suppose an economy which does not exist, and base it on assumptions regarding the nature of society and the human person which also are unsupportable, either in theory or in fact. Starting with the premise that the ultimate value is utility through market exchange, neoclassical economists have developed a theory of the firm that, in its extreme, excludes the existence of firms, or which has taken the majority of economic activity out of its purview (the transactions cost approach). It has set up as the ideal by which actual market outcomes are to be measured criteria that no actual firm could meet (and which only the smallest and least productive firms approach). Furthermore, it claims that any consumption of goods or services has equal validity (as long as it takes place through a competitive market). Given these conclusions, it is obvious why economists claim that market outcomes are always the best for any society, regardless of all evidence to the contrary.

The Challenge of Catholic Social Thought to the Firm

Unlike neoclassical economic theory, Catholic social thought is openly and explicitly based on a specific vision and set of value judgments. These are not hidden preconceptions, but instead are celebrated as pillars upon which all social formations and analysis need to be built. Catholic social thought presents a vision grounded in the Old Testament and comes to life in the Gospels, and it provides the explicit underpinning for the various encyclicals and other Church documents that make up the Catholic tradition in social teaching.[18] The core of this vision is the belief that

> God speaks to every reality. Whatever we are looking at whether it is an issue such as world hunger . . . or an economic system such as Capitalism, God does have something to say to that reality. Our world either is or is not in accord with God's ideal for it. Consequently it is important for us to come to know what God is saying to whatever reality we are examining. God speaks to these issues or situations in various ways: through the Bible, through the teachings of His Church, through the signs of the times and through the prophets who interpret those signs. . . . [W]e should listen to God in theological reflection and in prayer.[19]

One bedrock value of this tradition is the assertion of the dignity of all humans: "The dignity of the human person, realized in community with others, is the criterion against which all aspects of economic life must be measured."[20] This brief statement says a mouthful, for it is a call for a radically different conception of human nature and an equally different view of the nature of society. The dignity of the human person cannot be reduced to a calculus of utility and disutility, nor can society be reduced to the mere sum total of individuals. This view insists that the individual and the community are interconnected; neither can be reduced to the other, and society is neither mechanistic and individualistic (as is the society of neoclassical economic theory) nor completely organic (as is the society of vulgar Marxism).

Most important, Catholic social thought is based on different criteria of value. According to Catholic social thought, something has value if it moves us closer to God and lacks value if it comes between God and us. While market exchanges might reflect this value criterion in the case where individuals use it as the basis of their economic actions, this value criterion is not contingent on being a market outcome to give it legitimacy. Thus the value criterion for defining efficiency and equity must be based on the goals of protecting human dignity and promoting the common good (which encompass God's design for us) and not—as in neoclassical economic theory—on utility, either in consumption or in production (profits).

Economic theory defines efficiency in terms of market transactions and outcomes, profit and loss, underpinned by the mythical entities of utility and disutility. Catholic social thought proposes a different yardstick. It is not antigrowth or hostile to economic life (both common charges), but it opposes treating economic growth as an end rather than as a means. Thus, Catholic social thought offers a different vision of economic development and progress,[21] since it understands that to pursue productivity as a goal, without regard for the context of economic activity and its human dimension, is to miss the purpose of economic activity: meeting human needs. As the United States Catholic bishops state in *Economic Justice for All:*

> Productivity is essential if the community is to have the resources to serve the well-being of all. Productivity, however, cannot be measured solely by its output in goods and services. Patterns of production must also be measured in light of their impact on the fulfillment of basic needs, employment levels, patterns of discrimination, environmental quality, and sense of community.[22]

Catholic social thought draws the key distinction that humans can never be treated as only means to an end, for they are the ends. Thus, the treatment of workers as mere commodities to be used to maximize profits is objectionable. We can see a clear statement of this view in Pope Leo XIII's *Rerum novarum* (1891):

> The following duties bind the wealthy owner and the employer: not to look upon their work-people as their bondsmen but to respect in every person his or her dignity and worth. . . . They are reminded that . . . to misuse people as though they were things in the pursuit of gain . . . is truly shameful and inhuman. . . . Furthermore, employers must never tax their work-people beyond their strength, or employ them in work unsuited to their sex and age. Their great and principal duty is to give every one what is just. . . . to gather one's profit out of the need of another, is condemned by all laws human and divine. . . . Lastly, the rich must religiously refrain from cutting down the workers' earnings, whether by force, fraud or by unjust dealings.[23]

Thus, for Catholic social thought the concept of efficiency must be defined in terms of the meeting of human needs, irrespective of whether these needs are expressed in the market and including needs that are nonmaterial, such as spiritual needs or the need for social participation.

The tradition of Catholic social thought also proposes a very different conception of equity. The basis of equity in Catholic social thought is the common gift from God of the earth. It follows from this conception of equity that the minimum criterion of equity is that all share in this gift so that all can meet their basic, minimum needs. In Donal Dorr's admirably clear formulation, "God destined the earth and all that it contains for the use of all people and peoples. Furthermore, the right to have a share of earthly goods sufficient for oneself and one's family belongs to everyone."[24] This concept of equity is not a demand for perfect equality; it supposes, rather, the goal that all be ensured the means to a decent standard of living. The tradition of Catholic social thought also argues that greater equity is to the benefit of both rich and poor, and that there are gains to society from greater equity: "Excessive economic and social inequalities within the one human family, between individuals or between peoples, give rise to scandal, and are contrary to social justice, to equity, and to the dignity of the human person, as well as to peace within society and at the international level."[25]

Catholic social thought has, for the most part, staged a two-pronged attack on social justice issues. On the one hand, it has drawn attention to the many structural factors that lead to the abuse of human dignity and to social inequities. These factors require structural reform, most often in the form of national or international intervention. Here we would find Catholic social thought favoring such policies as minimum wage legislation and better trade terms for developing countries. Yet, equally important for the tradition is changing the hearts of individuals. Catholic social thought calls on each of us to look at every person as a fellow child of God, to see Christ in each as we conduct our business lives, our lives as owners, managers, workers, consumers, and voters. Thus it is a call for a new attitude toward the microaspects of our economic lives.

The call for structural reform grounded in personal conversions should ring especially loudly for those who manage the large bureaucracies that dominate modern capitalist economies and societies. As Donal Dorr has noted:

> We live in a stratified society where certain economic, political, cultural, and religious structures maintain and promote the dominance of the rich and powerful over the mass of ordinary people and peoples. These structures operate through agencies and institutions that are staffed mainly by middle-class people—those who provide the professional and commercial services of society. Whatever their private loyalties and values, these service people contribute to structural injustice through the kind of work they are doing. The possibility of making an 'option for the poor' arises for such people and it is mainly to them that the challenge is issued.[26]

Conclusion

Our last task is to highlight briefly what some of the differences would be between an understanding of the firm based on the underlying values of Catholic social thought, especially the conception of equity and efficiency, and the current dominant theory of the firm based on neoclassical economic theory and its value premises: utility as the ultimate good, and efficiency and equity defined purely as market outcomes (even if only abstract and not actual market outcomes).

In terms of theoretical influences, the first and most far-reaching difference between the neoclassical theory of the firm and a Christian theory lies in the latter's promoting an understanding of the firm based first on how firms actually behave and second on how they can best promote the goals of human dignity and the common good. A Christian theory would fully follow the maximum of Leo XIII: "There is nothing more useful than to look at the world as it really is—and at the same time look elsewhere for a remedy to its troubles."[27] As has been noted by many commentators, the net effect of the neoclassical theory of the firm is to act as an enabling myth, allowing large corporations to wield significant market power under the protection of the myth that competition keeps them in check. The vast majority of economic activity takes place in environments significantly different from the competitive market model economists use to explain and understand the economy, yet adherence to this model is necessary in order to support the view that market outcomes as such are efficient and equitable. It is thus an enabling myth and not a serious attempt to objectively investigate the economic behavior of firms. An understanding of the firm based on Catholic social thought would be more useful and more realistic.

A second major difference is the abandonment of the belief that the highest goal of the firm is to maximize shareholder value by any means allowed under the law. This often encourages the firm to violate many of the economic rights Catholic social thought asserts, some of which will be mentioned below. If one follows the view that the firm should maximize shareholder value as its primary goal, one then has to divorce the means to achieving this goal from the goal itself (the end). There are no limitations on how profits, and thus shareholder value, are maximized, outside of adherence to the law (setting aside the power of these vested interests to rewrite the law to suit their economic advantage—much of the illegal activity of the early 1980s that brought down the savings and loan industry was afterward made legal). The issue of whether this activity entails making goods and services that meet human needs is incidental and often accidental. Profits, as Thorstein Veblen noted in *The Theory of Business Enterprise*, can be just as easily maximized by limiting production to keep prices higher than their competitive level (Veblen called this industrial sabotage).[28] This use of market power is a significant factor in determining profit levels and is at the root of the various merger waves our economy has gone through in the past century.[29] In the past two decades we have seen that firms pursuing the goal of maximizing shareholder value have followed policies such as downsizing; going bankrupt to get out of union contracts; moving production to third-world countries in order to avoid environmental and workplace safety regulation; spending retained earnings (which should go to reinvestment in production capabilities) to buy back stock so as to artificially inflate share prices; artificially creating shortages to keep prices high; speculating in currency markets; raiding pension funds; and engaging in numerous other activities that pursue the goal of maximizing shareholder value but are contrary to promoting the common good.

Modern Catholic social thought, like the political economy of Karl Marx before it, has noted that one aspect of a capitalist economic system is the exploitation of labor to promote greater profits for the owners of capital. In this situation, the worker is being treated as a means to an end and not as the end itself. This is clearly contrary to Catholic social thought, which has consistently viewed the worker as the end itself. As John Paul II argued:

> It should be recognized that the error of early capitalism can be repeated wherever man is in a way treated on the same level as the whole complex of the material means of production, as an instrument and not in accordance with the true dignity of his work—that is to say, where he is not treated as subject and maker, and for this very reason as the true purpose of the whole process of production.[30]

This is the idea of the priority of labor over capital, that the economic system must serve people, and not the reverse.

Catholic social thought also asserts, more specifically, that workers should be paid a just wage, that the workers' subsistence cannot be equated with the wage that the market determines. This is a recognition that wages need to reflect social concerns and goals, such as a decent standard of living, and not merely what clears the market. It is also a recognition of the fact that, contrary to neoclassical economic theory, actual market prices (especially wages) frequently reflect market imperfections, such as market power, unequal information, and other factors that cause the real world to diverge from the mythical world of economic theory. Thus, in the real world, social, cultural, and historical factors play a strong role in determining income levels and wage rate (a point John Stuart Mill clearly understood). Catholic social thought merely asserts that one commonly held value, the right to a living wage, be explicitly included in the various factors that determine wage rates. Furthermore, Catholic social thought asserts the right of workers to form associations to protect their rights as workers. This is in contrast to the view of neoclassical economic theory, which states that unions are market imperfections, distorting market outcomes.

Finally, Catholic social thought, while recognizing and affirming the right of private property, also asserts the social nature of property: all property must be used to promote the common good. The basis of private property, as Saint Thomas Aquinas pointed out long ago, is that property often best serves the common good when it is privately held, so that private ownership is a contingent, not an unconditional right (see Alford and Naughton, chapter 2, and Cortright and Pierucci, chapter 7). As John Paul II has noted, all property is under a "social mortgage." It must be used toward the common good. By contrast, any restriction on the use of private property, according to neoclassical economic theory, is a hindrance to market mechanisms and a cause of inefficiencies.

Catholic social thought offers an analysis that is more realistic in its view of society and human nature and offers views of efficiency and equity that are more justifiable than the views generated by neoclassical theory. It presents a challenge to the orthodox theory of the firm by rejecting the underlying values upon which neoclassical economic theory is based. Starting with different value premises, Catholic social thought develops different conceptions of efficiency and equity, and thus questions many of the accepted premises supporting the goals and activities of firms in modern capitalism. If we want to have a more values-based and ethical economy, if we want to promote social justice, we must start by rethinking the place and role of the firm in our society and work toward instituting the values of Catholic social thought, which are the values necessary for a just society, into the operation of firms as well as the other economic units that comprise our economy.

Notes

1. The work of Clive Beed and Cara Beed is particularly useful in addressing the conflict between neoclassical economics and a Christian perspective on the economy. I recommend their article "Realism and a Christian Perspective on Economics," *Review of Political Economy* 9, no. 3 (1997): 313–33, as a good starting point. The various writings of Charles Wilber of the University of Notre Dame should also be signaled out for their insight into these issues.

2. Robert G. Simons, *Competing Gospels: Public Theology and Economic Theory* (Alexandria, Australia: E. J. Dwyer Pty, 1995), ix.

3. Joseph Schumpeter, *History of Economic Analysis* (New York: Oxford University Press, 1954), 41–42.

4. Gunnar Myrdal, *Political Element in the Development of Economic Theory* (New York: Simon and Schuster, 1954) and *Value in Social Theory* (London: Routledge, 1958).

5. I have argued the how and why of economic theory's move away from an empirical understanding of the economy in *Economic Theory and Natural Philosophy* (Aldershot: Elgar, 1992).

6. Marc Tool, *Essays in Social Value* (Armonk, N.Y.: M. E. Sharpe, 1986), 89.

7. Jeremy Bentham, *An Introduction to the Principles of Morals and Legislation* (London: Methuen, 1982), 11.

8. The move toward "revealed preference theory" does not change this fact, for what the preferences reveal is the attempt to obtain utility through market exchange. The theory assumes its conclusion (that individuals attempt to maximize) rather than demonstrates it empirically. The net effect of this theory is to remove the philosophically charged terminology of Bentham's utilitarianism without changing the content.

9. The theory of exchange assumes an economy in which all economic actors trade their initial endowments only. It thus excludes produced goods, money and time, uncertainty, as well as failing to explain the initial endowments. This is hardly an adequate basis for understanding a capitalist economy.

10. Geoff Hodgson, *Economics and Institutions* (Cambridge, England: Polity Press, 1988), 196.

11. Armen Albert Achian and Norman Demsetz, "Production, Information Costs, and Economic Organization," *American Economic Review* 62 (December 1972): 777.

12. Quoted in Malcolm Sawyer, *Theories of the Firm* (New York: St. Martin's Press, 1979), 5.

13. Yet, Machlup hit on the truth of the matter, for much of the theory of the firm is in fact designed to justify the neoclassical economists' theory of value, the heart of their vision and their value judgments. Here we see an obvious example of the ideological aspects of theory.

14. John Kenneth Galbraith, *The New Industrial State* (Boston: Houghton Mifflin Company, 1967).

15. Economists also use the analysis of Edgeworth Box to show how, given a level of output and an initial distribution of income, free trade will lead to the most efficient distribution of output. This explanation is even more unrealistic than the perfect competition story.

16. This is the concept of deadweight loss.

17. John Bates Clark, *The Distribution of Wealth* (1899; reprint, New York: Augustus M. Kelley, 1965).

18. For two excellent overviews on the relationship between business and faith, see J. Michael Stebbin's "Business, Faith and the Common Good" and Dennis P. McCann's "On Moral Business: A Theological Perspective," both in the *Review of Business* 19, no. 1 (Fall 1997): 5–8, 9–14. Also of interest is Patrick Riordan's "The Purpose of Business and the Human Good," *Review of Business* 19, no. 4 (Summer 1998): 4–10.

19. Seán Healy and Brigid Reynolds, *Social Analysis in Light of the Gospels* (Dublin: Folens and Co., 1983), 5–6.

20. U.S. Catholic Bishops, *Economic Justice for All* (1984), 28.

21. See Donal Dorr, *Option for the Poor* (Dublin: Gill and Macmillan, 1992), 180–87. See also Paul VI, *Populorum progressio,* and John Paul II, *Sollicitudo rei socialis.*

22. U.S. Catholic Bishops, *Economic Justice for All* (1984), 71.

23. Leo XIII, *Rerum novarum,* 16–17. See also Dorr, *Option for the Poor,* 24.

24. Dorr, *Option for the Poor,* 154.

25. Ibid., 158.

26. Ibid., 2.

27. Leo XIII, *Rerum novarum,* 14.

28. Thorstein Veblen, *The Theory of Business Enterprise* (New York: Viking Press, 1904).

29. Numerous studies have shown that market power and limiting competition, and not efficiencies from economies of scale, are the primary motivation for mergers.

30. John Paul II, *Laborem exercens,* 7.

6

The Shareholder Value Principle and the Purpose of the Firm

Limits to Shareholder Value

PETER KOSLOWSKI

The question whether the maximization of shareholder value is *the* criterion for the working of a firm has become a contentious issue in business. In July 1998 the German president, Roman Herzog, declared that "it is not acceptable that the price of the shares of a firm rises with the number of employees laid off" and admonished German business firms thereby not to maximize the shareholder value only, but to look at the purpose of the firm in a broader perspective.[1] On the other hand, the neoclassical theory of the firm contends that the firm works best when it fulfills the task of maximizing the shareholder value only. According to the financial theory of the firm, business concerns a union of investments on which return must be maximized.

The question at stake: can the purpose of the firm be described exhaustively by its task to render the maximum shareholder value to its shareholders? One simple but important objection comes to mind immediately: the joint stock company with many shareholders is only one type of firm, more common in America than on the Continent. In Germany, for example, a very large part of the economy is not organized on the basis of shares and shareholder ownership.[2] Medium-sized firms, of course, have owners, but they do not have shareholders in the sense required by the shareholder value principle. In the one-owner firm different purposes will often prevail than in the firm which divides ownership among many stockholders.

This essay will discuss the question whether the purpose of the firm can be described by the shareholder value maximization principle. It will examine why shareholder value moved to the center of the debate over management and corporate governance. It will investigate what the purpose of the firm is and whether shareholder value is instrumental or teleological for the firm. It will demonstrate that maximizing shareholder value is the central purpose of financial firms, because maximizing value is the firm's product and not merely an instrumental criterion of the firm's success. It will describe how shareholder value moved to the center of the debate through a "spillover" from the teleology of financial institutions to industrial firms, and how an inversion of teleology and instrumentality happened in the course of this spillover. The essay will analyze where the orientation on shareholder value can be useful and, finally, give some ideas about the place of the shareholder value principle in light of the differences over the concept of human motivation that characterize Christian denominations.

Shareholder Value Moves to the Center of Interest

Two developments have moved the topic of shareholder value to the center of debate. First, the competition for capital among firms and also among national economies has been intensified by the opening up and globalization of the world economy. In particular, the opening of formerly communist economies released demand that formerly had been blocked from the world capital markets by the iron curtain. The number of firms and economies competing for the same capital stock has, accordingly, increased. Just as labor must achieve a higher productivity if it comes under competitive pressure, so capital must increase its productivity if the scarcity of this factor and the competition for it increase.

As a result, investors expect a higher return on capital and increased shareholder value. Competitive pressure on capital markets causes an increase in performance and puts pressure on costs, resulting in a decrease in the capital intensity of production or in an increase in the productivity of capital since, in the world market, higher returns on capital can be earned in other places on the globe. The opportunities for investing capital in other places multiply, raising expectations for compensation on the part of investors. The world capital market multiplies the number of opportunities and possibilities for investment and thereby also raises the opportunity costs paid by those whose capital is used or invested inefficiently.

All advanced economies have come under pressure, both on the side of capital and on the side of labor, owing both to multiplying opportunities to invest capital and to an increase in the supply of labor. The opening of huge markets for investment and labor, particularly in China and East Asia, generates additional competitive pressure on the capital of the advanced economies.

The second development which has served to promote interest in the shareholder value principle concerns the relationship between capital owners and management. Increased opportunities to invest put the management or the owner-manager under competitive pressure. The multiplication of alternative uses also multiplies capital's possibilities for "exiting" a firm, permitting shareholders or capital owners to put pressure on the management through the threat of takeovers. This situation implies increased pressure on management to earn higher return on capital or higher shareholder value than before. The debate over the role of shareholder value belongs to a new discussion on corporate governance. Corporate governance must be improved—that is, management must meet the rising expectations of capital—by a stronger emphasis on shareholder value maximization.

The importance of the new international competition and resulting pressure on management is demonstrated by the Russian situation after the privatization of formerly publicly owned Soviet firms. Faced with a market environment, the former Soviet managers led their firms to bankruptcy. After this bankruptcy, however, a privatization came into being which favored the same managers who had brought their firms to bankruptcy and made them the new owners of firms they had already ruined. The Russian economy faced the difficulty that there were no other shareholders available who could put the former Soviet managers under pressure. At the same time, for various reasons and by different political measures, the Russian government did not allow international investors to put a healthy pressure on the former Soviet managers from the threat of takeover by international firms. By blocking international owners from the Russian market for corporate control on nationalist grounds, the most important chance to put the new owners (who were the old managers) under pressure has been missed. The example of post-Soviet Russia demonstrates that international competition for ownership of shares and for corporate control is one of the most important instruments for disciplining management available to a nation.

In summary, emphasis on shareholder value is a means of enhancing the efficiency with which investments are allocated in the world market, an effect which should be welcomed. Moreover, the shareholder value principle is at the same time an instrument to prevent shirking by management and by whole firms.

Shareholder Value as a Means of Controlling the Firm

The demand for profitability is the means to prevent shirking in the operations of all members of a firm. In Alchian and Demsetz's theory, the owner functions as the one who prevents the shirking of the firm's members, while the firm's profitability holds the owner to his duty to prevent the shirking of the other members of the firm.[3] If the owner does not fulfill his monitoring function, residual profit will decrease; he will be punished by decreased profits or even losses, and thereby be kept vigilant against shirking in his firm.

The shareholder value principle, with its emphasis on future cash flows, changes the perspective on residual profit. Profit is not measured anymore as a figure of the past but as an *expected* future residual. The firm must maximize the future profit, measured in dividends and the increase of the shares' market value. Management has to see that the future residual profit, after reduction of all costs, is maximized. Nevertheless, this orientation on a future residual profit, despite all the problems of forecasting a future return on investment, does not change the basic nature of profit.

Profit and shareholder value, seen from the point of the firm, are not the final purpose of the firm but an instrumental end. Profit and shareholder value are the means to prevent shirking and to make sure that all members of the firm deliver their contractual contributions to the firm in an optimal way, as agreed in the contract.

Among all of the different groups involved in the firm, only the shareholders make profit and the value of the shares their goal. For all other groups, this goal is interesting only as a means to secure the success of the firm as a whole. It is not a final end that they could adopt on their own. Only in a very mediated way, then, can shareholder value be considered to be the purpose of the firm. It is, first of all, the purpose of one group within the firm, the shareholders; its prominence among the goals of the other groups within the firm is justified solely by its function of disciplining the owners, who in turn discipline all other members of the firm.

Moreover, from the point of view of the firm as a social unit and organization, shareholder value cannot be considered to be *the* purpose of the firm. It is only one criterion of the firm's success. As the future residual, it can be considered to be a control variable for the other goals and purposes of the firm and for its success. The fact that shareholder value is a residual, and remains so even if it is projected into the future, precludes elevating it to the first principle or the first purpose of the firm. A residual control principle remains what it is: a control principle, and not the final end of an organization.

The Purpose of the Firm

The debate on shareholder value belongs to the consideration of the purposes or goals of the firm in the theory of business administration. For the problem of shareholder value, what is interesting about the partly scholastic distinctions drawn among the many goals of a firm is the idea that the firm should be a one-purpose institution, which is untenable. Every firm has many purposes. The various groups within a firm have their own purposes, which they try to realize in the firm. Labor expects high wages from the firm; customers expect optimal goods from the firm; shareholders expect maximum returns on their investment; the community expects high taxes and public benefit payments from the firm, and so on. Some of these goals are conflicting, like the goals of maximum wages and maximum profits; others can be complementary, such as quality products and high returns on capital.

If one wants to single out the first purpose or final teleology of the firm, it is clear that the goal of no one group among those constituting the firm can qualify as *the* purpose of the firm, since the other groups also have the right to pursue their purposes via the firm. If there is one overriding purpose of the firm, it must be a purpose that could be accepted as such by all groups connected with the firm; it must be a purpose common to all members of the firm and to the public. Since all members of the firm and all members of society are consumers in some way—either directly, as consumers of the firm's product, or indirectly, as consumers of the goods for which the firm's product is an input—one must conclude that the overriding purpose of the firm is to satisfy consumers with its products. Dennis McCann makes this point when he recalls Peter Drucker on the firm's purpose, creating a customer (see chapter 8).

All members of the firm are consumers and are therefore interested in maximum productivity leading to optimal products. However, not all members of the firm are shareholders. The shareholders' peculiar purpose, therefore, cannot be the purpose of all the firm's members. It can be deduced from this that the purpose of the firm is the production of optimal products, or of optimal inputs for other products, under the constraints that meeting the goals of the major groups within the firm or touched by the firm's operation supposes: paying adequate wages to workers, adequate dividends to shareholders, and adequate prices to suppliers.

The necessary condition for the existence of the firm, and thus the main purpose for which firms come into being, is the production of products, not the production of profits or shareholder values. This main purpose of the firm may only be realized if sufficient returns on investment are earned, and, in this sense, the realization of shareholder value is a condition for the realization of the main purpose of the firm.

However, it is not the first condition. The main purpose of the firm, the production of best products, implies that the firm must be productive and efficient. How this productivity and efficiency are reached is a secondary question. Since it is the purpose and task of the business firm to provide the public with the best products produced at the lowest opportunity cost, those conditions that best secure the realization of this purpose must be met. The means of securing the purpose of the firm are, however, not the primary purpose of the firm. If the purpose of the firm, the production of optimal products, can be achieved best by market efficiency and shareholder value maximization, they are obligatory means. If it can be achieved by other, more effective means, then these must be chosen. Productivity is an obligation of the firm independent of market efficiency.

It is an old principle of the Aristotelian natural law tradition, also dominant in Catholic social thought, that obligation arises from the nature of the matter: *obligatio oritur a natura rei*.[4] This principle is also central in Radbruch's philosophy of law. According to Radbruch, the idea of obligation in law derives from the purpose of the institutional realm the law is to regulate, from the principle of equal right, and from the principle of legal security (or secure expectation as to the law's content and enforcement).[5]

Applied to the theory of the firm, the principle that obligation derives from the nature and purpose of the matter or institution in question requires that the main ethical and legal obligation of the firm must be deduced from its first purpose, and not from the conditions which secure the realization of its purpose. This first purpose of the firm is, however, not the maximization of the residual profit and of share value in the stock market, but the production of optimal products under the condition that the secondary goals of its member groups or stakeholders also be realized.

It is the virtue of the stakeholder approach (discussed in more detail in section 2 of this volume) to bring back to the theory of the firm the idea of a multipurpose organization, as opposed to the single-purpose organization assumed by the financial theory of the firm. The stakeholder approach, however, cannot integrate the several goals of the various stakeholders, but leaves them to be negotiated on an equal level. Moreover, integration of the different stakeholders' goals with the overriding productivity goal of the firm is not developed in the stakeholder theory introduced by R. Edward Freeman.[6]

The stakeholders' goals are subordinate to the overriding purpose of the firm: the rendering of its specific products or services via the market, to the public. This principle implies not only that the stakeholders' claims on the total income of the firm are limited by the strategic power they can exert in the contest with the claims of the other stakeholder groups, but that they are limited by the claims the firm as such, and its persistence as an institution, make on all its member groups. The necessity for continuing production of first-class goods disciplines strategic negotiations among the different stakeholder groups, as it also disciplines the drive for residual profit or maximal shareholder value. It renders other goals subordinate, although shareholder value maximization might, as the residual, dominate among the several goals of nonowning stakeholders.

Shareholder Value as the Product and Main Purpose of Financial Firms

There is one group of firms whose production goal coincides with maximizing shareholder value: financial institutions. The product of a financial institution *is* the maximization of shareholder value; however, it is also the maximization of its customers' shareholder value. Among financial institutions such as investment banks, investment funds, life insurance companies, and pension funds, shareholder value is not only the residual measuring the performance of the firm, but the very product for which the firm has come into existence. These institutions exist to render to their customers the product or service of securing the maximum return on their investment. For financial institutions, maximizing shareholder value is the main purpose of the firm and the primary measure of its performance.

A person who gives her savings to an investment fund purchases from this firm the product of maximizing her shareholder value. The investment fund in turn achieves its purpose and optimally fulfills its obligation if it maximizes the customers' shareholder value—but not its own shareholders' shareholder value. In financial institutions and the financial services industry, shareholder value is not only the residual condition for the optimal working of the firm, but the very product of the firm, and therefore gains a particular importance beyond that which it holds in other firms.

Spillover Effects from the Financial Institution to the Industrial Firm

The Western economies are presently experiencing the effects of a transfer of institutional conditions from financial institutions to industrial institutions, which, in turn, promotes shareholder value as the only purpose of the firm. Since increase of customers' shareholder value is the product financial institutions sell, shareholder value is the central and pivotal criterion of their business operations and business success. Among financial institutions, shareholder value defines the purpose and sets the criterion or instrumental control variable of the industry.

The special conditions of the financial services industries have been transferred to industrial firms, prompting the assumption that shareholder value is not only the control variable, but also the main purpose of the firm's operations. That is to say, this spillover from the financial firms to the industrial firms has caused an "inversion" whereby the shareholder value principle ascends from (subordinate) control principle to (superordinate) purpose of the firm. Since, for financial institutions, the control principle is at the same time the purpose of the institution, one has been tempted to think that the dual role of the shareholder value principle—as the control principle and as the purpose of the firm—applies also to industrial institutions, despite the fact that in the former case "shareholder value" refers to the interest of customers and in the latter it refers to the interest of the firms' owners.

In the radical version of the shareholder value approach, as defended by Jensen and Meckling, among others, the inversion of the firm's purpose and of the firm's control principle is explicit.[7] The radical shareholder value approach takes the residual of the firm's success for the firm's final purpose. In fact, shareholder value realized is the bookkeeping for the firm's success, but it is not its final purpose.

The spillover from financial institutions to industrial firms is particularly visible in the career of the holding firm, the trend toward which, interestingly enough, has been reversed recently in spite of the dominance of the shareholder value principle. In the transformation of the industrial firm into a conglomerate and a holding firm which only serves to monitor investment funds in its different divisions, its headquarters functions as the firm's own financial service institution, ensuring that all its divisions yield the maximum shareholder value for the holding. The holding's headquarters gives, for that purpose, little consideration to the material purposes and products of the divisions themselves.

For the holding firm, shareholder value has become the purpose and the product of the firm, precisely as maximizing shareholder value is, for an investment fund, its original business and product: the products of the divisions have become only a means to secure shareholder value for the holding headquarters. The holding firm is thus a particularly good example of the inversion of means and ends. Its organization implies that the end of the firm, the product of the divisions, becomes a means to shareholder value for the holding, although shareholder value was originally the means for controlling costs and ensuring optimal productivity, that is, the best product at the least cost.

It is revealing that recent economic developments demonstrate that the holding structure is much less advantageous than it appeared to be several years ago. Industrial firms are finding it most profitable to revert to their original strength and main task, the production of the products of their core competence. They no longer view themselves as investment funds for their own capital and no longer take their divisions to be mere investment opportunities for the funds of the holding's equity.

Understanding shareholder value as a control principle, the holding firm no longer considers shareholder value to be its main purpose, but it need not thereby fail to secure its own optimal performance. Rather, understanding the shareholder value principle rightly as a control principle allows the firm's producing divisions to realize their optimal product and, thereby, optimizes the whole firm's financial performance. The large corporation can maximize its shareholder value only if it considers shareholder value to be not the purpose, but only the control principle of its operations.

It seems to be the virtue of the shareholder value principle as a control principle that it is self-fulfilling and self-enforcing, just so long as it is not erected into a substitute for the main purpose of the firm, since it does not promote maximum shareholder value if it is taken for the purpose of the firm. There is no tendency built into the shareholder value principle to cause by itself the inversion of means and ends, and to turn itself from the means of control to the firm's end or purpose.

Effects of the Inversion of the Means and Ends on Corporate Governance

The inversion by which maximizing shareholder value supplants optimal productivity as the firm's primary purpose turns management's primary task, production, into speculation, as the example of the holding firm has demonstrated. The idea that, by the invisible hand of the labor market and the firm's contractual obligations, the overall orientation to shareholder value necessarily realizes the common good of the firm does not hold. True, the industrial firm can maximize shareholder value only if it produces some useful goods and keeps the implicit contracts with its employees and customers in some way. It realizes these common goods of the firm, however, only "somehow" and "on the coattails" of shareholder value maximization, since the new overall purpose of the firm—again, maximizing shareholder value—is increasingly realized by mere speculation.

Since the price of shares in the stock market does not exclusively reflect the real value of the firm's productivity and performance, but is also subject to mere speculation, management has an interest in becoming involved in speculative manipulations of the value of the firm's shares and, therefore, of its shareholder value. This distraction of the management's attention (and intention) from the main purpose of the firm, its product or products, to the secondary goal of the firm, maximizing shareholder value, results in two detrimental effects. First, it creates perverse incentives for the management to take more interest in speculation than in production or, at least, to become too interested in speculation instead of concentrating on production. Second, it results in a certain "short-termism" in managing the firm, focusing management on shareholder value and returns on investment for every quarterly report. The "terror of the quarterly report" is intensified.

Incentives are central to any economic order, and it is one of the main arguments for the shareholder value principle that it creates efficient incentives for management to maximize the overall value of the firm. The incentives it creates, however, can prove perverse, that is, can deflect management's intention toward activities that are not in the long-run interest of the firm as such. If shareholder value becomes the overall purpose of the firm, managers have strong incentives to invest their attention and time in finding ways to manipulate the price of shares in the stock market, ways that are often not in the interest of nonshareholding members of the firm. The possible perverse incentives the shareholder value principle exerts on the management, if it is considered to be the only purpose of the firm, are considerable. They direct the resources of the management to unproductive instead of productive action.

The second effect, "short-termism," or an exaggerated attention to the short-term share price in the stock market, is also not in the long-run interest of the firm if profitable long-run strategies are hindered by it. It is important to note, however, that short-termism is not by itself an economically and ethically negative phenomenon. It might be necessary and ethically legitimate to liquidate an investment after a very short time, were it found to be the wrong decision or were it subjected to sudden adverse developments.[8] The temporal horizon of management's decision making and of shareholders' decision making can, however, be shortened unduly by an exaggerated emphasis on shareholder value maximization.

Effects of the Inversion of Means and Ends
of the Firm on Industrial Relations

The inversion of the principle of shareholder value maximization from a control principle to the main purpose of the firm treats the members of the organization of the firm as means for the end of maximizing shareholder value. Using the members of the organization as means for an end is not objectionable in itself. The Kantian formulation of the categorical imperative is that one should act in such a way that one never treats the other as means *only,* not that one should never use another person as a means for a legitimate purpose. The firm that makes shareholder value maximization its first purpose may not treat its members as means only, but it will be in danger of doing so, and it will give its members the impression that the firm regards them as means for this end only and not also as ends in themselves.

The principle of justice in the economy and in the firm is that payments and rewards for services rendered should be determined according to the value of the contribution rendered to the purpose of the organization or firm.[9] This is the content of Thomas Aquinas's principle *Suum cuique tribuere,* give to each what is owed to him. Everyone should receive what he contributes to the common purpose of the organization. This principle was also the deeper justification for the theory of income in the theory of marginal productivity. Its normative content is that the factors of production should be compensated according to their marginal product (see Clark, chapter 5, on marginal utility theory).

The principle that all members of the organization should be paid according to their contribution to the goal of the firm creates tension with the shareholder value principle, which tends to imply that the firm should concentrate, in its consideration of the principle that persons should be rewarded according to their contributions, on return payments to shareholders only.

The idea that residual profit belongs only to the entrepreneur or the capital owner has been questioned on the ground that the dispositive factors usually cited—for example, the assumption of risk—may not be solely responsible for the success of the firm, since labor's contribution to the success of the firm might also involve dispositive elements. However, if labor is not ready to share in residual loss, the imputation of residual profit primarily to the owners is justified.

That residual profit is imputed only to one group makes it necessary to strive for a stronger participation of the workers in the formation of capital, if they are also to participate in the residual profit and shareholder value. This issue is addressed by Gates's essay (chapter 12). The call for more workers' participation in the ownership of the means of production correlates to emphasis on shareholder value maximization. If, then, shareholder value moves to the center of the goals of the firm, it should also be the case that labor, as owner of shares, has a higher stake in the shareholder value created by the firm.

There is a sequence of disciplining principles in the firm and a sequence of controls that step in when one of the principles fails: the shareholders prevent the firm's members from shirking; the stakeholders discipline the shareholders and their claim to returns on capital and prevent them from believing that their goal is the only goal of the firm; and the stakeholders are disciplined by the purpose of the firm, the product, and by the principle of justice that all members of the firm should be compensated according to their contributions to the firm. The shareholder value principle and the shareholders discipline the firm; the stakeholder value principle and the stakeholders discipline and limit the shareholders; the purpose of the firm disciplines and limits both the shareholders and the stakeholders.

Merging Shareholder Value and the Managers' Interests

The shareholder value principle cannot be interpreted only as an increased control on the performance of the managers. Rather, the firm's overemphasis on shareholder value may also lead to a strategic alliance between shareholders and managers against other stakeholders. If the shareholders and managers form one stakeholder group with shared interests, the managers are tempted to decide in their own and their shareholders' interest to realize a higher share value at cost to the firm and to other stakeholders. An indicator for this process is the increase to the managers of British state-owned companies that have been privatized as joint-stock companies. The most striking effect of the privatization of these firms has been the multiplication of the managers' income.

As we have seen, shareholder value maximization creates incentives for managers to look more after profits from speculative gains than after profits from superior productivity and products. These incentives can become perverse, since the value of the shares in the stock market is not only the result of the management's or firm's real performance, but also of its perceived performance. Share price is influenced by others' mere speculation as well.

The speculative element in the price of shares and, hence, shareholder value renders problematic the linking of managers' salaries to the development of the market value of the firm's shares. If the firm's shares experience an increase in their value due to speculation in the stock market, and if management receives higher or additional income from stock options, management's attention is attracted more to the movement of share prices than to the operations of their firms.

A case study for this problem is the lawsuit against a stock-option plan Daimler-Benz AG proposed for its managers. One of the shareholders in the firm, Ekkehard Wenger, a professor of business administration, brought suit against the firm on the grounds that the plan violates the interests of the shareholders. Wenger argued that a conversion of stock options into real Daimler-Benz shares after three years, under the condition that the share price had risen by 15 percent during the period, is not acceptable, since a rate of increase of value at 5 percent per year involves no extraordinary performance by management if the average rate of increase in the stock market is just the same. A special remuneration dependent on the success of the firm could be justified only if the rate of increase in the price of the firm's share were higher than the average rate of increase in share value on the stock market.

The court at Stuttgart dismissed this action with the statement that "judging the managerial content of such a stock option scheme is not the task of the court."[10] The court's decision, however, does not close the question as to the managerial appropriateness of the scheme. Whether an *average* increase in the value of a firm's shares justifies additional income for its management via stock options, and whether such schemes may not induce in managers an exaggerated concentration on the price of the firm's shares, thereby creating perverse incentives, remain open to discussion.

Unequal Possibilities of Tax Evasion for Labor and Capital

We have noted how the opening up of world markets, particularly of the East Asian and Chinese markets, has necessarily led to a change in the relationship between income from capital and income from labor in the highly developed economies. Inevitably, capital has become scarcer, despite the phenomenon of the increased inheritance of capital.[11]

On the global scale, there is a scarcity of capital despite low interest rates, a fact also confirmed by high dividends and increases in the market price of shares. Globalization is not only the cause but also the result of an extension of the capital market by the demand for capital from those countries that are characterized by a high supply of labor and a high need for capital investment from the advanced economies.

To give an example: the interest rate for industrial credit in Russia was 48 percent per year in 1997 (summer), an indicator of an extreme scarcity of capital, but also an indicator of an economic order that does not yet work. Not only in Russia, with its extreme market conditions, but in the global market, the ratio between capital and labor income changed, and capital became more scarce than labor, a development that increased in turn the globalization of the use of capital and of capital investment.

The increase of capital income in relation to labor income is enforced by a phenomenon that also results from the globalization and enhanced mobility of capital: increased opportunities for tax avoidance in the advanced economies. This phenomenon results from the fact that capital income can avoid taxation much more easily than labor income, since capital is much more easily moved to locations where lower tax rates prevail. Labor is subject to the necessity of being enculturated and integrated into a community, whereas capital can float relatively freely around the globe.

The problem of tax avoidance, and the fact that capital income can avoid taxation more easily than labor income, is the Achilles' heel of the shareholder value approach. It renders necessary the formation of capital in the hands of workers. An increased ownership in the means of production by labor becomes urgent not primarily on consideration of income distribution, but since capital income increases more rapidly than labor income (as Gates argues in chapter 12). It is necessary, rather, since taxation becomes inequitable. If the capital owner and shareholder can avoid taxation to a higher degree than labor, by legal tax avoidance, the economy faces a challenge that is not prima facie a distribution problem, but a problem of the justice of taxation, owing to inequitable distribution of the tax burden. Taxation becomes regressive instead of being progressive or linear.

There is a growing consensus among economists that the higher mobility of capital on the global scale renders it impossible to maintain the tax state (*Steuerstaat*) that the advanced economies have practiced hitherto, particularly in continental Europe.[12] The tax base of countries with a high rate of taxation, such as Germany or Italy, is gradually destroyed by the ease with which the enterprise can change the location where it is taxed to low-tax countries. Germany is surrounded by small countries with low rates of taxation, such as Austria, Luxembourg, and Switzerland, that attract capital from the larger countries with high tax rates. Smaller nations are able to overcompensate for the decrease in tax revenue caused by the lower tax rate by an influx of additional taxable capital from nations with higher tax rates.

The question of how to balance the relative tax advantage capital income enjoys compared to labor income becomes pressing. The formation of shareholder value not only in those social strata that have been capital owning until now, but also in the hands of workers, takes on political urgency.[13] Since capital income will avoid countries with extremely high and even illegitimate rates of taxation, and since government can hardly address the phenomenon except by severe measures of social control, individuals from all social strata must become capital owners in order to enjoy the lower rates of taxation on capital income which result quasi-necessarily from the process of globalization.[14]

Inequality in income and uneven distribution of capital ownership will persist even under conditions of increased formation of capital owned by workers, but the degree of inequality in the taxation of total personal income will at least be reduced.

Shareholder Value and the Concept of the Market Order

The emphasis on shareholder value has repercussions for the understanding of market order. Shareholder value theory's preoccupation with future cash flow and with the expected returns on alternative investment projects direct the interest of the entrepreneur to new knowledge and new products promising high cash flows. The shareholder value concept discourages adaptation of the firm to given market conditions but encourages the creation of new products and the development of new markets. This emphasis on new, alternative opportunities for investment brings the shareholder value theory closer to the process theory of the market developed by the Austrian school of economics than to the theory of general equilibrium characteristic of neoclassical economics.[15] It also represents an important correction to the static idea of the economic order and of economic institutions that has become dominant in the theory of the economic order proposed by the German tradition of ordo-liberalism.

The shareholder value theory demonstrates that the static order suggested by the model of perfect competition must always be broken up by new, alternative opportunities for investment and that the market is a process in which capital flows to the best alternative uses— often completely new products and production processes. Investors must consider the relative market situation of the firm and look for opportunities to break up markets that are in equilibrium by entrepreneurial innovation and the repositioning of firms. The shareholder value theory is, in short, a formula for creating disequilibrium in the market.

Shareholder Value, Investment Funds, and the Unfaithfulness of Investment

If an integrated, world capital market is arising, and if the investors' obligation is to move their capital always, as quickly as possible, to that spot where it may realize a rate of return that is marginally higher than the return at its present location, the economy faces a problem of "economic unfaithfulness." Rendering the shareholder value principle the only economic criterion effects a quasi-ethical sanctioning of the total "unfaithfulness" of investment.

The problem of the unfaithfulness of investment is particularly aggravated by the increasing importance of anonymous pension funds. If pension and investment funds worked in such a way that they liquidated any investment at once, if they could achieve a rate of return that is 0.01 percent higher (after subtraction of all transaction costs), the resulting strategy might not be rational and efficient, since the unfaithfulness of the investment funds puts the firm they leave under pressure to find new shareholders.

A second questionable effect of the shareholder value principle concerns repercussions on the structure of human motivation. Making profit maximization the ultimate purpose of all economic activity avoids the debate and conceals the question whether the kinds of economic activity in hand are legitimate and whether there are economic activities that might maximize shareholder value but are not acceptable from an ethical point of view (see Gordley's critique of economists on this point in chapter 4). This effect originates from the inversion of means and ends in the conception of the firm caused by the shareholder value theory. If shareholder value maximization is made the ultimate goal of the economy and the first purpose of all firms, the distinction between legitimate and illegitimate kinds of profit formation is lost, since the actual purpose of the firm or of an economic activity is always made to be a means to the end of profit maximization. In other words, all other goals are subordinate to the first goal and duty of shareholder wealth maximization. The repercussions for the structure of human motivation are considerable.[16]

The effects of investment funds and their unfaithfulness differ between countries. Whereas in Germany pension funds play practically no role in the capital market, and the stock market is therefore not very lively, the pension funds are important players in the capital markets of the United States and Great Britain. The formation of pension funds should be encouraged in Germany to strengthen the capital market, but one must be aware that the highly impersonal investment strategy of the pension funds also has a problematic side.[17]

Since the managers of the pension funds do not invest for themselves but for others, they feel justified in a complete unfaithfulness toward the firms in which they invest. The managers of pension funds invest not as shareholders but as agents for other principals, and they invest for other people's old-age pensions. They can therefore exculpate themselves from any responsibility for the firms they invest in by pointing to the fact that they must maximize shareholder value in the interest of the pensioners and by claiming that any means to maximize shareholder value is justified by the goal of securing old-age pensions. This exculpation from responsibility for the consequences of investment decisions aimed solely at maximizing shareholder value is not likewise viable for shareholders who invest on their own account.

Any kind of fiduciary relationship, or acting on behalf of others and for their purposes, results in a reduction of moral obligation, since responsibility for the actions is shared and can be shifted between the principal and the agent. In the case of investment funds, responsibility for investment decisions is shared between the pensioners' claim to profitable old-age pensions—a goal that, superficially, seems legitimate beyond all question—and the reckless pursuit of shareholder value maximization by the fund managers.

The fact that, owing to their institutional arrangements, pension funds entertain an increased element of unfaithfulness in their investment decisions may be problematic not only from an ethical point of view, but also from the point of view of efficient allocation. It must be asked whether the investor, under the framework of the shareholder value principle, need not also have a duty to be faithful to a firm he has invested in up to a certain extent, even if this firm happens to be in a period of crisis. To some extent, the obligation to solidarity and the obligation to secure efficiency and shareholder value maximization must be weighed against each other. There is no simple solution to this question.

The question of faithfulness in investment is comparable to the problem of how the firm should manage personal crises of its workers: Can it fire them at once? Should it be obliged to give them a chance to recover from their crises? In both cases, the problem is very hard to quantify and invites no simple solution. The necessary faithfulness and the necessary unfaithfulness, or readiness to "exit," must be weighed— in investment and in labor relations—by a decision-maker who accepts personal responsibility for his decisions' consequences.

The Shareholder Value Principle and Catholic Social Thought

Inquiry into *the* purpose of the firm and into the right relationship of means and ends is a methodological approach typical of the natural right tradition and Catholic social thought. The idea that the firm has something like a "natural" purpose and that this purpose ought not to be made to be a means for another end will be subject to criticism from theories of subjective value. These theories claim that the human is free to set purposes, that there is nothing like a natural purpose, and that, therefore, there is nothing like a "natural" purpose of the firm.

There is some justification for this argument insofar as a person who is not interested in the purpose of the firm per se, but only in maximizing shareholder value, might be more successful and do more good than a person who is very much striving for the purpose of the firm and is not fixed on profit, but in the end neither achieves the purpose of the firm (producing a good product) nor high shareholder value. The former person might have *intended* solely to maximize the shareholder value, but may realize the social good of a good product as well, for example, through the influence of the shareholder value principle as a "control."

At this point, two distinctions are useful: the distinction between individual and social ethics and the distinction between single-purpose motivation and multipurpose motivation.

Catholic social thought, or social ethics, cannot compel individual economic agents to accept its concept of the order of purposes and make it their own, but it can show that for social institutions and for their ethical foundations it is better if the right order of goals is followed, even though the economic agents acting within these socioethical institutions retain the freedom to adopt a reverse order of goals. Again, the natural right tradition does not force everyone to have the same order of goals, but it can ground the right order of purposes and explain why institutions should adopt and propagate this order.

The fact that better results are sometimes achieved by bad motives and that bad results are sometimes achieved through good motives does not discredit the nexus between desirable motives and desirable results. It may be better, in single cases, to achieve good results by bad motives than to achieve bad results by good motives. For the justification of social norms, motives, and expectations—for social ethics—this fact does not shake the observation that it is better yet to achieve good consequences with good motives. The best state of affairs, seen from the point of view of social ethics, is still the one in which good results are realized by good motives.

The question of rightly ordered intentions brings the shareholder value principle into relation with certain denominational differences.

The idea that the maximum efficiency and common good of society are reached when individual economic agents adhere to their abstract concept of maximizing their own profit is linked to the Protestant idea of the sinner's incapability to do good. It is thereby also linked to different conceptions of original sin. The Protestant idea of social coordination supposes that people are so distorted by original sin, they cannot intend the common good as such. The common good can, therefore, only be reached as the invisible hand directs individuals' inevitably selfish intentions and needs to ends beyond them. This conception is particularly strong in Lutheran thought, where the human is considered to be so fallen that his will is a slave's will, being enslaved to its own selfishness. Nothing good can be expected from the direct intention of the human will.

Society, then, cannot be intentionally structured to achieve the common good. Rather, the common good can only be an indirect purpose or *dolus eventualis*—an effect not intended at all, but realized as the side effect of the pursuit of those selfish goals of which the fallen human is alone capable. Likewise, when shareholder value maximization is made the first purpose of the firm, the firm's common good, the good product and the fulfillment of the stakeholders' stakes in the firm, is made the side effect of the direct intention, or *dolus directus,* for the maximization of shareholder value, which is understood as private good.

For Protestant thinking, this is the best solution possible. Catholic social thought will find it second best, even under conditions of original sin, which make the human selfish and prone to value profit maximization above the purpose of the firm itself. In contrast to the Lutheran concept of original sin, which takes the human to be incapable of doing good by intention, the Catholic understanding of original sin holds that the human is able to do good intentionally, even under conditions of original sin. In the case of the purpose of the firm, this implies that the individual is still able to adopt the common good of this community, the firm, as his own, despite his tendency to value self-interest above all.

Catholic thought suggests that the human is a sinner, but that this sinner is still able to do good through the institutional framework at hand, in this case, through the firm, which must take into account sinful human nature. That shareholder value maximization represents the second-best solution implies that owners must pursue the purpose of the firm and their own purpose of shareholder value maximization at the same time, that they ought to consider the first purpose of the firm to be the good it produces, and that they ought to organize the firm accordingly.

The distinction between single-purpose and multipurpose motivation comes in here. That shareholder value is a control principle of the firm should not imply that the owner of the firm knows only one purpose, the maximization of shareholder value, but that he pursues the purpose of the firm and his own purpose of shareholder value maximization at the same time.

The motivational structure of the entrepreneur and manager can be described by the concept of the overdetermination of action, a concept that is also close to the understanding of the structure of human motivation in Catholic social thought. The concept of the overdetermination of action, of the *Überdeterminiertheit der Handlung,* was originally introduced by Sigmund Freud in his *Interpretation of Dreams:* our dreams are overdetermined by several motives overlying and overlapping each other.[18] Not only our dreams, but also our actions and even our economic actions are overdetermined by several motives.

The concept of the overdetermination and of overlapping determinants of economic action is more suitable for describing the firm's and the shareholder's purpose than the concept of the inversion of intentions and purposes, making the purpose of the firm only the means for shareholder value maximization. Shareholder value maximization should be the side effect of a good product and firm, not a good product and a good firm the side effects of shareholder value maximization.

Notes

1. Roman Herzog, interview with *Bild-Zeitung,* 28 July 1998, p. 2.
2. Cf. E. Gaugler, "Shareholder Value und Unternehmensführung" (Shareholder Value and Managing the Firm), in *Shareholder Value und die Kriterien des Unternehmenserfolgs,* ed. Peter Koslowski (Heidelberg: Physica, 1998).

3. Armen Albert Alchian and Harold Demsetz, "Production, Information Costs, and Economic Organization," in *Economic Forces at Work,* ed. A.A. Alchian (Indianapolis: Liberty Press, 1977), 73–110.

4. Luis De Molina, *De iustitia et iure* (Madrid, 1602). Cf. Peter Koslowski, *Ethik des Kapitalismus,* 6th ed. (Tübingen: Mohr Siebeck, 1998) and the English translation, *Ethics of Capitalism and Critique of Sociobiology: Two Essays* (Berlin, New York, Tokyo: Springer, 1996).

5. Gustav Radbruch, "Rechtsphilosophie," in *Philosophy of Right,* 8th ed. (Stuttgart: Koehler, 1973), 114.

6. R. Edward Freeman, *Strategic Management: A Stakeholder Approach* (Boston: Pitman, 1984), and "The Politics of Stakeholder Theory: Some Future Directions," *Business Ethics Quarterly* 4 (1994): 413ff.

7. M.C. Jensen and W.H. Meckling, "The Theory of the Firm: Managerial Behavior, Agency Costs, and Ownership Structure," in *Economics and Social Insitutions: Insights from the Conferences on Analysis and Ideology,* ed. Karl Brunner (Boston: Martinus Nijhoff, 1979): 163–231.

8. Cf. Peter Koslowski, *Ethik der Banken und der Börse* (Tübingen: Mohr Siebeck, 1997), and the abridged English version, "The Ethics of Banking," in *The Ethical Dimension of Financial Institutions and Markets,* ed. A. Argandona (Berlin, New York, Tokyo: Springer, 1995).

9. Cf. for this principle G. Schmoller, "Die Gerechtigkeit in der Volkswirthschaft" (Justice in the Economy), *Jahrbücher für Gesetzgebung, Verwaltung und Volkswirtschaft im Deutschen Reich* 5 (1881): 19–54. For the historical school of economics, cf. Peter Koslowski, *Gesellschaftliche Koordination: Eine Theorie der Marktwirtschaft* (Societal Coordination: A Theory of the Market Economy) (Tübingen: Mohr Siebeck, 1991); Peter Koslowski, ed., *The Theory of Ethical Economy in the Historical School: Wilhelm Roscher, Lorenz von Stein, Gustav Schmoller, Wilhelm Dilthey and Contemporary Theory* (1995; reprint, Berlin, New York, Tokyo: Springer, 1997); and Peter Koslowski, ed., *Methodology of the Social Sciences, Ethics, and Economics in the Newer Historical School: From Max Weber and Rickert to Sombart and Rothacker* (Berlin, New York, Tokyo: Springer, 1997).

10. Cf. "Niederlage für Daimler-Kritiker Wenger" (Defeat for Daimler's Critic Wenger), *Süddeutsche Zeitung* 185 (August 13, 1998): 17; as well as "Wenger unterliegt Daimler," and comment by Mathias Philip, "Aktien optionen" (Share Options), in *Hannoversche Allgemeine Zeitung* 188 (August 13, 1998): 9. The comment takes sides with Wenger against Daimler-Benz.

11. This marks an important change, particularly in Germany, where in Western Germany—but not in Eastern Germany—after the serious losses of wealth during and after World War II, a large transfer of wealth and capital by inheritance is now experienced.

12. Cf. Vito Tazi, "Globalization, Tax Competition and the Future of Tax Systems," in *Steuersysteme der Zukunft,* ed. G. Krause-Junk (Berlin: Duncker and Humblot, 1998), 11–27.

13. The governments of the high-tax states prove themselves to be more and more incapable of prohibiting the possibilities of tax evasion for capital income. They are comparably helpless against shifting capital income abroad for the purpose of tax evasion. The government can take two strategic options against this development. It can first move taxation from indirect taxes on income to taxes on consumption and direct taxes. This option results in the abolition of progressive taxation and is regressive in its effect on the low-income groups. The other option for government is to open the access to the kinds of income that are unavoidably taxed at a lower rate to groups that do not have this access so far, to labor. The disparities in taxation between capital or shareholder value on the one hand and labor income on the other hand cannot be sustained in the long run.

14. The effects of tax and the attempts to evade taxation was already an argument for the formation of capital in the hands of workers in the 1950s. Nell-Breuning, the most important thinker of Catholic social teaching in the German-speaking countries and coauthor (together with Gustav Gundlach) of the draft for the encyclical letter *Quadragesimo anno,* argued for the formation of capital in the hands of workers, since the high taxation on capital caused an overinvestment on the side of the capital owners in ways to avoid taxation and so led to economically useless investments only justified by the wish to save taxes. Cf. Oswald Von Nell-Breuning, "The Formation of Private Property in the Hands of Workers," in *The Social Market Economy: Theory and Ethics of the Economic Order,* ed. Peter Koslowski (Berlin, New York, Tokyo: Springer, 1998), 305 ff.

15. For this distinction in the theory of the market cf. A. Bosch, Peter Koslowski, R. Veit, eds., *General Equilibrium or Market Process: Neoclassical and Austian Theories of Economics* (Tübingen: Mohr Siebeck, 1990) and Peter Koslowski, *Prinzipen der ethischen Ökonomie,* 2d ed. (Tübingen: Mohr Siebeck, 1994).

16. The problem of the inversion of means and ends is formulated by Helen J. Alford and Michael J. Naughton in terms of the inversion between foundational (or instrumental) and excellent (or intrinsic) goods. Although one can see the importance of this distinction of human motivation, the idea that shareholder value is the foundational purpose of the firm and that other goals, such as fulfilling the stakes of other stakeholders, are excellent goods does not do justice to the fact that it is the foundational good of the firm to produce the optimal good (good in the sense of product), and not the optimal

shareholder value. The good product is, so to speak, the firm's foundational *and* excellent good. Cf. chapter 2 in this volume.

17. Cf. Rainer Fehn, "Schaffen Pension Funds über vollkommenere Kapitalmärkte mehr Beschäftigung?" (Do Pension Funds Create More Employment via More Perfect Capital Markets?), in *Shareholder Value und die Kriterien des Unternehmenserfolgs,* ed. Koslowski, 73–108.

18. Sigmund Freud, *Die Traumdeutung* (1900; reprint, Frankfurt am Main: S. Fischer, 1982).

Section II

Adding the Stakeholder
Model to the Debate

Introduction

At the midpoint of his careful survey "Modern Contract Theory and the Purpose of the Firm," Lee A. Tavis observes, "The shareholder and stakeholder theories of the firm"—theories which exhaust the present field—"have evolved with little recognition of, or input from, Catholic social thought."[1] On reflection, Professor Tavis's matter-of-fact observation appears as a stunning comment on the Catholic academy in the United States.

Nearly seventy years have passed since Adolph A. Berle, Jr., and Gardiner C. Means's *The Modern Corporation and Private Property* (1932) threw open the question, What is the business corporation's purpose? by tracing the implications, for "the traditional logic" of property and of profits, of the corporation's essential feature, namely, the separation of the managerial function (in Berle and Means's language, "control" or "active property") from ownership (shareholding, or in their language, "passive property").[2] Berle and Means concluded:

> the owners of passive property, by surrendering control and responsibility over the active property . . . [and] the controlling groups, by means of the extension of corporate powers . . . in their own interest[,] . . . have placed the community in a position to demand that the modern corporation serve not alone the owners or the control but all society.[3]

Their call for a concerted response from theorists already in possession of Pius XI's *Quadragesimo anno* (1931)—with its withering critique of

> [the] immense power and despotic economic dictatorship . . . con-
> solidated in the hands of a few, who often are not owners but only
> trustees and managing directors of invested funds[4]

and with its call for the reconstitution of subsidiary social institutions under a public authority alive "to the needs of the common good; that is, to the norm of social justice"[5]—might seem to have been sounded in the very voice of secular social economics. If so, the history both of corporate and of managerial theory since 1931–32 suggests that the invitation went largely unheard, or was declined, in Catholic quarters.

Hitherto, successive renewals of the invitation, marked by the promulgation of a continuing series of encyclicals, constitutions, and pastoral letters treating economic aspects of the "social question," have not evoked a more energetic response.[6] Sustained examination of the corporate economy and corporate practice by Catholic scholars, in the light of the principles of Catholic social thought, has been conspicuous for its paucity, if not for its absence.

In the meantime, the one theoretical development which, on first blush, seems to address comprehensively many concerns at the heart of the social question—that is, stakeholder theory—arrived on the scene self-described (in its normative form) as Kantian capitalism and has been elaborated without explicit reliance on the social character of ownership, subsidiarity, solidarity, the common good, just wages, or any other leading principle of Catholic social thought (see McCann's essay for the relationship of corporate organization to subsidiarity, chapter 8).[7]

It may be that the Catholic academy's neglect of the Church's social tradition is one more symptom of the fact that, through most of the last seventy years, differences among world socioeconomic systems overshadowed all differences in the realm of socioeconomic principle. That the tradition of Catholic social thought endorsed, for example, private ownership of the means of production, could well seem wholly decisive in a world divided between socialist-command and capitalist-market systems. That the Church approached the question of property via a fundamentally Thomistic notion of ownership at odds, in essential respects, with the post-Enlightenment concept of private property was a further fact apt to be overlooked or downplayed. Hence (to extend the example), the "prepolarized" reception of John Paul II's *Laborem exercens* (1981)—of the encyclical's (then) startlingly forceful reassertion of the traditional Catholic teaching that *"the right to private property is subordinated to the right to common use,"* that the promotion of living wages is a social obligation, and that labor enjoys a normative priority over capital[8]—saw a class of commentators wondering in print whether the pope from socialist Poland might be incapable of appreciating the institutions of market economies. A decade later, the same class of commentators was able to remark *Centesimus annus's* "endorsement" of the free market,[9] without troubling much over the fact that John Paul II offered his observations as part of a sustained reflection, continuous with *Laborem exercens* and *Sollicitudo rei socialis,* on the right-to-property's role in realizing the universal destination of material goods.[10]

A further decade—and a world—gone, perhaps *Laborem exercens, Centesimus annus,* and other documents of the Catholic social tradition can be read without added ideological "color." Even if so, however, how is their significance for broadly economic matters—including corporate governance and managerial practice—to be assessed? That is, does the tradition of Catholic social thought propose (as Kennedy and McCann wonder in chapters 3 and 8) no more than certain ethical principles by which the unavoidable social effects of economic "laws" can be (partly) blunted? Does it propose original insights into human action which suggest in their turn that—and how—the positive "laws" of economics and the techniques of managerial science *"can* be ordered to serve human flourishing and the common good"? Catholic scholars (and others) are waking to these questions' urgency, but are waking as well to the variety of plausible, sometimes contrary answers which can be given them. Even setting aside debate over their truth, little agreement yet exists on what the principles of Catholic social thought entail for the business organization and conduct of economic life.

In terms of the theory of the firm, the question of the kind of bearing Catholic social thought can, or ought, to claim—intrinsic or extrinsic, original (even radical) or supplementary—involves assessing its relationships to the rival theories which, by default, already occupy the field on their own account, the shareholder and stakeholder models. The essays on just such assessment which appear in the following section fall into no simple pattern. They belong emphatically to the present, "waking" stage of scholarly engagement and are thus essays in the original sense of that term: trial attempts or approaches; they differ from one another, often as strikingly as they differ from conventional thinking.

Diverse as their approaches are, however, our authors have in common the view that (1) the stakeholder theory of the firm and its management makes a serious claim to represent *the* normative alternative to purely financial *cum*-strategic (shareholder) theory and practice; (2) on this showing alone, any account of the firm grounded in Catholic social thought must situate itself—critically or complementarily, as a supplement or as an alternative—in relation to stakeholder theory; and (3) Catholic social thought commands a clear account of principles upon which stakeholder theory (at best) inchoately relies, or to which (at worst) it is incapable of giving consistent effect. This last point of agreement is, of course, also the point at which our authors begin to fall out among themselves. Their differences—taken together—provide a conspectus of the possible relations between Catholic social thought, stakeholder theory, and, inevitably, the financially driven, "strategic" thought which still dominates corporate decision making as the shareholder value principle.

Notes

1. See page 224 of this volume. See also the preface for further details on the lack of engagement between Catholic social thought and management.

2. See Adolf A. Berle, Jr., and Gardiner C. Means, *The Modern Corporation and Private Property,* 2d rev. ed. (New York: Harcourt, Brace and World, 1968), 293–313.

3. Ibid., 311–12.

4. Pius XI, *Quadragesimo anno* (Washington, D.C.: National Catholic Welfare Conference, 1942), 105; cf. 106–9.

5. Ibid., 110; cf. 79, Pius IX's famous formulation of the "principle of subsidiarity."

6. See *Pacem in terris* and *Mater et magistra* (John XXXII, 1961 and 1963), *Gaudium et spes* (Second Vatican Council, 1965), *Populorum progres-*

sio (Paul VI, 1967), *Laborem exercens* (John Paul II, 1981), *Economic Justice for All* (United States Catholic Bishops, 1986), *Sollicitudo rei socialis* (John Paul II, 1987), and *Centesiumus annus* (John Paul II, 1991).

7. See William M. Evan and R. Edward Freeman, "A Stakeholder Theory of the Modern Corporation: Kantian Capitalism," in *Ethical Theory and Business*, 3d ed., edited by T. L. Beauchamp and Norman E. Bowie (Englewood Cliffs, N.J.: Prentice Hall, 1988).

8. See John Paul II, *Laborem exercens*, in *The Encyclicals of John Paul II*, ed. J. Michael Miller, C.S.B. (Huntington, Ind.: Our Sunday Visitor Publishing Division, 1996), 14.2 (emphasis original), 19.1–19.6, 12.1–12.6.

9. See John Paul II, *Centesimus annus*, 32.4, 34.1, in *The Encyclicals of John Paul II*.

10. See ibid., 30.1–31.3.

7

Clearing Ground

Toward a Social Ethic of Corporate Management

S. A. CORTRIGHT

AND ERNEST S. PIERUCCI

In the context of the liberal regime, the questions "What are the social responsibilities of the business corporation?" and "To what normative standards should corporate decision making be held?" translate easily into the language of interests. So, to ask "In whose interests should the business corporation be operated?" or "Whose interests are corporate managers obligated to weigh? to serve?" may well seem to be a matter merely of framing the former questions in more precise terms.

Recent essays offering a thoroughgoing account of corporate responsibility in terms of the interests managers are obliged to weigh, and corporations to serve, have gradually taken shape as the "shareholder-stakeholder" conversation—or rather, as John Boatright reminds us, have emerged as a revival of that conversation. The conversation's beginnings date from the first systematic attempts at coming to grips with the rise of the corporate form and with the emergent power of the managerial class.[1] The revived shareholder-stakeholder conversation has proved at once compelling (compare its prominence in, even domination of, the literature) and stubbornly inconclusive (also compare the continuing ramification of the debate).

R. Edward Freeman, who is responsible (if any one person can be) for the conversation's revival, has placed on the record an assessment — rather, a diagnosis — of the state of the shareholder-stakeholder discourse. It is an odd and remarkable document. Freeman begins with the goal of "clarifying certain foundational issues" but ends with an exhortation to unabashed pragmatism, which he recommends as the only hopeful recourse against despair over impotent theoretical wrangling.[2] "From foundations to pragmatism" is an unusual itinerary.

Now, whatever one may make of Freeman's prescription, his diagnosis of the state of the conversation he has done so much to shape commands attention. Moreover, as Freeman himself advises, it represents mature reflection of some years' gestation and is indebted to wide consultation.[3] We propose, then, first to revisit crucial junctures in the revived shareholder-stakeholder conversation, taking Freeman as our guide.

Pictures from a Conversation

Freeman's diagnosis is as straightforward as could be desired. First, received business theory and received normative theory alike move in tacit obedience to his "separation thesis": the discourse of business and the discourse of ethics can be separated, so that such sentences as "x is a business decision" have no moral content, and such sentences as "x is a moral decision" have no business content.[4] As a result, conventional thinking about business tends ineluctably to play some variation on the theme that, as the corporation exists "to enhance the economic well-being, or serve as a vehicle for the free choices, of the owners,"[5] corporate managers are functionaries whose obligations begin and end with their fiduciary duties to shareholders. Managers are obligated, because corporations exist, to preserve and extend the property interests of shareholder-owners; consideration of other interests, including interests advanced on normative grounds, can at most constitute "a side-constraint on the maximization of stockholder wealth, justified only if a greater good or other moral end is served."[6] The separation thesis, then, forges an iron link between property rights and a purely strategic, unattenuated shareholder theory of management.

Second, the whole point of the revived stakeholder-shareholder conversation has been—from the side of stakeholder theory—to deny the separation thesis and its immediate entailments, and to rethink business theory in a moral context.[7] To the extent, however, that the latter project has been translated into making out theoretical grounds for the reconciliation of discrete, technical-*cum*-strategic business thinking, on the one hand, with normative thinking, on the other, it has covertly relapsed into—or rather has never escaped—the very dichotomy it was intended to deny or to dissolve. As a result, the conversation has descended into an impotent round of distinction meeting counterdistinction, growing at once "richer"—that is, increasingly recondite and complex—and more barren—that is, more academic, in the invidious sense forever captured by the phrase "*merely* academic."

The root, then, of Freeman's palpable impatience is this: even if, on the basis of recent theoretical gains, we can (as Freeman concludes) "safely say that the stockholder theory is or should be intellectually dead," in practice it refuses to die, no matter how many versions of stakeholder theory have been thrust, by eager hands, through its heart.[8]

Now, as Freeman formulates it, the separation thesis represents a conceptual dichotomy and suggests an epistemic "option."[9] For, if "the discourse of business and the discourse of ethics *can* be separated" (albeit at the price of an intractable conceptual dualism), then the two can also be treated inseparably.[10] As Freeman reads them, certain of the revived stakeholder-shareholder conversation's developments combine to issue a pressing invitation to exercise the option.

First in importance among these developments is the finding of Thomas Donaldson and Lee E. Preston:

> The plain truth is that the most prominent alternative to the stakeholder theory (i.e., the "management serving the shareholders" theory) is morally untenable. The theory of property rights, which is commonly supposed to support the conventional view, in fact—in its modern and pluralistic form—supports the stakeholder theory instead.[11]

Unless, however, "modern" is a synonym for "sound," this would-be categorical declaration slightly outruns Donaldson and Preston's argument. They themselves state the case more circumspectly before the conclusion just cited:

> [But] if a pluralistic theory of property rights is accepted, then the connection between the theory of property and the stakeholder theory becomes explicit. All the critical characteristics underlying the classic theories of distributive justice are present among the stakeholders of a corporation, as they are conventionally conceived and presented in contemporary stakeholder theory.[12]

Now, the positive correlation between contemporary stakeholder theory and contemporary property theory contrasts with a telling disjunction of shareholder theory from property theory. For it is characteristic of virtually all versions of the latter to hold

> the notion that property rights are embedded in human rights and that restrictions against harmful uses are intrinsic to the property rights concept [, which] clearly brings the interests of others (*i.e.,* of non-owner stakeholders) into the picture . . .[13]

so that

> the contemporary theoretical concept of private property clearly does not ascribe unlimited rights to owners and hence does not support the popular claim that the responsibility of managers is to act solely as agents for the shareowners.[14]

These considerations, finally, represent the outlines of an argument that, unlike the shareholder theory, "the stakeholder theory can be normatively based on the *evolving* theory of property."[15]

The second development concerns the judgment that, but for the pervasive influence of the separation thesis, many of the apparently normative disagreements which have turned shareholder-stakeholder discourse into a manufactory of proliferating, competing interpretations and positions would simply show up moot and fade away into desuetude. Such is the fate Freeman foresees for the positions resulting from the "stakeholder paradox" discerned by Kenneth E. Goodpaster, and for the competing "third position" proposed by John Boatright.

Goodpaster introduces the issue with this uneasy conclusion: "it seems essential, yet in some ways illegitimate, to orient corporate decisions by ethical values that go beyond strategic stakeholder considerations to multi-fiduciary ones."[16] He goes on to explicate the paradox:

> [i]t can be argued that multi-fiduciary stakeholder analysis is simply incompatible with widely-held moral convictions about the special fiduciary obligations owed by management to shareholders . . . for the obligations of agents to principals are stronger or different in kind from those of agents to third parties.[17]

The paradox thus enjoins a distinction between opposed versions of stakeholder analysis: there appear (in Goodpaster's phrases) both a "strategic stakeholder analysis," or "business without ethics"—namely, the exercise of exclusive, fiduciary duties to manage relations with a firm's stakeholders for the economic advantage of shareholders or of the firm itself—and a version representing "effective loss of the private sector with a multi-fiduciary stakeholder synthesis," or "ethics without business."[18] Goodpaster takes the critical position that stakeholder theory generates the paradox by supposing that only countervailing fiduciary duties to customers, suppliers, neighbors, and other groups closely affected by corporate decisions—that is, stakeholders—can place strategic business practices driven by fiduciary duties to share-holders on a consistently normative footing. His positive position to the contrary holds, accordingly, that

> The foundation of ethics in management—and the way out of the stakeholder paradox—lies in understanding that the conscience of the corporation is a logical and moral extension of the consciences of its principals. It is not an expansion of the list of principals, but a gloss on the principal-agent relationship itself. Whatever the structure of the principal-agent relationship, neither principal nor agent can ever claim that an agent has "moral immunity" from the basic obligations that would apply to any human being toward other members of the community.[19]

That is to say, ethical (albeit nonfiduciary) obligations are owed by managers to all, and fiduciary obligations to some, so that

What remains is a practical paradox, not a theoretical one. Directors and officers must see themselves both as trusted servants of the corporation and its shareholders (a kind of partiality) *and* as members of a wider community also inhabited by the corporation, its shareholders, and many other stakeholder groups.[20]

The assertion that the stakeholder paradox reduces to a practical, nontheoretical challenge to managers in their workaday decision making is addressed to John Boatright, whose inquiry, "What's so special about shareholders?"—namely, that their status may appear as the *fons et origo* of managers' fiduciary duties—leads him to "a third position, somewhere between Goodpaster's view and the stakeholder approach."[21]

This *via media* opens up as Boatright accepts (with Goodpaster) the principle that the fiduciary duties owed by managers to shareholders (and, Boatright would add, not merely to shareholders) are irreducibly different from ethical or legal duties to nonshareholders and shareholders alike.[22] However, Boatright argues that the difference can be grounded neither in shareholders' equity claims as owners nor in an expressed or implied contract between management and shareholders, nor yet (as Goodpaster would have it) in the claim that managers act as the legal agents of the shareholders.[23] In search of the required ground, Boatright is driven to revisit the origins of the shareholder-stakeholder conversation, and so to the exchange between E. Merrick Dodd, Jr., on the one side, and Adolf A. Berle, Jr., and Gardiner C. Means, on the other.

Common to Dodd, Berle, and Means was the realization that the corporate form consists in divorcing shareholders' ownership from management's control, thus radically circumscribing shareholders' claims in equity. For Dodd, the emergence of control as the unitary vehicle of genuinely corporate action suggested:

If the unity of the corporate body is real, then there is reality and not simply legal fiction in the proposition that the managers of the unit are fiduciaries for it and not merely for its individual members, that they are . . . trustees for an institution [namely, related and beholden to many constituencies] rather than attorneys for the stockholders.[24]

Berle and Means were more impressed, as Boatright reminds us, by the twofold consequence of the "divorce." [25] On the one hand, shareholders' surrender of control to corporate management means "they have released the community from the obligation to protect them to the full extent implied in the doctrine of strict property rights." [26] At the same time, management's accession to control apart from ownership has

> cleared the way for the claims of a group far wider than either the owners or the control. They [the shareholders and the control group, namely, management] have placed the community in a position to demand that the modern corporation serve not only the owners or control but all society. [27]

As opposed to Dodd's, Berle's controlling insight was that the scope of management's fiduciary obligations is the obverse of the scope of management's discretion: "When the fiduciary obligation of corporate management and 'control' to stockholders is weakened or eliminated, management and 'control' become for all practical purposes absolute." [28] For Berle, accordingly, management's fiduciary obligations in law—to shareholders and other parties (such as creditors)— figure as the political community's "check" against the rise of a "social-economic absolutism of corporate administrators [which], even if benevolent, might be unsafe." [29] The construction of "the economic commonwealth which industrialism seems to require" is an ongoing act of public policy making, for which fiduciary controls on corporate managers serve as instruments. [30] In that connection, courts and legislatures have found that regulating managerial discretion under "the strict profit-maximizing imperative that the law of fiduciary duties imposes" works for the public benefit. [31] In practice, Boatright notes, considerations of public policy have engendered distinctions in law between managerial decisions that are, and those that are not, held to the strict fiduciary standard. In light of these distinctions, the *matter* of the stakeholder paradox may be restated in straightforward, unparadoxical form:

> It is illegitimate to orient corporate decisions that bear on the fiduciary duties of management by ethical values that go beyond strategic stakeholder considerations to include the interests of other

constituencies, but it is essential to orient other corporate decisions by these values.[32]

Now Freeman (to resume his argument) would have us interpolate into the Goodpaster-Boatright exchange some such reasoning as follows.[33] These two accounts yield opposed positions (positions opposed to one another and to so-called multifiduciary stakeholder theory) only if (from Goodpaster's side) managers have an ethical obligation to be partial to their principals' interests by consulting their business sense alone when their principals' interests are at stake, and only if (from Boatright's side) the managers' obligation to consult their business sense alone is legally imposed on them in specific situations. Goodpaster and Boatright can work out their opposed positions, then, only if both hold (albeit on differing grounds) that practical rationality dictates a separation of business from ethics, that the separation thesis captures a feature of practical rationality.

When Freeman declares, "if you give up the Separation Principle . . . then the argument between Goodpaster and Boatright is beside the point,"[34] we must add, beside the point for a reconceived business ethics, one which is responsive both to the implications of contemporary property theory (Donaldson and Preston) and to the reduction of shareholders and stakeholders alike to claimants before the tribunal of public policy (one reading of Boatright). We may then interpret: "if you give up the conventional stand-point . . . there is disclosed a new point to business ethics," namely, "reinventing the corporation and describing and redescribing the complex human beings who work in the corporation."[35] How it comes about that a principle which, for Goodpaster and Boatright, belongs to the rational consideration of human activity becomes for Freeman something one both *can* and (with inducement) *ought* simply to give up—an option, a standpoint— is a question to which we will return.

The impatient, hortatory note which colors Freeman's review of the shareholder-stakeholder conversations arises, we suggest, because Freeman discerns an impending sea change in the corporate property relation which promises consequences as far-reaching as those confronted by Berle and Means in the wake of the separation of corporate ownership from corporate control. The "signs of the times" are written in the fact that, just when stakeholder theory is emerging as a corollary to the changing analysis of property, the stakeholder is emerging as a metaphor—more exactly, as a synecdoche—for a new, successor form of moral embeddedness for what Freeman calls "the human process of joint value-creation,"[36] that is, for the corporate economy.

The work of invention and redescription to which Freeman summons business ethicists and business theorists alike amounts to designing conceptual models of emerging social relations that are already adumbrated in the metaphor of the corporate stakeholder:

> our task is to take metaphors like the stakeholder concept and embed it in a story about how human beings create and exchange value. . . . Redescribing corporations means redescribing ourselves and our communities. We cannot divorce the idea of a moral community or of a moral discourse from the ideas of the value-creation [sic] activity of business.[37]

The latter injunction is, in Freeman's language, a call to pragmatism. There are as many "normative cores" to be inscribed in narrative accounts of joint value-creation as there are political—that is to say, architectonic—standpoints occupied by those who can make out a "stake" in the process.[38] Hence,

> Seeing the stakeholder idea as replacing some shopworn metaphors of business with new ones . . . is to give up the role of finding some moral bedrock for business. . . . The cash value of our metaphors and narratives is just how they enable us to live, and the proof is in the living.[39]

So Freeman reads the signs of the times and construes their demands. In the next section, we return to incidents in the shareholder-stakeholder conversation by way of offering an alternative reading of those signs.

Rereading the Signs

Our rereading of the signs rests in part on points of agreement with Freeman, Boatright, and Goodpaster. With Freeman (and with Donaldson and Preston), the question "Who is a stakeholder?" or "Whose interests ought to count with corporate managers?" can be most clearly answered as a corollary to the theory of property (or, as we will put it, as a corollary to one's conception of the property relation among persons, including corporate "persons"); accordingly, one's conception of the managerial function will be largely determined by one's conception of the property relation. With Boatright, the revived shareholder-stakeholder conversation still moves within parameters first laid down by Berle and Means and supposes in particular the decomposition of the "atom of private property" (to use Berle and Means's phrase) accomplished by the separation of corporate control from corporate ownership. With Goodpaster (and Holloran), at stake in the shareholder-stakeholder conversation is the distinction of the private from the public realm, and that distinction goes to the heart of received notions of personal liberty, and thence to fundamental notions of the purposes of community and of general justice.[40]

Our rereading rests in further part on an appreciation of the shareholder-stakeholder conversation which is suggested by these points. By way of conveying that appreciation, we will revisit those incidents of the conversation in which the points emerge.

Let it be the case, as Berle and Means argue, that the corporate form in itself

> calls for analysis . . . in terms of social organization . . . [since] it involves a concentration of power in the economic field comparable to the concentration of religious power in the mediaeval church or of political power in the nation state . . . [while] it involves the interrelation of a wide variety of economic interests.[41]

Still, the notion of the corporate stakeholder could not arise apart from further argument that the corporation is in some sort indebted to the public trust and is in some sort or degree a public institution. For the stakeholder advances a claim of right, and such a claim must represent an enduring interest, since the claim is to be answered by a managerial obligation to foresee, assess, and adjust corporate activity in its light. Presumably the corporate stakeholder, unlike one's disaffected next-door neighbor, does not figure simply as someone with a casual complaint against someone else's use of property. There must be a standing set of expectations on both sides of the stakeholder-firm relationship.

The further argument will be enabled by a consequence of the property relation's decomposition into the discrete forms of passive ownership and active control to which Berle and Means first drew attention:

> the owners of passive property, by surrendering responsibility and control over the active property, have surrendered the right that the corporation be operated in their sole interest, — they have released the community from the obligation to protect them to the full extent implied in the doctrine of strict property rights. . . . [T]he controlling groups, by means of the extension of corporate powers, have in their own interest broken the bars of tradition which require that the corporation be operated solely for the benefit of the owners of passive property. . . . They have placed the community in a position to demand that the modern corporation serve not alone the owners or the control but all society.[42]

Berle and Means's language—"They have released the community from the obligation" and "placed the community in a position to demand"— may suggest a community once restrained by antecedent obligations, now free to pursue wholly new courses. In fact, Berle and Means's argument might better be read as the observation that the community's new position results from no shift in its fundamental purposes, but from a shift in the corporation's relation to those purposes.

As embodied in the polities forged by the Enlightenment, the purposes of community had long been

> to protect men in their own. Only where property interests conflicted with some very obvious public policy did the law interfere. Its primary design was protecting individual attributes of individual men,— their right to property, to free motion and locomotion, to the protection of individual relationships entered into between them.[43]

To claim these protections and to find a place within the scope of these purposes, the "corporate individual" can no longer appeal *pro forma,* in the persons of its shareholders or of its managers, to "the traditional logic of property" but must, Berle and Means contend, justify the uses of "active property" by linking these uses directly to the normative values of the community. [44] These justifications—which become familiar as representatives make the case for corporate interests in various legal and legislative forums—run the gamut, from appeals to utility, to liberty, to desert, and so on. Corporate property rights come to consist in appeals that win legal recognition.

On the one hand, the community is released from an obligation to defend corporate property relations as if they were on all fours with personal property relations. On the other hand, corporate management must show that corporate uses are compatible with the community's avowed ends. In this sense, then, a reversal of a burden of obligation has taken place between the corporation and the political community at large. The traditional logic of property extends a presumption of legitimacy to the economic activity of private, individual persons; the corporate individual, by contrast, must earn the sanction of law for its undertakings. [45]

The shareholder-stakeholder or corporate interests–public interests conversation commences, then, with the "socialization" of corporate property relations; that is to say, it commences when the exercise of corporations' social responsibilities are seen as justificatory, and when in consequence the granting of legal protections to corporate property relations betokens that those relations serve the public interest. [46] Berle and Means end their argument (with the observation "It remains only for the claims of the community to be put forward with clarity and force") where the shareholder-stakeholder conversation begins. [47]

The later shift from a public interest view of corporate responsibility to a stakeholder view, a shift which at once revives and redirects the conversation, rests on two adjustments to Berle and Means's account: (1) public interest in the uses of active corporate property bears analysis into the interests of various "corporate publics"—consumers, employees, suppliers, and so on; (2) as active corporate property relations take shape in a "bundle" of legal rights, the question of correlative obligations surfaces in the new form which is noted and outlined by Donaldson and Preston: any of the corporate publics may press their claims against the corporation on the same normative bases—utility, liberty, desert, and so forth—advanced by the corporation in justification of its claims. [48]

With the first adjustment, the corporate stakeholder comes on the scene as heir and beneficiary of the socialization of corporate property relations. With the second, the stakeholder's interests are set normatively on all fours with those of shareholders and of the corporate "individual" itself. It remains only for stakeholders' normative claims to achieve embodiment in law, and stakeholders will have been promoted to owners (in all but name, at least) of active corporate property. [49] Put another way, the corporation will have been transformed into the agency of a limited public, and managers into trustees for that public.

This transformation of the corporate form is, of course, what Goodpaster's "multifiduciary stakeholder synthesis"—ethics without business—envisions, and it is what his argument from the stakeholder paradox is calculated to forestall. These facts would be of the same passing interest to us that they are to Freeman, were it not the case that the class of arguments upon which Freeman presumes—in particular, the class of arguments foreseen by Donaldson and Preston—will be found compelling if and only if the class of arguments from which Goodpaster draws are also found compelling, for they are the same class of arguments.

At root, to hold property is to be at liberty: it is to dispose of the means necessary to execute designs, to satisfy preferences, and to fulfill purposes. Property rights themselves go toward securing and ordering that liberty, amidst the welter of designs, preferences, and purposes that play out in civil society. For the establishment of one's own at once secures a definite scope for one's unilateral activity and draws limits to it. Further constraints, in law and in moral principle, on the use of property go to the legal or moral rectitude of designs, the tolerabilty of preferences, or the worthiness of purposes. These constrain the uses of property by way of supervening over property rights: Waldo's vehicle is no less fully, no less rightfully at his disposal when he uses it in a holdup than when he uses it for delivering Meals on Wheels (as quite a separate matter, Waldo is no less rightfully commended for his deliveries than jailed for his withdrawals). [50]

Freeman, Donaldson, Preston, and others are explicitly unwilling to let the interests of consumers, employees, and others closely affected by corporate uses of property ride on the side constraints which hedge the uses of property generally. The desiderated normative stakeholder theory looks neither first nor principally to remove or to ameliorate whatever obstacles to stakeholders' pursuit of their own well-being may be attributable to corporate activities. Normative stakeholder theory, rather, looks to make corporate activity a vehicle for executing stakeholders' designs, for satisfying their preferences, and for fulfilling their purposes.

Now, of course, the business corporation is already a vehicle for all these things, but only as an organized occasion for the confluence of emphatically free purposes, designs, and preferences, and only through the mutual exercise of largely unconstrained liberties to associate and to conclude contracts. As such, the corporation is also an organized occasion for the summary rejection of some purposes in favor of others, and the frustration of some designs as the condition of pursuing others. If there is one motive driving the stakeholder side of the shareholder-stakeholder conversation, it is the conviction that summary corporate decision making is in fact arbitrary corporate decision making, and that arbitrary decision making—certainly when it impacts interests beyond those of the decision makers—is a normative anomaly, a failure of practical rationality.[51] For while not every preference, design, or purpose can be realized, all can be accorded a voice and heard; and all *should* be heard, because *human communities and their sub-parts exist to affirm and, so far as possible, foster individuals' pursuit of their (often conflicting) preferential interests.*

Hence, for Freeman, Donaldson, Preston, and others, the problem of grounding stakeholder theory normatively reduces, like all true problems, to a re-analysis of the terms in which it is stated, so as to produce the solution definitively, that is, as a matter of definition.[52] As a matter of definition, then, the stakeholder emerges as one whose interest in corporate decision making is the moral equivalent of the corporation's own interests in the use of corporate property, and so must be weighed with (and against) other interests—namely, shareholders' interests—whose common measure is their basis in property. The idiom in which stakeholders' "voices" are to be heard is the language of distributive justice, but the argument that is cloaked in the idiom is, as above, an argument from liberty.[53]

Now, what lends to strategic corporate decision making its summary character is that corporations' organizing purposes are, typically, very sharply—which is to say, narrowly and prosaically—drawn: say, "to manufacture and market soap at a profit to shareholders." The elegant, short argument in §3 of Goodpaster and Holloran's "In Defense of a Paradox" depends largely on pointing out that this narrowness, which is so instrumental to the actual realization of purposes, is itself an expression of substantial (as opposed to formal) liberty, of voiced interests actually being realized (as opposed merely to being weighed). From this point of view, the working enterprise is a triumph of practical rationality.

So Goodpaster and Holloran argue that the grounding of corporate officers' fiduciary obligation to weigh first, and with partiality, interests which go to the corporation's expressed objectives lies

> in consideration of liberty (for the corporation and its shareholders), fairness (in respecting the corporation as having political rights), relationship (in management's acceptance of its role in furthering the corporation objective) and in community.[54]

As they explicate it, the "consideration of liberty" goes to the use of property, within the constraints of community, by persons in voluntary association (inviting others' participation, by contract, in their undertakings), to realize their chosen objectives. But this "consideration of liberty" goes further: it appears also in a politic forbearance, which is slow to interfere with these exercises of liberties, which is articulated as respect for the distinction between the public and the private, and which is found "lying close to the heart of the human feelings that give rise to governments."[55] The "feelings" in question are the obverse of the rooted view that *human communities and their subparts exist to affirm and, so far as possible, foster individuals' pursuit of their (often conflicting) preferential interests.*

The criterion of practical rationality which informs Goodpaster and Holloran's argument is just the criterion that informs Donaldson and Preston's program of argument. Donaldson and Preston's claims against the moral tenability of shareholder theory notwithstanding, no practical reasoning from either side can overcome a dichotomy which proceeds from opposed valuations of a shared criterion of practical rationality: each side must concede the practical rationality of the other's position. So far as they are coherent and consistent, the arguments from each side can serve only to emphasize the root disagreement. A neutral resolution would require denying the foundational "liberty criterion" altogether, and with it both arguments. Short of that, were we asked to decide between them, we could choose between these courses of reasoning on many grounds. One ground only would be denied us: we could not affirm one over the other on the basis of its superior practical rationality. In the first place, then, our appreciation of the revived shareholder-stakeholder conversation leads us to suspect that the conversation is irresolvable in its own terms.

In the second place, our appreciation suggests that the ultimate disagreement between stakeholder theorists and shareholder theorists concerns the nature and aims of the liberal regime to which both are beholden, even before it concerns the nature and aims of the business corporation. Accordingly, if either shareholder or stakeholder theory exhausts the possibilities, the choice between them may come down to a raw question of allegiances. So at length we are brought circling back to Freeman, who also proposes that stakeholder theory represents a fundamental choice against shareholder theory, made in light of proposals concerning the kind of socioeconomic regime under which we should prefer to live; but who suggests further that attention to what we have called the signs of the times will persuade that the choice is, after all, virtually nugatory, since "stockholder theory is an idea whose time has come and gone . . . [it] is or at least should be intellectually dead."[56]

Freeman's odd language of constrained choice and imperative preference stands among the features of his "diagnosis" to which we earlier drew wondering attention in connection with his polemic against the separation thesis.[57] On the one hand, according to Freeman, the thesis is a *thesis:* it represents an epistemic option, one choice among theoretical approaches to management; on the next hand, it is a kind of habitual rationalization for the "merely academic" preoccupations of conventional business ethics and for the moral obtuseness of strategic business theory;[58] on the third hand, it is the conceptual linchpin of a superseded theory of management, so that to cling to it is to court irrelevance. Though an admitted option, it is—just count the hands—not much of one. We are thus invited to reverse our earlier question, so as now to ask: How could a Goodpaster or a Boatright regard the thesis except as a piece of shopworn baggage, to be speedily jettisoned?

Freeman's language should ring familiar. It is the rhetoric of street politics, the idiom that partisans of opposed standpoints use to pry one another loose from their allegiances. The object is to move one's opponent off his position to or toward one's own by sheer weight of contrary opinion or by the demonstration that his position is untenable— is outmoded or outflanked by changing circumstances, or is just too silly for words. Hence, the question arises: *from* what and *to* what positions are we to be thus moved?

From Classical Liberalism . . .

There should be no difficulty recognizing the context in which a consistent presumption in favor of separating business decisions from ethical decisions is itself a principle of practical reasoning, a rational habit of thought. As to that context, in William James Booth's admirable summary:

> The attributes claimed for it are familiar: an economy whose actors are considered equals and a system indifferent to their noneconomic attributes; a contractarian, voluntaristic institutional context for exchanges; and the view that the public authority should not decide among preferences—that one is entitled to live one's life "from the inside," selecting and ordering one's preferences according to the good as one understands it and seeking to engage the voluntary cooperation of others in one's pursuit of them.[59]

The context in point, then, is that "new form of moral embeddedness for the economy" which marks the achievement of Polanyi's "great transformation" and inaugurates—if the term is to have a relatively precise meaning—modernity.[60] This normative sense of "embeddedness" supposes, and must not be confused with, a concomitant institutional embedding of the economy: in a system of property rights embodied in law; in recognized and enforceable contractual forms; and, in general, in political institutions which respond to the supposition that "any interdiction of what is voluntarily agreed to among persons must be taken, in the first instance, as a *prima facie* evil . . . and must be understood as a normative loss."[61] Such a loss may be justified as the cost of meeting some compelling exigency or of promoting certain other values than liberty; it remains, however, a loss and is recognized as a loss.

The core, or nexus, of normative principles which informs the context and its institutional framework is summoned to realize what we may call the "liberal ideal": that, by rational assent to the core principles, persons who otherwise embrace widely divergent and incompatible notions of human well-being and well-doing will be enabled at once to live out their notions and to constitute a peaceable society: one free of invidious distinctions in political status; one in which access to the means of living out one's notion of the human good is universal. These core principles can, then, be usefully summed as "classical liberalism" or (perhaps more descriptively) as "individualistic liberalism."[62]

Read in the context of the classical liberal ideal, what Freeman calls the separation thesis may be renamed the "liberty warrant," and may be expressed this way: decisions which dispose of private property, and thus support the pursuit of individual preference (business decisions), are distinct and separable from decisions respecting the exercise of the like autonomy by everyone (ethical decisions). That is to say: business decisions belong to the much wider array of human activities which reduce essentially to the selection, ordering, and pursuit of individual preferences. Since they proceed under differing (and sometimes incompatible) notions of the human good, such activities are "extranormative" per se. In fact, normative rules exist to protect and to enlarge the sphere of such activities. To say, then, that business decisions are separate from ethical decisions is simply to remark on their differing but allied functions: business decisions effect (ultimately) individual preferences; ethical decisions restrain the human propensity to overreach.[63] Their separation *effectuates* the substantial liberties—which is to say, the human dignities—of the classical liberal regime.

In this light, what Freeman laments as a habitual rationalization appears as a rational habit, that is, as a grounded predisposition and prejudgment in favor of the proliferating variety of individual preferences and of the corresponding variety of voluntary enterprises aimed at their pursuit, and against regulative claims made in the name of social or general interests, whether advanced normatively or institutionally, by philosophers, politicians, or policy makers. This, then, is the habit whose expression as public philosophy is high regard for the distinction between what is private and what is public, on the ground that that distinction is functionally equivalent to the distinction between the realm of human liberty and dignity and the realm of necessary coercion. Perhaps we may summarize by observing that in a polity dominantly imbued with this habit, Boatright, for example, could afford to rest his version of shareholder theory on the legal niceties of public policy.[64]

The strength of one's allegiance to the public philosophy of classical liberalism is, as Goodpaster and Holloran's argument implies, likely to be measured by one's qualified or unqualified assent to the proposition that to hold property is to be at liberty.[65] Locke provides the classic statement of this idea:[66]

> every man has the property of his own *person:* this no body has any right to but himself. The *labor* of his body, and the *work* of his hands, we may say are his. Whatsoever then he removes out of that state that nature has provided, and left it in, he hath mixed his labor with, and joined to it something that is his own, and thereby makes it his property. . . . [T]his excludes the common right of other men: for this *labor* being the unquestionable property of the laborer, no man but he can have a right to what that is once joined to, at least where there is enough, and as good, left in common for others.[67]

This and allied passages from Locke's *Second Treatise of Government* have, of course, been subjected to extensive analysis to demonstrate their inconclusiveness as justification for the institution of private property.[68] However inconclusive, the passage nonetheless signals what it is Locke wishes to justify: a liberty in things—the "run," if you will, of things—which is exactly parallel to one's unconstrained, obligationless "run" of one's own body,[69] so that possession is to the individual what, as Locke argues, the institution of property is to civil-social order, namely, an expansion of actual liberty, of liberty-in-action.[70]

The subjection of things to one's exclusive, arbitrary preference descends, to repeat, from classical liberalism as the *meaning* of possession. This subjection is completed as a (Lockean) right by all others' unqualified obligation to refrain from exercising their preferences (asserting their interests) over one's possessions.[71] The point bears emphasis: unless others' obligation holds despite any preponderance of interests which might be adduced to the contrary, this classical-liberal sense of ownership-as-liberty is rendered merely nominal. The whole point of institutional or legal rights in property is to give sure effect to *others'* obligation, both by suasion, or custom, and by law, or coercion.[72] Accordingly, the property relation reduces finally to a relation among persons (and not *to* things): it consists in the establishment, for and among individuals, of private "spheres of liberty" whose boundaries are composed of things—namely, properties—which are, in their turn, extensions (in no metaphysical sense) of individuals, for they are subjected exclusively to individuals and are reserved to individuals' use as are individuals' bodies.

For those to whom property thus means liberty of action, the legal institution of property rights, the definitions of the kinds and extents of ownership, and the intersection of property rights with other legal rights and with the obligations of citizenship, will weigh (in Robert Nozick's phrase, once more) as "side constraints" on an original and antecedent liberty.

. . . To Liberal Individualism

There should be little difficulty in recognizing the context in which purely strategic corporate decision making shows up as a normative anomaly. It is, first, a context built upon the fiction of individuals.[73] "Individuals" are the human agents whose voluntary agreements (in forms ranging from functional communities of interest to formal contracts) move the social-political and economic realms. They function as "bearers of preferences"—that is, as bearers of strictly "first person" expressions of desires or needs, but also as bearers of moral, political, and social desiderata.[74] Preferences thus stand, without further qualification, as the ultimate reasons for individuals' actions and as the ultimate premises of their practical reasonings, which are, therefore, normatively

"opaque" one to another.[75] As MacIntyre notes, the immediately resulting social context for individuals' pursuit of their preferences exhibits
striking

> parallels between human beings in the social and political realm
> and the institution of the market, the dominant institution in a
> liberal economy. . . . In markets, too, it is only through the ex-
> pression of individual preferences that a heterogeneous variety of
> needs, desires and goods conceived in one way or another are
> given a voice. The weight given to an individual preference in the
> market is a matter of the cost which the individual is willing and
> able to pay; only so far as an individual has the means to bargain
> with those who can supply what he or she needs does the indi-
> vidual have an effective voice. So also in the political and social
> realm it is the ability to bargain that is crucial. The preferences of
> some are accorded weight by others only in so far as the satisfac-
> tion of those preferences will lead to the satisfaction of their own
> preferences. Only those who have something to give get. The dis-
> advantaged in a liberal society are those without the means to
> bargain.[76]

On the one hand, on every level and in every arena of commerce
among individuals, social exchange is dominated by continuous mutual interrogations (opinion polls, market surveys, offers and counter-
offers, and so forth) aimed at ascertaining the shape, kind, and extent
of respondents' preferences: of their positions, of the relative positions of
positions, of the strength of their position, and so forth. On the other
hand, the bargaining positions thus publicly advanced have the significance of "counters": they are without normative-qualitative distinction; they are, again, opaque one to another.

We have stressed the mutual opacity of individual preferences in
order to render as transparent as possible the demands that those
whose concern is to advance and implement their preferences must
make upon the various arenas of public bargaining. It will be, first, of
the essence that all transactions, and not merely market commerce,
proceed under agreed canons. Given the heterogeny of the public arenas and of the sorts of satisfactions they offer, the canons in question

will vary materially. Nevertheless, uniformity will be most important in two connections.

First, canons of bargaining must be such that each participating individual or group has assurance that under them he, she, or they will prove as effective as possible both in voicing and in implementing preferences.[77] In particular, the weighing of competing preferences, the methods of tallying relative weights, and the criteria for granting rights to implement preferences must feature market-like clarity and market-like openness. On this the social function devolves.[78] Second, at their normative core—namely, the rules of distributive justice[79]—canons of bargaining must be framed to guarantee participation in the social function for the disadvantaged: no one's preference lacks merit—none can—so none should be left unvoiced; the rules must also protect individuals' and groups' freedom both to express and, so far as their weight and the effectiveness of their bearers' bargaining permits, to implement preferences.[80]

In a public culture organized thus for the pursuit of ultimately individual preference, then, the extension and refinement of bargaining canons will tend to dominate the ethical dimensions of social life. For this reason, ethical and what we call procedural thought will coalesce: questions of right and wrong will become questions of "the right way" and "the wrong way" to advance one's interests. As a further consequence, because disputes of normative import will tend to take on a procedural cast, and because a claim to general, public agreement will be the usual warrant for a resolution, courts (bearing the public's confidence by definition) and legislatures will become arbiters of first resort. In this sort of culture, as MacIntyre remarks, "The lawyers, and not the philosophers, are the clergy."[81]

Finally, as the summative consequence of the foregoing tendencies, ethical progress will be seen to consist both in the extension of explicit, rationalized bargaining canons to new or heretofore unrationalized forms of transactions, and in the continuing explication and refinement of recognized canons; statute law will follow (and lead) apace. The parallel development of rationalized modes of bargaining and their legal embodiments will assume the character of social progress, or socialization. Overall, a spirit of evangelical egalitarianism will mark these developments, since they will be seen as extensions of full participation, under the aegis of distributive justice, in the social function.[82] Obversely, unrationalized forms of transactions will increasingly appear unjust.

What Donaldson and Preston call "the evolving theory of property" figures in this context as a transformed meaning for ownership. The legal analysis of ownership into a bundle of distinct (and largely separable) rights emphasizes property's role in organizing individual—namely, bargaining—relationships. Indeed, the owned object may almost seem to disappear behind a web of claims made by rights-holders upon the performance or forbearance of rights-regarders.

As in the market, ownership lends weight to individuals' and groups' voicing of their preferences, so quite generally the liberty associated with rights in property becomes principally a liberty or power of "voice," rather than a power of personal action: it becomes a liberty to command or demand, that is, to take up a certain sort of bargaining position (sometimes, a dictatorial one). This shift appears with particular clarity in the form of Berle and Means's account of the ownership exercised by control over active corporate property, which (on their analysis) already reduces to "a set of relationships under which one individual or a set of individuals hold powers over an enterprise."[83] Needless to say, such relationships invite rationalization.

Moreover, in the context of this regime, a present exercise of ownership suggests itself as the implementation of a prior claim of preference, assigned via the weighing of such factors as need, desert, and promise. A sea change in the very meaning of ownership waits on the analogous redefinition of specific property rights—understood as claims to future use (for example, expand the plant), to future alienation (put the plant up for sale), or to future profit (discontinue department A next year and reinvest the savings)—as claims to preference requiring a present weighing of affected interests.[84]

If the egalitarian spirit accounts for stakeholder theorists' élan and cements their allegiances, the transformation of property relations is the lever by which they may yet move the world of corporate management.

Conclusion

The socialization of corporate property relations, which (as Berle and Means conceived the case) was the admission that the public should be invoked to constrain corporate uses of property, is not wholly inconsistent with the traditional, classical-liberal conception of ownership. It can be understood as a supervention on the part of the public authority in pursuit of goods or values other than liberty that claim a place among the ends of a pluralistic community[85]—a necessary constriction, but not a wholesale invasion of the private sphere. (For their part, Berle and Means were inclined to present socialization as a phase in the historic democratization of all human institutions, while foreseeing the eventual transformation of corporate control into a quasi-agency of democratic government.)[86]

Not so the socialization (or resocialization) supposed by stakeholder theorists: its effect is to transform corporate liberty of use into an obligation to act precisely according to the preponderance of discrete, (ultimately) individual interests at variance both with one another and with the corporation's strictly economic purposes. Its aim is to complete the rationalization of what Berle and Means identified as "active corporate property" into a direct vehicle of the social function. The straightforward "means-ends" decision making fostered by the pursuit of purely economic objectives is to be replaced by a new managerial rationality: the corporation itself is to become the locus of bargaining among variant and competing interests. Managers will broker, tally, and weigh those interests, with a view to deciding which will be implemented, if all cannot be. They will do so under rules that are, ostensibly, matters of agreement among the individuals whose interests are represented, but are just as likely to turn out to be matters of legal fiat.

In pursuit of the basic, normative questions with which we began, contemporary shareholder theorists and stakeholder theorists reason from shared standards of practical rationality to contrary answers. Our first rereading of the signs of the times, then, is this: stakeholder and shareholder theories faithfully reflect deeply and publicly held values of the liberal regime; the shareholder-stakeholder conversation (which occasionally shows the colors of partisan debate) is a token that the liberal regime is at odds with itself.

Second, there is no prima facie reason to suppose that the shareholder-stakeholder conversation can be resolved normatively in favor of either side. Moreover, if the results of our epitome of the arguments, from distributive justice, available to stakeholder theorists (such as Donaldson and Preston) and the liberty-based arguments available to shareholder theorists (such as Goodpaster and Holloran) hold, there is good reason to suppose that the conversation cannot be resolved within the limits of practical reason set for it. Against the supposition that the conversation might yet be resolved by some original argument drawn within those limits stands the history of the conversation hitherto. Below, we will argue that Freeman's inducement to give up what he calls the separation thesis is, at best, disingenuous. (However, we do not believe it would disingenuous of Freeman or of anyone to suggest that stakeholder theory, shareholder theory, and the conversation between them were best given up.)

Third, Freeman's proposal to resolve the shareholder-stakeholder dispute by a pragmatic *coup d'audace* promises merely to continue the conversation by other means. If we are correct, Freeman cannot argue against the rationality of allegiances to the principles descending from liberalism's historical sources, nor does he: the one inducement to give up the separation thesis that he cannot and does not offer is that the separation thesis is practically incoherent. No more could Goodpaster argue that Freeman's fundamental egalitarianism is practically incoherent. That is why Freeman treats the separation thesis as allegiance to a position, and exerts himself to dissolve the allegiance and move readers off the position.

What Freeman can and does do is offer the outlines of a program to translate the normative interests that some philosophers, jurists, and activists cherish against corporate business activities into legislative and otherwise political bargaining positions, but these are to carry the added weight of retaining for rhetorical purposes their normative fancy-dress. In this new form of moral "embeddedness" for the corporate economy, we are all to be stakeholders, not in this or that corporation, but in the corporate form itself, provided we can find our voice and get the courts and legislatures to listen.

But will they? What are the allegiances "out there" to the distinction between the public and private realms, or to the notion that even such merely legal individuals as corporations may, subject to the usual side constraints, do what they will with their property? We shall know the answer once we have played out the shareholder-stakeholder conversation again, this time in the courtrooms and legislative hearing rooms.

Finally, if we are correct, no normative conclusion concerning our opening questions that avoids a declaration of allegiance to one side or the other in the shareholder-stakeholder conversation can be drawn from our argument.

The shareholder and stakeholder theories jointly exhaust the resources of liberalism, as a form of practical rationality, for addressing the normative dimension of business. These theories exhaust liberalism's resources not by way of presenting decisive, exclusive alternatives, but by way of irresolution: both are consistent expressions of liberalism; the decision between them is a normative toss-up. Meanwhile, they foster conflicting practices and endorse conflicting prescriptions which likewise present normative toss-ups. Their effect is thus precisely the reverse of ethical. They cannot aid in establishing a consistent ethos of corporate management; they can only detain us in endless debate over foundations they cannot lay.

Notes

1. John Boatright, "Fiduciary Duties and the Shareholder-Management Relation, or, What's So Special about Shareholders?" *Business Ethics Quarterly* 4, no. 4 (1994): 393.

2. R. Edward Freeman, "The Politics of Stakeholder Theory: Some Future Directions," *Business Ethics Quarterly* 4, no. 4 (1994): 409–21.

3. Ibid., 419 n. 1.

4. Ibid., 412.

5. Ibid., 411.

6. Ibid., 412.

7. Ibid.

8. Ibid.

9. Ibid., 413.

10. Ibid. (emphasis added).

11. Thomas Donaldson and Lee E. Preston, "The Stakeholder Theory of the Corporation: Concepts, Evidence, and Implications," *Academy of Management Review* 20, no. 1 (1995): 88.

12. Ibid., 84; Donaldson and Preston clearly accept the so-called pluralistic theory, but—beyond citing the authority of "the most respected

contemporary analysts of property rights"—they leave the question of the pluralistic theory's soundness in abeyance.

13. Ibid., 83.

14. Ibid., 83–84.

15. Ibid., 83 (emphasis added).

16. Kenneth E. Goodpaster, "Business Ethics and Stakeholder Analysis," *Business Ethics Quarterly* 1, no. 1 (1991): 63.

17. Ibid.

18. Ibid., 67.

19. Ibid., 68.

20. Kenneth E. Goodpaster and Thomas E. Holloran, "In Defense of a Paradox," *Business Ethics Quarterly* 4, no. 4 (1994): 428.

21. Boatright, "Fiduciary Duties," 404–5.

22. Cf. ibid., 400–1, 403.

23. Cf. ibid., 394–400.

24. E. Merrick Dodd, Jr., "For Whom Are Corporate Managers Trustees?" *Harvard Law Review* 45 (1932): 1160.

25. Cf. Boatright, "Fiduciary Duties," 401.

26. Adolf A. Berle, Jr., and Gardiner C. Means, *The Modern Corporation and Private Property* (New York: Macmillan, 1932), 355 (cited in Boatright, "Fiduciary Duties," 401).

27. Ibid., 355–56 (cited in Boatright, "Fiduciary Duties," 401).

28. Berle, Jr., "For Whom Are Corporate Managers Trustees?" 367 (cited in Boatright, "Fiduciary Duties," 402).

29. Ibid., 372 (cited in Boatright, "Fiduciary Duties," 401).

30. Ibid. (cited in Boatright, "Fiduciary Duties," 402).

31. Boatright, "Fiduciary Duties," 402.

32. Ibid., 404.

33. Cf. Freeman, "Politics of Stakeholder Theory," 412–13.

34. Ibid.,413.

35. Ibid., 418.

36. Ibid., 415.

37. Ibid., 418–19.

38. Cf. ibid., 413–15.

39. Ibid., 418.

40. Cf. Goodpaster and Holloran, "In Defense of a Paradox," 427.

41. Adolf A. Berle, Jr., and Gardiner C. Means, *The Modern Corporation and Private Property,* rev. ed. (New York: Harcourt, Brace and World, 1968), 309–10.

42. Berle and Means, *Modern Corporation,* 311–12.

43. Ibid., 296.

44. Cf. ibid., 293–98.

45. Writing in 1967, Berle takes the logic of this position to its proximate conclusion in one direction: "Corporations are essentially political constructs. Their perpetual life, their capacity to accumulate tens of billions of dollars in assets, and to draw profit from their production and sales, has made them part of the service supply of the United States. Informally, they are an adjunct of the State itself" (Berle and Means, "Property, Production and Revolution: A Preface to the Revised Edition," in *Modern Corporation,* xxvi).

46. Compare Evan and Freeman's principle of corporate *legitimacy* (our emphasis): "The corporation should be managed for the benefit of its stakeholders: its customers, suppliers, owners, employees and local communities. The rights of these groups must be ensured, and, further, the groups must participate, in some sense, in decisions that substantially affect their welfare" (William M. Evan and R. Edward Freeman, "A Stakeholder Theory of the Modern Corporation: Kantian Capitalism," in Tom L. Beauchamp and Norman E. Bowie, eds., *Ethical Theory and Business,* 3d ed. (Englewood Cliffs, N.J.: Prentice Hall, 1998), 103.

47. Berle and Means, *Modern Corporation,* 312.

48. Cf. Donaldson and Preston, "Stakeholder Theory," 81–85.

49. Commenting on the implications of the proposition that "stakeholder theory can be normatively based on the evolving theory of property," Donaldson and Preston observe, "One need not make the more radical assertation that such stakes constitute formal or legal property rights" (ibid., 83, 85). Their observation is true and somewhat disingenuous; one need not make the claim, as it can be left to the eventual decisions in the courts or legislatures.

50. In this connection, we would argue that when contemporary property theorists follow legal theorists by including, without qualification, an obligation to refrain from harmful uses among the "bundle" of rights-claims that go to make up the concept of "full, legal ownership" common to mature liberal regimes, they commit a philosophical solecism. The philosophical concept of rights in property does not incorporate legal or moral approval of the uses to which property may be put. Rather, the liberty that property subserves is itself limited by the norm of general justice classically expressed by Locke in the *Second Treatise of Government* (Indianapolis, Ind.: Hackett Publishing Co., 1980) at II.6: "reason . . . teaches all mankind, who will but consult it, that being equal and independent, no one ought to harm another in his life, health, liberty or possessions." The "legal incident" to property rights which proscribes harmful uses thus figures philosophically as the public authority's

reminder to all that it will treat holding property as liberty, not license. Cf. Lawrence C. Becker, *Property Rights: Philosophic Foundations* (Boston, London, and Henley: Routledge and Kegan Paul, 1980), 18–19 (following A. M. Honoré, "Ownership," in A. G. Guest, ed., *Oxford Essays in Jurisprudence* [Oxford: Clarendon Press, 1961], 107–47). Again, for Donaldson and Preston, "that restrictions against harmful uses are intrinsic to the property rights concept clearly brings the interests of others (*i.e.,* of non-owner stakeholders) into the picture" ("Stakeholder Theory," 83).

51. This apprehension is foreshadowed by Berle and Means's urgent concern that "under the leadership of the dictators of industry"—whose motives are more likely analogous to those "of an Alexander the Great seeking new worlds to conquer" than to those of the profit minded, traditional tradesman—control is likely to achieve a concentration of economic power in the corporate form which threatens a "social-economic absolutism of corporate administrators" (*Modern Corporation,* 306–8).

52. Cf. Eva T. H. Brann, "The Student's Problem," a lecture delivered at St. John's College, Annapolis, Maryland, September 9, 1967; reprinted in S. A. Cortright, ed., *What Is It to Educate Liberally?* (Moraga, Calif.: Saint Mary's College of California, 1996), 66–79.

53. Thus Donaldson and Preston ("Stakeholder Theory," 83–85) foresee, e.g., arguments establishing "the stake of people living in the surrounding community . . . based on their need, say, for clean air," which would invoke the characteristic of need in warrant of a utilitarian demonstration that corporate interests should be pursued only so far as their realization would leave the realization of implicated interests overall unaffected or enhanced. This and other examples drawn from effort (to establish employees' stake as a warrant in an argument from desert) or from promise (to establish customers' stake as a warrant in a contractarian argument) are summoned to serve the principles "that stakeholders are identified by *their* interests in the affairs of the corporation and that the interests of all stakeholders have intrinsic value" (ibid., 81; emphasis original). Unsurprisingly, the intrinsic value of stakeholders' interests translates into the proposition that expectations of benefit, which motivate all participation in corporate enterprise, should get equal consideration (see ibid., 68).

54. Goodpaster and Holloran, "In Defense of a Paradox," 427.

55. Christopher Stone, "Corporate Vices and Corporate Virtues: Do Public/Private Distinctions Matter?" *University of Pennsylvania Law Review* 130, no. 6 (1982), cited in Goodpaster and Holloran, "In Defense of a Paradox," 427.

56. Freeman, "Politics of a Stakeholder's Theory," 413.

57. See pp. 143–144 of this essay.

58. Thus Freeman states, "As long as the discourse distinguishes 'business' and 'ethics,' we will need business ethicists to make it up as we go along . . . and as long as business ethics is separate, business theorists are free to make up supposedly neutral theories, such as agency theory, which can be used to justify a great deal of harm" ("Politics of Stakeholder Theory," 412).

59. William James Booth, "On the Idea of the Moral Economy," *American Political Science Review* 87, no. 3 (September 1994): 661.

60. Ibid.

61. Ibid., 662.

62. We borrow the second of these terms, and adapt important elements of our subsequent characterizations of the transformations of liberalism's normative core, from Alasdair MacIntyre, *Whose Justice? Which Rationality?* (Notre Dame, Ind.: University of Notre Dame Press, 1987), 335ff.; our appreciation of classical liberalism's historical roots in the seventeenth century is much indebted to Daniel Kolb, "Natural Law and the Heart of Virtue," a paper presented at the second annual John F. Henning Conference on Catholic Social Thought, "In Work, Leisure and Worship: The Person in Catholic Social Thought," Saint Mary's College of California, Moraga, Calif., February 21, 1998.

63. Thus, again, Locke's norm of general justice (see above, n. 50) descends as "virtue entire" from the historical sources of liberalism; cf. Kolb, "Natural Law," 10.

64. The *other* reading of Boatright; see earlier discussion.

65. Cf. Goodpaster and Holloran, "In Defense of a Paradox."

66. Although we present this view of the property relation via Locke, it is true that no one among the first anatomists of liberalism saw with greater clarity, or drew attention to the view more insistently, than Hegel, that property *is* arbitrary personal liberty realized; cf. Hegel, *Philosophy of Right,* trans. T. M. Knox (Oxford: Oxford University Press, 1967), §§40–41, 44, etc.

67. Locke, *Second Treatise,* V. 27 (emphases original).

68. Cf. Lawrence C. Becker, *Property Rights: Philosophic Foundations* (London: Routledge and Kegan Paul, 1977), 33ff.; in addition to his own criticisms, Becker reviews those of Proudhon, Henry George, J. S. Mill, Robert Nozick, and others.

69. Cf. ibid., 37, where Becker comments on Locke's contentions: "it is wisest to regard them [property rights] as simply summations of one's rights to life and liberty" (again, Becker's interest goes here to the insufficiency of Locke's argument as a philosophical justification for the institution of private property).

70. Cf. Locke, *Second Treatise*, V. 32–51, and Kolb, "Natural Law," 18.

71. That the classical liberal sense of possession and rights-in-property is still with us appears, e.g., in Jeremy Waldron, "Property Law," in *A Companion to Philosophy of Law and Legal Theory*, ed. Dennis Patterson (Cambridge: Blackwell Publishers, 1996). Waldron's explication bears comparison point-by-point to Locke's: "The person to whom a given object is assigned by the principles of private property . . . has control over the object: it is for her to decide what should be done with it . . . [S]he is not understood to be acting as the agent or official of society. Instead, we say that the resource is *her property* . . . it is as much *hers* as her arms, legs, kidneys and corneas . . . [H]er right to decide as she pleases applies whether or not others are affected by her decision" (6; emphases original); and again: "an individual's right to make decisions about a thing has two elements. First . . . it implies the absence of any obligation to use or refrain from using the object in any particular way. . . . Second, private property implies that other people . . . *do* have an obligation— an obligation to the owner—to refrain from occupying, using, modifying, consuming or destroying the object" (7; emphasis original); and finally: "Private property involves a pledge by a society that it will continue to use its moral and physical authority to uphold the rights of owners" (9).

72. Cf. Locke, *Second Treatise*, IX. 124, X.138, and Kolb, "Natural Law," 14–15.

73. The point is merely that individuals seem rather to be made than born: to act one's part as an individual is a kind of achievement, and failure to perform as expected is a matter for various degrees of censure.

74. Cf. MacIntyre, *Whose Justice? Which Rationality?* 338.

75. The view that human agents just are, so to speak, bearers of arbitrary preference to market is, of course, a constant of liberalism, historical and present. Thus Locke (*An Essay Concerning Human Understanding* II.xxi.5; cited in Kolb, "Natural Law," 11): "The mind has a different relish, as well as the palate; and you will as fruitlessly endeavor to delight all men with riches or glory . . . as you would satisfy all men's hunger with cheese and lobsters; which though very agreeable and delicious fare to some, are to others extremely nauseous and offensive; and many people would, with reason, prefer the griping of an hungry belly, to those dishes which are a feast to others. . . . For as pleasant tastes depend not on things themselves, but upon their agreeableness to this or that particular palate, wherein there is great variety; so the greatest happiness consists in having the greatest pleasure, and in the absence of those which cause any disturbance, any pain. Now these to different men are very different things. . . ." John Rawls (*A Theory of Justice* [Cambridge, Mass.: Belknap Press, 1971], 554) remarks further what Locke, though it is an ex-

tension of his reasoning, neglects, namely, that "the mind's relish" differs with times and circumstances, and at most times also with itself: "Human good is heterogeneous because the aims of the self are heterogeneous. Although to subordinate all our ends to one end does not strictly speaking violate the principles of rational choice . . . it still strikes us as irrational or more likely as mad. The self is disfigured and put in the service of one of its ends for the sake of system."

76. MacIntyre, *Whose Justice? Which Rationality?* 336.

77. MacIntyre (ibid., 337) convincingly argues that this sort of effectiveness emerges as a central, organizing value of the liberal regime.

78. We suggest that the sense of the social at work in both classical and contemporary liberalism is captured by the uncompromisingly classical liberal economist Ludwig von Mises (*Human Action: A Treatise on Economics,* 3d ed. [Chicago: Henry Regnery Co., 1966], 683–84), speaking on "the meaning of private property in the market society": "In the market society the proprietors of capital and land can enjoy their property only by employing it for the satisfaction of other people's wants. . . . Ownership is an asset only for those who know how to employ it in the best possible way for the benefit of the consumers. It is a *social* function" (emphasis original). One may well wonder what would be lost to von Mises's point were "market function" substituted for social function. The two seem hardly distinguishable, unless the market is the type of every social function. But what the market prototypically does, and what is uppermost in von Mises's mind, is to weigh or tally preferences with a view to deciding which should be satisfied when all cannot be: *that* is the type of the social function under any form of liberal regime.

79. Modern writers refer frequently to distributive justice but rarely to commutative justice, since in a culture preoccupied with trading interests and preferences off against one another, the latter category is absorbed into agreeable exchanges; that is, as a category, it goes the way of "just price."

80. Cf. MacIntyre, *Whose Justice? Which Rationality?* 337–38.

81. Ibid., 344.

82. Cf. ibid., 342–44.

83. Berle and Means, *Modern Corporation,* 2d ed., 305.

84. Something along these lines is, of course, what Donaldson, Preston, Freeman, et al. foresee, and it is indicative of their allegiances that early work on the prospects turns already on proposals over how the relevant rules of bargaining should be framed and, just as importantly, over how "to spell out [the] principles in terms of model legislation" (Freeman, "Politics of Stakeholder Theory," 418).

85. Cf. Booth, "Moral Economy," 662.

S. A. Cortright and Ernest S. Pierucci

86. Thus, in the first connection (Berle and Means, *Modern Corporation,* 2d ed., 319): "Such a great concentration of power and such a diversity of interest [as are represented in the corporate form] raise the long-fought issue of power and its regulation—of interest and its protection. A constant warfare has existed between the individuals wielding power, whatever form, and the subjects of that power. . . . Absolute power is useful in building the organization. More slow, but equally sure is the development of social pressure demanding that the power shall be used for the benefit of all concerned. This pressure . . . is already making its appearance in many guises in the economic field." And in the second connection: "It is conceivable,—indeed it seems almost essential if the corporate system is to survive,—that 'control' of the great corporations should develop into a purely neutral technocracy, balancing a variety of claims by various groups in the community and assigning to each a portion of the income stream on the basis of public policy rather than private cupidity" (ibid,. 312–13). Berle and Means did not explain either (1) how such a role in the conflict among closely held interests of interested groups could ever be played out purely "technically," that is, as opposed to politically, or (2) why such a role should not signal the absorption of the state into corporate "control" rather than the reverse. To his credit, Freeman sees both problems and looks to solve them at a stroke.

Business Corporations and the Principle of Subsidiarity

DENNIS P. MCCANN

One of the most challenging questions to emerge from this volume of essays is whether Catholic social thought contains, at least implicitly, a distinctive, substantive view of the modern business economy and the management of business corporations. If the answer is yes, then our task is to make that view explicit, starting from an understanding of its theological basis, so that it can inform our participation in today's discussions about organizational behavior, management, and business ethics. If the answer is no, then our inquiry into Catholic social thought can and must restrict itself to defining and promoting a merely ethical agenda within the accepted limits of conventional theories of business corporations and the modern business economy. Prior to this essay, I had resigned myself to seeing the contribution of Catholic social thought as a merely ethical agenda. Those who take Catholic social thought seriously could and should be at the forefront among those promoting high moral standards in business conduct, with particular sensitivity to the needs of the poor. Now, however, encouraged by the first two years of the International Symposium on Catholic Social Thought and Management Education, out of which the essays have been formed, I feel that it may be useful to raise once again the first possibility. Does Catholic social thought contain its own paradigm for understanding business corporations, and however latent at present, does this paradigm offer superior potential as a theoretical model for understanding business management and for teaching business ethics?

In order to open a discussion of this general hypothesis about Catholic social thought, I have chosen to focus on what I consider to be the topic within the tradition which is most likely to offer evidence of a distinctive paradigm. I wish to investigate Catholic social thought's principle of subsidiarity, for here, if anywhere in the tradition, is a protean statement of the tradition's distinctive understanding of society, and of the right ordering of relationships among the various institutions that constitute society.

I will proceed to investigate the principle of subsidiarity in three steps: (1) a brief review of the discussion of this principle in the official documents of Catholic social thought, which will show that the principle is explicit in relationship to the social order, particularly on the role of the government in the pursuit of social justice, but mostly implicit in its reference to other institutions; (2) an outline of a hypothesis regarding the latent theological assumptions governing the principle of subsidiarity, intended to provide good reasons for thinking that the principle is generalizable over the entire spectrum of human associations, including the Church and modern business corporations; and (3) a sketch of the theory of the business corporation latent in the principle of subsidiarity, based on a critical reading of Peter Drucker's classic, *The Practice of Management* (1954). The critical correlation of the principle of subsidiarity with Drucker's view of business organizations will not, of course, definitively answer the question whether Catholic social thought contains a distinctive understanding of business. But it will at least suggest, I hope, the utility of the principle of subsidiarity as a heuristic device for assessing the strengths and weaknesses of various comprehensive theories of business relative to the tradition of Catholic social thought, and thus advance the agenda of this volume.

Let me try to persuade the reader of the relevance of this line of inquiry by offering an analogy from the current state of theory in business ethics. Among the most attractive attempts to put business ethics on a firm theoretical foundation is Thomas Donaldson's proposal for extending classical social contract theory as a theory of business corporations or "productive organizations."[1] If business corporations can be regarded as conforming to the logic of the social contract, Donaldson suggests, then certain practical proposals for a comprehensive understanding of business ethics, such as the use of stakeholder theory to warrant the range of moral obligations and social responsibilities operative in business, can be put on a firmer theoretical or philosophical foundation.[2] However attractive this proposal, we must recognize that there are certain fundamental difficulties involved in uncritically grafting the social contract–stakeholder theory onto Catholic social thought. The most fundamental of these is the methodological atheism which animates the social contract tradition. It is hardly accidental that the social contract theory, as articulated by Thomas Hobbes and Jean Jacques Rousseau (though developed in a form less hostile to traditional Christian ethics by John Locke), is meant to provide a rational basis for public moral consensus completely severed from any recognition of God's existence or of the moral structure of human existence which he has created in us. Social contract theory is meant to provide a basis for public morality *etsi Deus non daretur* (as if God did not exist).

While some Christians working in the field of business ethics (for example, Chewning, Eby, and Roels) have ignored this difficulty and endorsed the social contract perspective as linked to stakeholder theory, Catholic social thought cannot afford the luxury of theological naiveté.[3] Catholic social thought must be methodologically as well as substantively committed to the biblical faith in God. It must rest explicitly on the premise of classical Christian theism, or it does little to serve the debate over the nature and purpose of business. In addressing the challenge raised by Donalsdon's approach, for example, the task is either to reconstruct the social contract–stakeholder theory so that it becomes compatible with Christian faith, or to look once again to the resources of Catholic social thought (grounded as it is in the Church's understanding of both Scripture and tradition) for an appropriately theistic understanding of the moral basis of social order and, by extension, of business or "productive organizations."

My proposal is that the principle of subsidiarity may provide the most useful point from which to consider which of these options is the most promising path for further reflection. The question is, then,

Does the principle of subsidiarity provide insight into the nature of business corporations that is both more theoretically adequate and more practically relevant than Donaldson's reconstruction of stakeholder theory within the social contract tradition? Here are my reasons for thinking it does.[4]

The Principle of Subsidiarity: What It Is and What It Is Not

The history of the principle of subsidiarity in Catholic social thought is deceptively simple. In the papal magisterium, it first is mentioned explicitly in Pope Pius XI's encyclical *Quadragesimo anno* (79), then developed by Pope John XXIII in both *Mater et magistra* (53), and *Pacem in terris* (140), and recently reaffirmed by Pope John Paul II in *Centesimus annus* (48). The principle was also invoked once, very briefly, in Vatican II's *Gaudium et spes* (86), and was discussed extensively in eight different passages in the pastoral letter of the United States Catholic Bishops, *Economic Justice for All: Catholic Social Thought and the U.S. Economy* (19, 99, 101, 124, 297, 308, 314, and 323). All of these citations refer to the social order and the role of the government in it; nevertheless, the principle was also applied to the organization of the Church itself in the final document of the Extraordinary Synod of Bishops, held in Rome in 1985, "The Church, in the Word of God, Celebrates the Mystery of Christ for the Salvation of the World," which found in the principle some promising insight into the Church's self-understanding as a "communion," as well as some practical suggestions for how that insight could be translated into appropriate programs of institutional reform.[5]

So much for the simple part. What makes this simplicity deceptive is that in its original formulation in *Quadragesimo anno,* the principle is described as "a fundamental principle of social philosophy, fixed and unchangeable," and yet Pius XI's encyclical marks its first formal appearance in the history of authoritative Church teaching! The gist of it, arguably, is implicit in the idealized version of the social order of medieval Christendom articulated in the encyclicals of Pope Leo XIII (1878–1903), which inaugurated the modern papacy's sustained attention to the "social question." But the precise origins of the term "subsidiarity" remain obscure, at least to me, though the question probably can be resolved by further research into the social thought of the papal advisers who drafted the encyclical. Here, however, is the famous citation from *Quadragesimo anno* in which the principle of subsidiarity is first formally introduced:

> Nevertheless, it is a fundamental principle of social philosophy, fixed and unchangeable, that one should not withdraw from individuals and commit to the community what they can accomplish by their own enterprise and industry. So, too, it is an injustice and at the same time a grave evil and a disturbance of right order, to transfer to the larger and higher collectivity functions which can be performed and provided for by lesser and subordinate bodies. Inasmuch as every social activity should, by its very nature, prove a help to members of the social body, it should never destroy or absorb them.[6]

History suggests that the principle of subsidiarity, however fixed and unchangeable in essence, was first articulated in the context of Pope Pius XI's struggle to distinguish Catholic social thought from the philosophy of corporatist institutional development that had been advocated under the banner of Italian Fascism. Subsidiarity, therefore, was originally meant to define the limits appropriate to state intervention in the social order, in order to protect and preserve the Church's own role in, for example, education and other aspects of social development.

The most illuminating commentary on the operative meaning of the principle of subsidiarity remains the United States Catholic bishops' pastoral letter, *Economic Justice for All,* if for no other reason than the fact that no other official document comments so extensively on the principle. Though some of the pastoral letters' critics, including Michael Novak, have invoked the principle of subsidiarity in order to resist or narrow the bishops' interpretation of John XXIII's doctrine of economic rights, the bishops use the term to frame the challenge of implementing the pastoral letter's set of "moral priorities for the nation," centered on the so-called preferential option for the poor. The bishops quote the principle in full, an unusual degree of emphasis, as they invite the collaboration of persons situated in different institutional settings with respect to the economy.

As *Economic Justice for All* reminds us, "This principle guarantees institutional pluralism. It provides space for freedom, initiative, and creativity on the part of many social agents. At the same time, it insists that all these agents should work in ways that help build up the social body."[7] When the bishops turn specifically to the role of "citizens and government," once again the principle of subsidiarity helps spell out the limits of public policy intervention with respect to the moral priorities they outline: "government should undertake only those initiatives which exceed the capacities of individuals or private groups acting independently." Lest their readers, particularly neoconservatives such as Novak, miss the nuances implicit here, the bishops go on:

> This does not mean, however, that the government that governs least governs best. Rather it defines good government intervention as that which truly "helps" other social groups contribute to the common good by directing, urging, restraining, and regulating economic activity as "the occasion requires and necessity demands."[8]

Here the bishops are commenting directly on *Quadragesimo anno* (79) and doing so in terms that are consistent with the overall development of the principle of subsidiarity in the papal magisterium.

A less conventional though highly promising constructive application of the principle of subsidiarity emerges further in the pastoral letter's groundbreaking chapter "A New American Experiment: Partnership for the Public Good." The principle is invoked three times: once with reference to the significance of mediating structures in developing economic "partnerships" at a local or regional level, and twice with reference to similar developments at both the national and the international level.[9] The focus thus shifts from limiting government intervention to identifying and nurturing the range of private, professional, and quasi-governmental associations that are capable of entering into nonadversarial patterns of collaboration with government. The role envisioned for such mediating structures, with reference to both economic development and the institutionalization of moral responsibility, does seem to represent a fresh application of this "fixed and unchangeable" principle.

Indeed, the details of the "New American Experiment" in which the principle is constructively applied carry over into a consideration of the ethical significance of new forms of corporate governance for individual business firms and certain industries. The experiments proposed range from innovative styles of corporate management to employee stock ownership plans, all of which are intended to foster a greater sense of accountability through increased participation throughout the enterprise, consistent with the pastoral letter's overall theme of justice as participation (see chapters 12 and 13 of this volume). Indeed, the bishops endorsed these experiments not just for their moral promise, which is considerable, but also for their potential to "enhance productivity, increase the profitability of firms, provide greater job security and work satisfaction for employees, and reduce adversarial relations."[10] They also recognize, however, that such efforts may be at risk because of the inordinate pressures of investors too obsessed with immediate returns to allow the innovations adequate time for a fair trial. While the bishops acknowledge the principle of fiduciary responsibility, they also call for a reexamination of the problem of corporate governance "within the bounds of justice to employees, customers, suppliers and the local community."[11] These issues, of course, lie at the heart of an adequate theology of the corporation and of the constructive role that the principle of subsidiarity may play in its development.

The extension of the principle of subsidiarity, outlined in these admittedly fragmentary descriptions of the "New American Experiment," might seem like a straw in the wind, were it not for a simultaneous though unrelated development at the Extraordinary Synod of Bishops held in Rome, October 1985. The synod's final document, "The Church, in the Word of God, Celebrates the Mysteries of Christ for the Salvation of the World," observed that the principle might help clarify certain points of ecclesiology, especially with regard to Vatican II's notion of collegiality. Again, the synod did not articulate the theological presuppositions animating the principle of subsidiarity, but it did thus confirm that the principle's range of application was not to be limited to a narrow focus on the role of the state in society. Invoking the principle of subsidiarity in the context of the Church's own constitutional development, as Richard McBrien has noted, means opening a path toward the institutionalization of greater accountability of the Church's central administration to the needs and aspirations of local churches. [12] Here, too, the point is that the principle may be a remarkably concise way of symbolizing the Catholic tradition's tacit ideal of the social order—of any legitimate social order—to be discerned in any institutional setting and used to evaluate that setting's ultimate organizational effectiveness.

This brief review of the history of the principle of subsidiarity suggests that the line of doctrinal development in Catholic social thought has extended the principle of subsidiarity from political first principles to the theory and practice of economic development, and lately to ecclesiology. The pattern of extension suggests that the principle of subsidiarity is generalizable, and thus applicable to an even larger range of social institutions. Such generalizability may simply be a sign of the cryptic nature of the principle. Perhaps it is simply Catholic social thought's equivalent of a Rorschach test, a vague idea that can be read in many different ways. But perhaps not. If it is anything more than a Rorschach test, its conceptual basis, particularly its theological basis, needs to be made explicit.

The Principle of Subsidiarity and Trinitarian Theology

Elsewhere I have argued that the principle of subsidiarity may be regarded as a practical corollary of the Church's faith in the Holy Trinity. [13] The Trinity, of course, symbolizes the nature of the community of Divine Persons revealed in Jesus Christ's unique status as the Son of God, the Word Incarnate, and in the mission of the Holy Spirit, which is accomplished through his faithful interaction with the will of the Father. Traditional Trinitarian theology, as represented, for example, in the Athanasian and Nicene Creeds, confesses not only the perfect equality or reciprocity characteristic of the relations internal to this community of Divine Persons primordially bonded to one another in love, but also the radical subordination of all other persons and things, who in faith and hope must acknowledge the objectivity of their absolute dependence upon the divine life unfolding within the Trinitarian community.[14] Formally considered, then, the Holy Trinity—in Catholic social thought, at least—serves as the ultimate template of all social relationships, the key to all that we can know of their ultimate significance. As such, it reveals a distinctive pattern of both egalitarian and hierarchical relationships, which are distinguishable and justifiable as functional necessities, that is, as manifest to us in the unfolding of the divine life, "in which we live and move, and have our being" (Acts 17:28). In short, the divine life is one of identity, except for the distinguishable roles that each Trinitarian Person plays in the mystery of salvation. God's own initiative in overcoming sin, through the grace unleashed in this world by the mission and ministry of Jesus Christ, accomplishes salvation in and for us through our diverse interactions with each of the Divine Persons. We become sharers in the divine life through participation in the sacraments that communicate the mystery to us, but not as equal partners. Faith remains the acknowledgment of our absolute dependence on, or radical subordination to, the divine life.

Though my evidence for such an assertion can remain only speculative, I contend that the pattern of divine life communicated in our graceful relationship to the Trinity is not simply encoded in our souls, as many of the ancient Fathers asserted, among them, notably, St. Augustine of Hippo. My hypothesis is that there are *vestigia Trinitatis*—traces of the Trinity—everywhere, if only we care to look for them. Even considered as a hypothesis, if the classical understanding of Christian faith is affirmed, the reality of God—God's own distinctive way of being what Christians confess God to be, "Creator and Lord of the universe"—must be manifest in some way in the very structure of reality as we know it. If St. Augustine was right to recognize that the distinctively Trinitarian pattern of divine life is inscribed in the exercise of human intelligence—in our distinctively human capacity for knowledge and love—should it not also be possible to discover similar traces in the organization of human institutions, at least in our aspirations for them?

Despite their diversity, institutions not only aspire to community, but also achieve whatever degree of social order and moral accountability they afford through the interweaving of egalitarian and hierarchical exigencies. If it is theologically legitimate to discern one important trace of the Trinity in the dynamisms of the human mind and heart, it seems no less legitimate to discern another in the proper ordering of human institutions. Besides, such a hypothesis seems required, if human institutions are to be regarded theologically, in Protestant theologians James M. Gustafson and Elmer W. Johnson's apt phrase, as "aspects of Divine governance in the world."[15] If the governance affirmed is already God's own work before it is consciously accepted as our own, then the divine life must somehow already be encoded in the institutions where we test and fulfill our vocations. Such, I am arguing, is the Trinitarian theological perspective that is tacitly presupposed in the principle of subsidiarity.

Such a theological affirmation of the meaning of human institutions by no means canonizes them, as if thereby they become sinless and unassailable. Just as the Trinitarian psychological template is obscured by the routinely ambiguous and inevitably sinful outcomes of human knowing and willing, so not all forms of organizational development necessarily convey faithfully the organizational template of divine life. The point of the principle of subsidiarity, however, is to provide us with critical leverage against such obscurities. Properly functioning institutions, to the extent that they adhere to the principle of subsidiarity, will render the Trinitarian social template less obscure than it otherwise might be. Like all things, like all of us, such human institutions remain radically subordinate to the Trinity, no matter how transparent they become in reflecting the pattern of organizational development implicit in the community of divine life.

It is worth recalling in this context that both the Trinitarian community of Divine Persons and the principle of subsidiarity exhibit something like a preferential option for egalitarian relationships. Perfect reciprocity is the objective norm, the ideal to which we aspire; and forms of subordination, that is, routine interventions by a hierarchy of "higher" organizations, are justified only to the extent that they actually empower the "lower" forms, individual persons as well as communities, to achieve their own distinctive purposes.[16] The full unfolding of the divine life in history, after all, was occasioned by the Original Sin of our first parents. And as the Roman Catholic liturgy of the Easter Vigil reminds us, without that "happy fault" (*O felix culpa . . .*), it is hard to see how we would have apprehended—or would have been apprehended by—the divine life in its fullness. The Trinitarian community of Divine Persons has intervened to save us from ourselves, just as "higher" institutions are called into being by the dysfunctions of individuals and by the "lower" forms of community engendered in the vicissitudes of our disordered history.

What is at stake here can only be suggested at this point. First, as the previous remarks indicate, Catholic social thought may already contain a template for developing a theology of the modern business corporation, namely, the principle of subsidiarity; but second, the critical potential latent in this principle will be realized only when its unstated theological premise is articulated; that premise, third, is rooted in the mystery of the Holy Trinity, which is ultimately the sole object of genuinely theological reflection. Even in Catholic social thought, then, a theological understanding of the modern business corporation must be about God first of all, or it is about nothing at all. If the principle of subsidiarity provides us with an authentic template for the social order, it does so because its truth is first about God's relationships with us before it is about the proper scale and scope of human relationships and social institutions. Granted, in invoking the principle, neither *Quadragesimo anno* nor the United States Catholic bishops' pastoral letter on the economy makes this point.

Nevertheless, the point can be inferred from a consideration of the pastoral letter's discussion of solidarity and participation. The bishops' discussion of solidarity is explicitly Trinitarian:

> Only active love of God and neighbor makes the fullness of community happen. Christians look forward in hope to a true communion among all persons with each other and with God. The Spirit of Christ labors in history to build up the bonds of solidarity among all persons until that day on which their union is brought to perfection in the Kingdom of God. Indeed Christian theological reflection on the very reality of God as a trinitarian unity of persons—Father, Son, and Holy Spirit—shows that being a person means being united to other persons in love.[17]

Solidarity, in short, is an achievement not to be taken for granted. It is the fullness of community to be realized ultimately in the love "brought to perfection in the Kingdom of God." The principle of subsidiarity is a signpost along the path toward that fullness. It helps us to distinguish which strategies for organizational development are likely to advance the cause of solidarity, and which are likely only to generate obstacles to solidarity.

Equally suggestive, though less theologically articulate, are the pastoral letter's remarks on social participation. If solidarity is the end state or envisioned outcome of human socialization, participation signifies the process involved in getting there. Participation is the object of social justice that, in the bishops' view, specifies the end of justice as a whole, encompassing within the economic sphere both commutative and distributive justice: "Social justice implies that persons have an obligation to be active and productive participants in the life of society and that society has a duty to enable them to participate in this way."[18] Clearly, achieving social justice requires an assessment of institutions with respect to their success in empowering persons for participation. Once again the principle of subsidiarity, and the Trinitarian template of the social order latent in it, seem presupposed in the United States Catholic bishops' specific way of framing the definition of justice in terms of social participation.

The polar opposite of the social participation stressed in the pastoral letter, which the bishops name "marginalization," helps to clarify the meaning that the term "structures of sin" might have in Catholic social thought. Marginalization is the general category defining all those conditions, especially those caused by various forms of "discrimination in job opportunities or income levels on the basis of race, sex, or other arbitrary standards,"[19] that exclude persons and communities from full participation in society. Past institutional arrangements that have contributed to the marginalization of persons and communities are truly "structures of sin," not just in the sense that they perpetuate evil, but also insofar as they impede or make a mockery of that solidarity which will, in the perfection of the kingdom of God, help manifest the mystery of the divine life. The principle of subsidiarity may thus be useful both for identifying various forms of marginalization, to the extent that these are a result of disorders in the routine exercise of institutional power, and for transforming these same institutions in the direction of the ideal of solidarity.

The Modern Business Corporation and
the Principle of Subsidiarity

Even if the points argued in the first two sections of this paper—
(1) that the principle of subsidiarity is open to generalization beyond
its original use in defining the limits of government intervention; and
(2) that the principle of subsidiarity may reflect the ideal pattern of
human social relationships implicit in our ongoing participation in the
divine life of the Holy Trinity—were completely persuasive; even if
both of these points could be accepted, one would still be entitled to
ask, "So what?" What practical difference does any of this make in our
attempts to understand, whether normatively or descriptively, the nature of modern business corporations? Since I do believe that the principle of subsidiarity can and ought to make such a difference, I will now
suggest some of the areas in which this difference can be appreciated.

The difference I hope to point out is evident, first, in the United
States Catholic bishops' pastoral letter on the economy, where the bishops directly address the concerns of "Owners and Managers" of businesses.[20] Nevertheless, the significance of what they say there requires
further critical reflection on the available theories of business management, the most compatible of which is, in my view, Peter Drucker's
classic, *The Practice of Management*.[21] The principle of subsidiarity, in
its present stage of development, may not represent a substantively distinct understanding of business as business, but it may help clarify
which, among competing theories of business, are the most consistent
with the overall agenda of Catholic social thought.

The U.S. Catholic bishops' specific exhortation to the owners and
managers of businesses provides an invitation to new collaboration
between bishops and business people. The bishops' hopeful and constructive approach is a far cry from the suspicions against business that
Catholic social thought often harbored in the past. The invitation to
collaborate is based, first, on a teleological definition of business in
terms of its role in achieving the common good (see Alford/Naughton
and Melé, chapters 2 and 9), and second, on a recognition that such an
understanding of business should enable Christians to understand
their business practice as an opportunity to exercise a "vital Christian
vocation."[22] Business has thus now become theologically significant for

Roman Catholics, as it has long been for Protestants, particularly in the Calvinist traditions.

The bishops' teleological definition of business is worth considering, not only for what it says, but for what it doesn't say. The bishops' words are taken from Pope John Paul II: the businessperson is affirmed as one "whose function consists of organizing human labor and the means of production so as to give rise to the goods and services necessary for the prosperity and progress of the community."[23] This is a very general definition, somewhat reminiscent of Thomas Donaldson's category of "productive organization." But it makes no mention of the role of profit making in the ways in which a business is organized in order to fulfill its goals of giving rise "to the goods and services necessary for the prosperity and progress of the community." The manner of giving rise, as it were, is left unstated. This is a crucial omission that must be remedied if the principle of subsidiarity is to inform a persuasive understanding of business.

Nevertheless, the definition, even in its present form, implies that business, like all other human institutions or "mediating structures," provides a distinct kind of assistance to persons seeking to live in community (see Fort, chapter 11). Business fulfills an economic function, in that it makes it possible for persons to satisfy their material needs by helping them to produce, obtain, and use scarce material resources at costs that are lower than otherwise they would be, were individuals to seek to satisfy these needs on their own. Economy, that is, the generation of wealth through exchange relations, is achieved precisely because business is the institution in which human capacities for social cooperation and competition are deployed as human labor and the means of production.

As the template for ordering all social relationships toward the common good, the principle of subsidiarity specifies both the possibilities and the limits of economic institutions. If the bishops' own definition of business fails to affirm the constitutive role of profit, and thus must be corrected by the principle of subsidiarity, which implicitly affirms profit as a necessary means to the end of wealth creation, other definitions are also implicitly corrected by the principle's teleological understanding of business. A most useful instance comes in the shape of Milton Friedman's classic definition, "The purpose of a business is to maximize profits." This financial theory of business, in my view, is defective in a way that inversely mirrors the reason why the bishops' own definition is defective: it fails to think through the constitutive role of profit, by treating it—contrary to the understanding of most businesspeople and to the actual practice of most owners and managers—as an indisputable absolute. Why would one want to maximize profits? Are profits an end in themselves, or do they require some reference to other, higher ends in order to have any meaning at all (see Gordley, chapter 4)? Friedman's definition, like the bishops', may be teleological; but, like the bishops', Friedman's teleology remains truncated until profit making is seen—as the principle of subsidiarity demands—in terms of its overall role in achieving the common good.

More promising than either of the foregoing, in my view, is Peter Drucker's equally famous definition of the purpose of a business: "There is only one valid definition of a business: to create a customer."[24] The power of this definition becomes apparent as one follows Drucker's thinking about what a customer is, and what is required from a business in order to create a customer. A customer is somebody, a person or institution, who comes back for more, that is, someone with whom the business seeks to enter into an ongoing relationship. Marketing and innovation, as Drucker says, are the two basic functions of a business, and both of them are driven by the need to make and keep customers.[25] Drucker's theory is as fresh and relevant today as it was more than two generations ago, when he first formulated it. From this protean insight into the relational character of a business, he goes on to rethink the ideal managerial structure of a business that is, in fact, fulfilling its purpose by creating customers.

A business that is thus fulfilling its purpose must be organized in such a way as to enable employees to understand and respond to the needs of customers. Such an organization will (1) be organized for "business performance"; (2) "contain the least possible number of management levels"; and (3) enable "the training and testing of tomorrow's top managers."[26] It will be characterized, in other words, by a structure that Drucker calls "federal decentralization," and that eliminates the need for, as it checks the growth of, conventional bureaucracy. The layers of hierarchy that continue to exist within such an organization function as a hierarchy of support and service to those employees who are authorized to interact directly with customers. The organization may still be shaped like a pyramid, but the pyramid will be inverted, both in theory and in practice.

I could go on, but I think enough has been said to suggest that Drucker's business organization exemplifies major elements operative in the principle of subsidiarity. The business firm itself is conceived as a "subsidium"—an aid or help—insofar as it facilitates making and maintaining a certain form of social relationship, namely, that between the firm and its customers; moreover, the inner structure of the organization is geared to focusing the firm's resources on developing that essential relationship. The organization is not self-perpetuating, nor does it tend to use business relationships simply in order to fulfill other ends, such as celebrating status for its own sake or exercising power as a form of domination. The managerial hierarchy is at the service of those who serve the needs of the customers, and in that it is justified—entirely in keeping with the principle of subsidiarity—just so far as such service and support is actually required.

Finally, because a business is still a business, Drucker cannot and does not ignore the role of profit. The purpose of a business may not be to make a profit, but profit remains, for Drucker, "the test of the validity" of the business, in that it determines how successfully the firm meets its own objectives for economic performance. Profit, in Drucker's view, is not an absolute, but a shifting goal determined by the environing social conditions, as registered at any given moment by the vicissitudes of the financial markets: "For the problem of any business is not the maximization of profit but the achievement of sufficient profit to cover the risks of economic activity and thus to avoid loss."[27] Drucker's reason for this view of profit is teleological, and he puts it provocatively: "That Jim Smith is in business to make a profit concerns only God and the Recording Angel. It does not tell us what Jim Smith does and how he performs."[28] The profit motive, in short, explains both too much and too little about a business. It is meaningless apart from an understanding of the purpose of a business, of this particular business, and the means organized for fulfilling this purpose. All of which, since it is driven by the need to make and retain good relationships with customers, seems consistent with, and a useful exemplification—however sketchy for now—of how to define business consistently with the principle of subsidiarity (see Koslowski, chapter 6).

Social Contract or Subsidiarity: Alternative Paradigms?

Let me conclude with a few remarks on the differences between Donaldson's social contract theory of business and the theory of business that seems to be implicit in the principle of subsidiarity. At the level of first principle or method, the difference is most apparent: social contract theory is methodologically atheistic, and subsidiarity is emphatically theocentric—in fact, classically Trinitarian, if my analysis of its theological assumptions holds up. This methodological difference, however, inevitably betrays a substantive difference: the principle of subsidiarity assumes that human persons are inherently social, and naturally so, as creatures of a personal, Trinitarian God whose own Being is irreducibly social. Social contract theory, by contrast, assumes that human persons are inherently autonomous, rational individuals, naturally committed to no higher moral compass than their own self-interest. The difference this difference makes, of course, is a matter for philosophical debate. My own view is that a very important truth about human persons in community depends upon recognizing this difference. Catholic social thought, on this point, gives a compelling answer to the manifold errors of modern individualism, which are just as pernicious in management theory and business ethics as they are in theology and philosophy.

At the level of concrete application, however, there may be few, if any, serious differences. Especially when grafted onto stakeholder theory, social contract theory does yield an agenda for business ethics and management education that clearly means to resist the worst failings of economistic or narrowly financial theories of business. Management will be urged to balance or optimize the competing claims of all legitimate stakeholders, even though neither stakeholder theory nor social contract theory have provided much insight into how to prioritize fairly among those competing claims. The same must be said of any theory of business generated from the principle of subsidiarity, at least as our comprehension of the principle presently stands. Recognizing the subsidiary function of business in relation to the common good may be sufficient to neutralize the inordinate claims of investors, but it may not offer any special insight into prioritizing competing claims among legitimate stakeholders, at least not without developing the subsidiary view of business in terms of the other substantively normative theories of human personhood and community that are prominent in the repertoire of Catholic social thought.

On one point, however, the subsidiary view of business may make a genuinely practical difference. The social contract theory, as far as I can tell, implies no preference for any particular set of managerial theories and practices. It does not, because it simply is not focused on the internal dynamics of human institutions. Of course, one could attempt to deduce a preferred management structure and a style of corporate culture from the nature of Donaldson's "productive organizations," but the deductions, it seems to me, would clearly be contrived and strictly ad hoc.[29] The principle of subsidiarity, on the other hand, is itself the expression of a robustly theological understanding of human persons and communities, and includes rather significant resources for understanding the internal dynamics of both. In light of the innovative applications of subsidiarity in the United States Catholic bishops' pastoral letter on the economy, the principle does seem to entail a clear preference for participatory styles of management and for strategies of organizational development that enhance innovation, responsiveness, and accountability, similar to those advocated in Drucker's theorizing about business. The more thoroughly the case for participatory management styles and structures is grounded in a coherent and persuasive account of human nature and of its ultimate significance in relation to God's own activity in the world, the better off we all are likely to be, at least when "we" represents the contributors of this volume and the community of those who have invested time and talents in this ongoing series of symposia on Catholic social thought and management education.

Notes

1. Thomas Donaldson's proposal is first presented in *Corporations and Morality* (Englewood Cliffs, N.J.: Prentice Hall, 1982), 36–59. Later it forms the core of his approach, as seen in "The Moral Foundations of Multinationals," in *The Ethics of International Business* (New York: Oxford University Press, 1989), 44–64. More recently, Donaldson and Thomas W. Dunfee

have attempted to give this perspective paradigmatic status in business ethics in "Towards a Unified Conception of Business Ethics: Integrative Social Contracts Theory," *Academy of Management Review* 19 (April 1994): 252–84; and Dunfee has gone on with N. Craig Smith and William T. Ross, Jr., to argue the paradigm's superiority for understanding marketing ethics in "Social Contracts and Marketing Ethics," *Journal of Marketing Ethics* 63 (July 1999): 14–32. In my view, Donaldson's apparent success in offering a comprehensive paradigm for business ethics must raise the kind of questions that I seek to address in this essay. Stated concretely, does Catholic social thought provide the makings of an alternative to integrative social contracts theory (ISCT), or should its role be merely marginal to ISCT, that is, limited to offering scattered moral advice that is confirmed, rejected, or ignored by the superior paradigm?

2. Thomas Donaldson and Lee E. Preston, "The Stakeholder Theory of the Corporation: Concepts, Evidence, and Implications,"*Academy of Management Review* 20 (January 1995): 65–91.

3. Richard C. Chewning, John W. Eby, and Shirley J. Roels, *Business through the Eyes of Faith* (San Francisco: Harper San Francisco, 1990).

4. For a good summary of subsidiarity, see Michael E. Allsopp, s.v. "Subsidiarity," *The New Dictionary of Catholic Social Thought,* ed. Judith A. Dwyer (Collegeville, Minn.: Liturgical Press, 1994), 927–29.

5. Hereafter, the official documents are cited by paragraph number from David J. O'Brien and Thomas Shannon, eds., *Catholic Social Thought: The Documentary Heritage* (Maryknoll, N.Y.: Orbis Books, 1992).

6. Pius XI, *Quadragesimo anno,* 79.

7. U.S. Catholic Bishops, *Economic Justice for All: Catholic Social Thought and the U.S. Economy* (1986), 51 (see note 5 above).

8. Ibid., 62.

9. Ibid., 308, 314, 323.

10. Ibid., 300.

11. Ibid., 152.

12. See Richard P. McBrien, "An Ecclesiological Analysis of Catholic Social Teachings," in *Catholic Social Thought and the New World Order,* ed. Oliver F. Williams and John W. Houck (Notre Dame, Ind.: University of Notre Dame Press, 1993), 176.

13. Cf. Dennis P. McCann, *New Experiment in Democracy: The Challenge for American Catholicism* (Kansas City, Mo.: Sheed and Ward, 1987), 129–38.

14. What I am sketching here is based upon the remarkable renascence in Trinitarian theology among Roman Catholic systematic theologians recently. Cf. Karl Rahner, *The Trinity,* trans. Joseph Donceel, with an introduction by

Catherine Mowry Lacugna (New York: Crossroad Publishing Co., 1997); Catherine Mowry Lacugna, *God for Us: The Trinity and Christian Life* (San Francisco: Harper San Francisco, 1993); Anne Hunt, *The Trinity and the Paschal Mystery: A Development in Recent Catholic Theology*, New Theology Studies 5 (Collegeville, Minn.: Liturgical Press, 1997). Much of this development, particularly among Catholic feminist theologians, has been stimulated by Mary Daly's radical critique of Trinitarian theology, *Beyond God the Father: Toward a Philosophy of Women's Liberation* (Boston: Beacon Press, 1976), which has found a substantively Catholic yet authentically feminist response in Elizabeth A. Johnson's *She Who Is: The Mystery of God in Feminist Theological Discourse* (New York: Crossroad Publishing Co., 1993). If my sketch linking the principle of subsidiarity with Trinitarian faith is to carry any weight theologically, it will have to address the issues regarding Trinitarian theology raised by these and other Catholic authors.

15. James M. Gustafson and Elmer W. Johnson, "The Corporate Leader and the Ethical Resources of Religion: A Dialogue," in *The Judaeo-Christian Vision and the Modern Corporation*, ed. John W. Houck and Oliver F. Williams (Notre Dame, Ind.: University of Notre Dame Press, 1982), 320.

16. This normative version of social relationships converges remarkably with some of the central insights of the Confucian tradition in Chinese moral philosophy. During my tenure as University Fellow at the Centre for Applied Ethics at Hong Kong Baptist University in 1998, I was privileged to hear two papers by Chinese Christian scholars that explicitly acknowledge and explore this convergence: one, by a Protestant, Edwin C. Hui, "Jen and Perichoresis: The Confucian and Christian Bases of the Relational Person"; the other, by a Roman Catholic, Joannes Sun, "Are All Human Beings Persons?" at the international symposium "Bioethics and the Concept of Personhood." Proceedings of the conference will be published by the Centre. Though neither author proceeds, as I do, to explore explicitly the implications of Trinitarian theology for social theory, their understanding the convergence of the Christian theology of the person with the Confucian tradition naturally and inevitably raises the question of "institutionalization," or the implicit moral template, as I am raising it here. For in the classical texts of the Confucian tradition, it appears not to be possible to consider personal relationships in complete or psychological abstraction from the social or organizational settings in which they concretely unfold.

17. U.S. Catholic Bishops, *Economic Justice for All*, 64.

18. Ibid., 71.

19. Ibid., 73.

20. Cf. ibid., 110–18.

21. Peter Drucker, *The Practice of Management,* Perennial Library Edition (New York: Harper and Row, 1986).

22. U.S. Catholic Bishops, *Economic Justice for All,* 117.

23. Ibid., 110.

24. Drucker, *The Practice of Management,* 37.

25. Ibid.

26. Ibid., 202–4.

27. Ibid., 36.

28. Ibid.

29. The previously mentioned essay by Thomas W. Dunfee, N. Craig Smith, and William T. Ross, Jr., "Social Contracts and Marketing Ethics," illustrates this point. The integrative social contracts theory, it seems, does represent an agenda for internal change in corporate decision-making structures, but the agenda is derivative from certain models of normative discourse ethics, such as that offered by Juergen Habermas, which arguably are not normally understood as part of the social contract perspective.

9

Not Only
Stakeholder Interests

*The Firm Oriented toward
the Common Good*

DOMÈNEC MELÉ

As explained throughout this volume thus far, the shareholder and stake-holder approaches serve as the two dominant competing frameworks for the orientation of management. These theories give support for multiple purposes: first, to describe and predict behavior in manage-ment and corporate governance; second, to identify the relationship between firms' managerial orientation and corporate performance—profitability, growth, and so forth—and thus to serve as an instrument for the formulation of strategic prescriptions; and third, to give a nor-mative foundation to management.

Although interrelated, these three aspects—descriptive accuracy, in-strumental power, and normative validity—are quite distinct.[1] There is a significant difference between the first two aspects (descriptive and pre-dictive) and the third (prescriptive). The former express conditions for obtaining certain results ("If you want to achieve—or to avoid—result R, then do A") and contribute to efficiency-enhancing decision making. The normative approach, on the other hand, prescribes how to act up-rightly (as in the Aristotelian tradition: "I ought to do A because it is

190

good" or "I must avoid B because it is bad"). In other words, shareholder and stakeholder models take both a strategic approach and an ethical one.

In this essay, I propose to point out certain deficiencies in the normative arguments for the stakeholder approach as Alford and Naughton have done for the shareholder approach (see chapter 2). I then outline a new approach based on the classical idea of the common good, which entails an appropriate identification and ordering of management responsibilities.

The Stakeholder Approach: Some Underlying Roots

The stakeholder model was proposed to counter the long-standing dominance of shareholder theory. This model takes into account the interests of those groups who can have some effect on the firm or may be affected by the firm's actions. The first theoretical development of this approach was carried out by R. Edward Freeman in 1984, although stakeholder theory and its applications originated considerably earlier.[2] It started in strategic management literature, but in the last decade, this model has spread considerably to other fields.[3] In fact, the bibliography available is now quite extensive.[4]

In recent years, Freeman, alone and with other collaborators, has deepened his initial work by enlarging it, clarifying certain aspects, introducing modifications, and giving new proposals.[5] In addition, Donaldson and Preston have provided a set of precise theoretical arguments as a base for this theory.[6] Later, Donaldson and Dunfee positioned the responsibility of the corporation in the context of an implicit contract with society.[7] In spite of these developments, the normative stakeholder approach has its critics.[8]

Literature on the stakeholder approach is plentiful, and an exhaustive study of it would exceed the space available here. Still, we may outline certain postulates generally accepted by authors who work with this theory:

1. It is acknowledged that those affected by business activity are autonomous agents with interests and rights. This entails a series of normative implications for management.

2. The business firm is conceived of as a vehicle for coordinating the interests of the various groups involved.

3. Property rights are legitimate but not absolute. Other, more important rights may transcend them. Many current property theories are consistent with this approach.

4. The firm's purpose is to try to satisfy the stakeholders' expectations and demands while safeguarding the company's survival.

5. The executive manager has multifiduciary duties to all the groups involved in the firm's progress, not only to shareholders.

6. The corporation ought to be managed to the benefit of its stakeholders (customers, suppliers, owners, employees, and local communities) and also according to the interests of the corporation. Thus a responsibility arises to consider all the effects of a decision for the groups involved, having an eye to the firm's survival as well.

7. Decisions must be made while keeping in mind the claims and expectations of the groups involved. By virtue of their autonomy, interests, and rights, the stakeholders should in some way participate in decisions that would substantially affect their own well-being.

8. To resolve conflicts of interest, one must weigh the interests of stakeholders according to some normative theory that establishes criteria or procedures for settling such conflicts.

Although the stakeholder model developed in opposition to the shareholder model, it is critical to note that the two approaches have some common roots. As developed in Cortright and Pierucci's essay (chapter 7), at the root of both approaches is a vision of the person as an individual who forges relations and links with others only for the sake of his own interests. Both, therefore, basically seek to answer the question: In whose *interests* is a company to be managed? The first responds: those of the shareholders; the second, those who have some stake in company decisions, including shareholders.

Both theories, then, unfold narrowly within what Cortright and Pierucci call a "logic of interests."[9] The question could, instead, be the following: How should a company orient its management? One could also ask: What *responsibilities* are entailed in managing a firm? Adopting either of these questions would mean rising above the "logic of interests" to enter a "logic of responsibilities."

Such a logic respects the obvious existence of interests but moves beyond considerations of interest to a broader perspective than the conventional theories employ—and, above all, it responds better to the human condition. Although the human being is frequently moved by interests, he is also capable of relating to others in a way that transcends pure interest, seeking just, solidarity-driven or even friendly relations. These latter respond to an ethical category called *sociability*, the exercise of which develops the agent's human qualities and facilitates social harmony.

In fact, acting only for the sake of interest does not lead to human flourishing, which is linked to relations of interdependence among persons. After all, the person is a social being: he lives in society and has need of other people for his well-being. By helping each other, people become specifically—humanly—better. A manager, for instance, might behave by respecting people and serving their needs, or by seeking only his own self-interest, failing to respect fundamental human rights and using people as a mere means to his objectives. In the first case, this manager improves as a human being; in the second, he debases himself.

Taking sociability into account leads to a view of society quite different from that which informs the stakeholder (as well as the shareholder) model. Society is not simply a group of individuals with individual interests, lacking any links except those forged for the sake of a hypothetical social contract (see Hobbes, Locke, Rousseau, Rawls). Nor is society a sort of organism in which the individual and his autonomy practically disappear into the collective (Hegel, Marx).

Consideration of sociability leads to the realization that society is formed by a group of people united by a principle greater than questions of reciprocal interest. People are united by a nexus of solidarity, not only of contract. They associate within intermediate societies or communities—among which are business organizations—and thus a social network is formed, which gives society its tone and consistency (see Fort, chapter 11). Consideration of the relationships among intermediary communities, and between these and political society, suggests that society ought to foster a common good for all its members and parts. Otherwise, society would lose its *raison d'être*. The common good is achieved through the cooperation of those who make up society, whether individuals or associations—including business firms.

The Common Good Approach

The notion of the common good is quite intuitive. Nevertheless, we must examine what we understand by "common good," since the term is not always used, or understood, univocally. For a family, a harmonious atmosphere is a common good. The same could be said of a company: remaining competitive, boasting executives and employees who are diligent, motivated, and cooperative, maintaining a good corporate reputation or a solid financial situation—all these are aspects of the common good of a company's members. In a global context, it belongs to the common good, for example, that problems with the ozone layer—the greenhouse effect—be mitigated or avoided; that the oceans be clean, the transport routes secure for the flow of merchandise; that biological weapons cease to pose a threat; that appropriate steps be taken against the nuclear threat; and so on.

The common good, in short, encompasses everything that is conducive to the human flourishing of each person in a community—such as a family or a civil society—and to the flourishing of the association as a whole. The common good is universal, distributive, and communicable to many without belonging exclusively to anyone. The common good, thus understood, is not the sum of individual interests, nor of general or majority interests, but is something that transcends particular interests. It is a good in which all can participate, and thus "common"—although not everyone participates to the same degree or in the same way.

The Catholic social tradition considers the common good as the basic reference point for any human society, and for business as well.[10] In this regard, John Paul II does not hesitate to affirm that the Church "recognizes the positive value of the market and of the enterprise, but at the same time points out that these need to be oriented towards the common good."[11]

The concept of the common good is abstract but neither vague nor at all irrelevant. It consists fundamentally not of concrete rules for particular situations, but of solid principles that aid reflection upon changing situations in business and society. Summarizing a long tradition,[12] three essential elements of the common good could be named:

1. Respect for people and their inalienable, fundamental rights, so that all persons can realize their vocation.
2. Social well-being and group development (this includes legitimate interests, which may vary according to the persons who claim them, but are always subordinate to human development).
3. Stability and security within a just order: that is, social peace.

Although there are certain commonalities to the stakeholder and common good approach, they differ significantly on the following first principles.

Dignity and Development of the Person

The common good approach, first of all, takes into account respect for the dignity and inalienable human rights of each person, as well as the conditions for human development overall. "In virtue of a personal dignity," John Paul II has written, "the human being is always a value as an individual, and as such demands to be considered and treated as a person and never as an object to be used, or as a means, or as a thing."[13] This affirmation recalls one of the well-known Kantian imperatives, but at its root the pontiff's hypothesis is different. The "human dignity" referred to here derives from the philosophical position that the person is conscious and free, able to know the truth and act accordingly, and called to develop as a human being, that is, called to human flourishing. Moreover, it rests above all on profound theological foundations.[14] These include the recognition of the person's autonomy—as in Kant— but especially the need for human flourishing, through a right exercise of freedom.[15] In other words, a human being is not merely an autonomous person with certain imperative duties separated from his human flourishing, but is a being in continuous development who needs the human good as its point of reference.[16] Full human development is oriented according to the reality and vocation of the person seen in his totality, namely, according to his interior dimension.[17]

The Firm: A Community of Persons in Society

Sociability explains the human practice of living in society and sharing natural communities such as the family and the political organization.

Economic firms originate with the free will of entrepreneurs and their collaborators. However, at the root of the firm is not only the person's freedom but also his sociability.

Societies contribute to the satisfaction of human needs and desires. In corporations, individuals can satisfy their economic and psychological needs. At the same time, they receive and give help by cooperating with others (labor) or by supplying material resources (capital). This cooperation makes possible development of individual capacities as well as harmonious flourishing in a community of interdependent human lives.

Accordingly, the firm involves unity among its members: they share in a common effort, are ruled by a common authority, and work in cooperation. In the firm, of course, there are "stakes," but not only stakes. Its members are also joined in multiple *nexuses*. These nexuses may exist for the sake of interests (economic or otherwise) or psychological benefits (pleasant peers, work climate, culture, and so on). There are also other nexuses, of a moral kind, which are distinct from interests. Among these, the experience of belonging and of commitment to the firm's mission demands solidarity, the will to justice, loyalty, a spirit of service, and so forth. These moral nexuses can contribute greatly to the firm's soundness. At the same time, action motivated by the moral values that underlie these attitudes contributes to the human development of the subjects who act—and so shape themselves—within the firm.

For all these reasons we may affirm that a business is a community of persons, forged by their work. As John Paul II explains:

> It is characteristic of work that it first and foremost unites people. In this consists its social power: the power to build a community. In the final analysis, both those who work and those who manage the means of production or who own them must in some way be united in this community.[18]

The community of persons who make up the business firm is interdependent with other groups (suppliers, customers, the employees' families, for example) and is itself a part of society. The firm, in a certain sense, can be conceived of as a community that is interwoven with others and thus exerts its activity throughout all of society. John Paul II appears to be basing his thought on this fact when he expresses the intriguing idea of the formation of "ever widening circles" in society on the basis of work in the firm:

> people work with each other, sharing in a "community of work" which embraces ever widening circles. . . . It is his disciplinary work in close collaboration with others that makes possible the creation of ever more extensive *working communities* which can be relied upon to transform natural and human environments.[19]

Like any other community, the company has a common good in which all its members may participate (see Kennedy, chapter 3).

The Purpose of the Firm: Specific Service to the Common Good

The business firm, like any other human community, must serve the common good. The firm is born in society, develops there, is thus a part of society and, by its social nature, should contribute to society's common good. If a company only made use of society, it would be like a parasite; if it caused harm, it could be compared to cancerous cells within an organism. In either case it would forfeit its moral legitimacy.

An attentive look at business reveals that its activity touches society in various ways, which may be favorable to, or may be opposed to, the common good:

1. By means of the product or service offered. The firm contributes to the common good by the production and promotion and sale of products and services that are genuinely useful for human development, and by offering and selling them under just conditions. It is well known, moreover, that business activity makes access to goods and services possible to a greater number of people than would be the case if there were no business firms. These products, along with the activities related to their sale, affect people's manner of living, whether by the use of a product or by the effect of the advertising, promotion, and sales carried out by the company.
2. By means of work performed within the company. The company contributes to the common good by the creation or maintenance

of jobs under fair conditions, through means that lend greater efficacy to human activity.

3. By means of the organizational culture and leadership. Human development is fostered by an appropriate organizational culture and leadership. The absence of these two factors could promote human deterioration.

4. By means of creating channels for investment. The firm provides a channel for good use of available resources through investment of capital in activities useful to people. The market, to which the firm is subject, stimulates innovation, an efficient use of available resources and an effective organization of work. One must caution, however, that the use of these resources may also erode the common good if the investment is not directed toward products that contribute to human development.

5. By means of creating and distributing economic value added. The firm contributes to the common good by generating and distributing wealth and by providing the opportunity for others (suppliers and customers) to do the same. The distribution of value added also favors the common good if carried out equitably. Along with the generation of value, there may be a negative impact on the natural environment contrary to the common good (the abusive consumption of natural resources, pollution, inappropriate waste disposal, and so forth).

6. By means of providing continuity to the company itself. This continuity is also favorable to the common good insofar as it makes the previous kind possible, while allowing the activity of other companies, institutions, or communities that benefit the activity of each firm.

The business that functions in the ways indicated contributes to making society more just as, through a chain of interdependencies, its activity touches all of society. Thus, business activity redounds to the common good—the good of all—although some receive its effects more immediately than others. Recalling that orientation to the common good is what lends the firm its moral legitimacy, these modes of affecting society will be acceptable to the degree that they do not erode the common good but contribute to its realization.

The Right to Property and Its Social Function

The property right is a legitimate one, but certain responsibilities are inherent in it, including responsibility not only for actual harm caused, but also for omissions, for failing to provide benefits to others derived from its proper use. The property right is a genuine right, but not an absolute one, since it has intrinsic limitations.[20]

Advocates of the stakeholder approach support their view by the non-absolute character of the property right and by the existence of rights that take precedence over it. Thomas Donaldson and Lee Preston contend that property rights are to be justified by underlying principles of distributive justice.[21] They also hold that the normative principles of distributive justice that underlie contemporary, pluralistic theories of property rights support stakeholder and undermine shareholder theory. However, their reasoning is somewhat problematic.[22] It could be argued that private property is not an absolute right, but relying on contemporary theories of property means basing one's argument on something subject to the contingencies of history. Should these theories veer toward a more absolutist understanding of property, (normative) stakeholder theory would collapse.

Traditional teaching on the common good acknowledges the right to property, but conceives of it not as absolute, but as a right that ought to be subordinated to the common needs of human development: that is, to the pursuit of the common good. The reason: property has to do with "things," and thus has an inherently instrumental character. It is in service to the common good that the social function of property resides, a function repeatedly proclaimed by natural law philosophers[23] and stressed in the Catholic social tradition.[24]

The social function of property is especially relevant to the means of production. Property is instrumental to company development and fulfills an important social function, regardless of its owner's purpose. Business activity enables a greater number of people to gain access to goods and services: without the company this would not be possible, or at least would not be achieved efficiently. Providing this access requires efficient use of resources and an appropriate work organization (see Gates, chapter 12).

Obligations of Justice and Solidarity

Stakeholder theory recognizes a duty toward shareholders, but as one duty among many, since the manager is deemed to have multifiduciary obligations toward all stakeholders. The difficulty is that the existence of these fiduciary duties is nothing but a hypothesis which is at best problematic.

A second difficulty with stakeholder theory concerns the identification of the parties who count as stakeholders. According to Freeman, a stakeholder is "any group or individual who can affect or is affected by the achievement of the organization's objectives."[25] This is a definition that lends itself to numerous errors. Some authors identify as stakeholders a few groups of people closely linked to the company, such as shareholders, employees, clients, suppliers, and the local community. Others adopt a still narrower criterion and exclude, for instance, the local community and suppliers. Still others (following Freeman) employ a broad criterion, considering as stakeholders absolutely everybody who could exert influence on or be affected by the firm's activities, including occasional consumers, competitors, pressure groups, the media, or even (presumably) terrorist groups who might perpetrate a kidnapping.

In the face of the original definition's ambiguity, new ones have been devised. Mitchell, Agle, and Wood have compiled a lengthy list of stakeholder definitions.[26] The confusion is heightened because normative and strategic considerations appear to be intermingled. There are authors, nevertheless, who specify criteria such as legitimate claim, legitimate interest, action impact, or legal claim, although they too fail to explain the grounds of the moral legitimacy of their criteria.

The common good approach holds that fiduciary duties owed to shareholders ought to be harmonized with the common good. This principle requires that corporate affairs be managed with the common good in mind, and that stakeholders receive fair treatment.[27] From the elements included in the common good and enumerated above, there emerges a set of obligations of justice and solidarity.

Justice leads us to give each person his rights (*ius sui*). There are many ways to understand justice, but in the context of our reflections so far the most appropriate is the one proposed by Aristotle and, following him, Thomas Aquinas. John Finnis provides a helpful modern version of this tradition of justice.[28] In sum, we can distinguish three types of justice:

1. General justice, which focuses primarily on the obligations of each individual or group to the common good of a given organization, institution, or community.
2. Distributive justice, which deals with the obligations of the ruler or recognized authority of a community to provide for any of the members of that community according to their contributions or needs, without favoritism or whim.
3. Commutative justice, which regulates exchanges between persons and groups in accordance with strict respect for their rights. Commutative justice dictates carefully respecting the rights of the person (human rights), keeping promises and commitments, abiding by free and fair contracts, safeguarding property rights, paying debts, making restitution for real injustices, and so on.

Solidarity involves a sort of "friendship" among interdependent parties which transcends the logic of stakeholder claims and competing interests. "Solidarity" expresses the aforementioned general obligation to strive for the community's common good as much as possible. There is a "solidarity *ad intra*" of the firm, which requires the collaboration of all the firm's members for its common good, and a "solidarity *ad extra*," which requires the firm to contribute to the common good of civil society according to its capacities and opportunities.

Antecedent and Consequent Responsibilities

Moral obligations entail responsibility for performing or omitting actions that can and should be performed, as well as responsibility, in some cases, for the consequences of one's actions. Although the stakeholder approach was developed to make up for the inadequacies of the shareholder theory's treatment of ethical responsibility, it too finds itself wanting on this subject. Both theories limit managerial responsibility to the effects of decision making in the interests of shareholders or stakeholders. Limiting responsibility in this way, however, is questionable. As

C. Llano points out, there is one responsibility proper to action (antecedent responsibility) and another proper to its effects (consequent responsibility).[29]

Moral theology, following Thomas Aquinas,[30] emphasizes the moral object or the morality of the action chosen—and therefore antecedent responsibility. John Paul II insists that "the morality of the human act depends primarily and fundamentally on the 'object' rationally chosen by the deliberate will."[31] Concerning consequences, one must keep in mind that when bad effects arise from an action, there are no apparent grounds for extending responsibility beyond foreseeable and (thus) avoidable effects which are accepted in order to achieve something good—something better than refraining from action altogether. On the other hand, it would be difficult to accept responsibility that was only based on a rationalist apriorism, such as responsibility limited a priori according to the effects on shareholder or stakeholder interests. According to the *Catechism of the Catholic Church,* "an effect can be tolerated without being willed by its agent. . . . A bad effect is not imputable if it was not willed either as an end or as a means of an action. . . . For a bad effect to be imputable it must be foreseeable and the agent must have the possibility of avoiding it."[32]

We may conclude, then, that responsibility in the firm depends primarily on the morality of the action performed or rightly omitted. Actions are to be evaluated according to the obligations of justice and solidarity listed earlier, and by their consequences for any affected parties (for example, pollution in industry or layoffs due to company restructuring), but these consequences are only imputable if they are not disproportionate to the achievement of a greater good, and if they are really foreseeable and avoidable.[33]

Order among Responsibilities

To establish right order in the exercise of responsibilities, we may introduce several principles related to the common good. First, one must fulfill the duties of strict justice, those derived from the absolute rights of persons and of legitimate contracts. Otherwise no other form of justice would be possible. The person has priority over things, since persons possess a certain absolute value, whereas things are instruments:

"Even prior to the logic of the fair exchange of goods and the forms of justice appropriate to it, there exists *something which is due to the person because he is a person,* by reason of his lofty dignity."[34] As John Paul II has noted, one application of this principle to the area of business asserts the primacy of persons in the production process and in relation to the finished product (see Murphy and Pyke, chapter 13, on the production process).

> We must emphasize and give prominence to the primacy of man in the production process, *the primacy of man over things.* Everything contained in the concept of capital in the strict sense is only a collection of things. Man, as a subject of work, and independently of the work that he does—man alone is a person.[35]

Second, in case of conflict, the common good takes priority over the particular good when these goods are of the same genus. This principle, taken from Thomas Aquinas, stipulates that the good of the whole, of the community—to which individuals belong as parts—is specifically different from and superior to the good of the parts (individuals' and associations' particular goods), because the common good allows for a higher level of perfection for all members of society.[36] This principle differs from the utilitarian principle in that it seeks not the interest or satisfaction of the majority, but the greater human good for all. In other words, prioritizing the common good might mean the sacrifice of private interests for the sake of the good of all. This primacy does not exclude seeking private goods as long as they are compatible with the common good. Moreover, this primacy only affects goods of the same genus. For instance, the principle might allow cutting salaries in order to save the company, thus subordinating the particular good (salaries) to the common good (the company's survival): in both cases economic goods are at issue. However, according to this principle, the need to overcome a company's economic difficulties (an economic good) could not be construed as an excuse to commit fraud (an act contrary to a moral good), or to force executives to work to the point of damaging their health or of failing to fulfill their family responsibilities (moral goods), for these goods differ generically from economic goods. Of course, to liquidate assets to the sole advantage of the shareholders or of management (bonds associated to profits) would also violate this principle, if by doing so we put the company's continuity at serious risk, thus subordinating the common good to private interests.

Third, the order of priority in solidarity ought to be determined by a certain type of unitive nexus among all persons or independent groups. This principle is inspired by the Christian idea of the order of charity.[37] Love is universal; nonetheless, there is an obligation to "love some more than others." Specifically, "we should measure the love of different persons according to the different kinds of union."[38] This principle is, then, a matter of common sense: it is not rational to abandon one's children to look after strangers, or to give one's only life preserver to another when one's brother is drowning.

By way of applying the principle of order of priority in solidarity to the company, we can affirm that the responsibilities of each to others depend on the unitive nexuses that link individuals or social groups with the firm, as a community of persons. Although it might not be possible to attend to requests that go beyond strict justice, it would still be necessary to prioritize the most immediate among them according to the existing nexuses.

Again, although it is difficult to state definitively who does and does not belong to the community of persons that is the firm, different degrees of membership could be defined according to the kind of unitive nexus into which each individual or group enters within the community. The following distinctions express (with flexibility) the degrees of membership, which may diverge from the legal definition.

1. Core members: Those managers, employees, or shareholders who are strongly committed to the company (they could be classified according to their loyalty, effort, participation, and persistence as shareholders, their identification with and efforts for the company, services rendered for the good of the company, and so forth);

2. Peripheral members: People involved with the company, with a certain degree of commitment to it, but a slight one (temporary workers, ephemeral shareholders, ordinary customers and suppliers, and so forth);

3. External interdependent groups: Those who are linked to the firm by a very weak commitment, or are not committed at all but are

related to the firm in specific ways (the local community, fortuitous clients, consumers, and so forth); competitors could also be included here, insofar as they share cooperative objectives about non-competitive matters.

Regarding the order of priority in solidarity, C. Llano has suggested a model of "responsibilities in concentric circles," in which circles or scopes of responsibility can be developed and arranged in levels, as follows: "me—family—company—industry—society."[39] The subject's responsibility depends on the "profession" or function he exercises. Llano's work rests on that of other authors, among them the German philosopher Robert Spaemann, who affirms: "It is not necessary for each citizen to direct all his actions immediately to the common good: his contribution to community welfare consists in the first place of assuming the specific responsibilities inherent to his condition."[40]

If we follow this suggestion and keep in mind the degrees of membership enumerated, we can trace, in each particular situation, concentric circles of responsibility, which can aid in determining the respective priority of legitimate, conflicting interests.

Orientation to the common good, as we have pointed out, encourages us to consider the company as one community within society. It does not permit us to ignore the secondary effects of the objectives attained by management, as the shareholder model does (when these effects are allowed by law and are not avoided by voluntary constraints). The concentric-circles criterion "relies on the consideration of secondary— and even tertiary—effects, which are represented by the series of circles; on consciously warning of the repercussions that one circle can have for others."[41]

Fourth, one must resolve conflicts of interest through practical wisdom. Under the shareholder approach, decision making is evaluated according to certain very simple (though, as noted, problematic) criteria. With the stakeholder model, the process becomes more complicated. When the interests of two or more groups conflict, the case is similar to situations that arise in society at large: continual conflicts of interest, submitted to some power that acts as arbiter. No wonder, then, that advocates of this approach seek normative justification for resolving such conflicts in political philosophy, turning to normative theories such as utilitarianism, procedural justice, or social contract theory.

All these justificatory strategies suffer from the deficiencies inherent in the theories selected. In their effort at normative justification, Freeman and Evan introduce an argument inspired by John Rawls's celebrated work, *A Theory of Justice.* Freeman and Evan suppose that firms consist of sets of multilateral contracts among stakeholders that must be administrated by managers. All parties affected by a contract have a right to bargain over the distribution of the effects of managerial decisions. To resolve conflicts between claimants, they suggest applying Rawls's "veil of ignorance" decision procedure, so as to induce "fair contracting" with all stakeholders.[42] This theory is questionable for several reasons: the existence of a set of contracts entailing claims to specific performance is not proven; the company and its stakeholders do not stand to one another as elements of a political society; and the theory offers no ethical justification for its reliance on Rawls (recall the well-known communitarian criticisms of his theory). Finally, there is the very problematic hypothesis that businesses are composed of a multilateral web of contracts, and that stakeholders have a right to participate in a company's decision making.

Other proposals are also problematic. Thus, Meznar, Chrisman, and Carroll have linked stakeholder management to business strategy, adopting a utilitarian ethical approach.[43] Others have employed the feminist "ethic of care."[44] R. A. Philips proposes the principle of fairness ("fair play"), and E. Schlossberger develops a theory of the dual investor.[45] All of these proposals suffer from the problems inherent in their chosen theories. Moreover, all adopt a normative theory fairly uncritically, thus risking becoming trapped in what Robert C. Solomon has called an "unabashed relativism," in effect advising managers, if you are utilitarian, you'll do this; if you're Kantian, you'll do that; if you're . . .[46]

Kenneth E. Goodpaster, alone and with his collaborator, Thomas E. Holloran, holds that managers owe certain fiduciary obligations to the owners and other, moral but nonfiduciary obligations to other stakeholders.[47] R. Edward Freeman disagrees, insists on a multifiduciary relationship between management and stakeholders, and suggests that the stakeholder theory could be aligned with various ethical theories according to the demands of circumstances and the interests various stakeholders are concerned to promote.[48] Again, Freeman's position invites an "unabashed relativism" and therefore threatens to undermine the whole project of finding ethical norms for management.

When oriented by the pursuit of the common good—as opposed to competing systems of normative "rules"—decision making is guided by the obligations of justice and solidarity, according to the order of priorities indicated. There is no "mechanical" rule to be followed. In practice, the possible cases are extremely varied, and prudential evaluation—that is, practical wisdom—is always needed.[49] Indeed, each case is unique, but there are universal principles to be applied to each concrete situation.[50] Ethical rationality requires ease in following what is in harmony with human goodness in each situation; this, in turn, necessitates an intellectual habit that brings about a certain connaturality with the human good.[51] That habit is prudence (practical wisdom). It is developed by individual acts that embody it and is supported by moral uprightness and human virtues. It is not a question of abstract knowledge or of rote application of "techniques" for decision making.

Prudence is the polar opposite of arbitrariness. It demands painstaking analysis of the situation, prediction of consequences, reflection, and counsel. In cases of conflicting interests, especially if any doubt is present, it urges listening to the parties involved and, especially, asking the advice of some upright person (one who is competent in the field) in order to establish appropriate priorities and select the best alternative. The nature or urgency of legitimate rights may also suggest a certain order of priority when resolving such conflicts. Legislation ought to facilitate deciding rightly in especially delicate cases, given that not all managers possess sufficient practical wisdom and rectitude of intention to arrive independently at a just resolution.

Conclusion

A. Argandoña suggests that the notion of the common good could provide a foundation for stakeholder theory.[52] He thus seeks to connect this theory with the tradition of the common good, which would be an improvement. However, the common good—in my judgment—rather than grounding the stakeholder theory which, as we have seen, genuinely is based on a "logic of interests," allows us to transcend that theory, though without abandoning concern for stakeholders.

Although this treatment of the subject has hardly touched its depths, I have attempted to show that the stakeholder approach to strategic management suffers from seriously weak anthropological and ethical foundations (the same could be said of the shareholder approach). Both approaches, however, incorporate potentially useful intuitions, such as the shareholder model's account of managers' fiduciary duties to owners (although these, "unattenuated" shareholder theory notwithstanding, are not absolute duties), and the stakeholder model's account of management's responsibility toward those who have a serious "stake" in the company (although it is flawed by conceptual ambiguities and lacks a properly normative foundation).

As this essay has argued, there are a number of differences between the stakeholder and the common good approaches (see the summary, fig. 1), including (1) philosophical anthropology, (2) property rights, (3) nature of the firm, (4) purpose of business, (5) duties, (6) corporate responsibilities, (7) order among responsibilities, and (8) resolving conflicts of interest.

Helen Alford and Michael Naughton explain in their essay (chapter 2) that the theory of the common good seems to correspond better to human nature because it takes into account the essential human trait of sociability. The ethics underlying this theory have an important objective reference: human beings and their development, or human flourishing, in which the notion of the common good is rooted. Even granting that concrete knowledge of these concepts may be difficult to attain, one must acknowledge that they provide a solid ethical reference point, free of the drawbacks of multiple rationalistic options. Although a few attempts have been made to bring a common good perspective to business management, in the context of corporate social responsibility[53] and corporate social performance,[54] or in the context of international commerce,[55] further development is urgently needed for a broader implementation of this approach.[56]

Figure 1. Normative Bases for Stakeholder and Common Good Approaches

Normative Bases	Stakeholder Approach	Common Good Approach
1. Philosophical anthropology	Human beings are autonomous agents, independently pursuing interests and exercising rights.	Human beings with individual interests and rights are fitted to flourish together in community.
2. Right to property	Right to property is non-absolute, but may supersede other, more fundamental human rights; it derives from, and rests on, current theories of property.	Right to property is non-absolute, and is subordinate to other, more fundamental human rights; it rests on property's social function, for promotion of the common good.
3. Nature of the firm	The firm is a vehicle for coordinating the discrete interests of various groups involved with or in its activities.	The firm is a community of persons, connected by interests and other nexuses, seeking their own and others' good via work.
4. Purpose of business	Business exists to satisfy claims and expectations, while making a profit sufficient to support the firm's ongoing activities.	Business exists to promote the common good by generating and distributing specific goods or services, including profits.
5. Duties of the firm	Management owes potentially conflicting, fiduciary duties to a variety of stakeholders (clients, employees, suppliers, et al.) and to the organization as a whole.	Management must observe commutative, distributive, and general justice, and must promote solidarity within the organization and in society at large.
6. Special corporate responsibilities	Managerial decisions must both take account of all stakeholders' interests according to fair (mutually agreed) procedures and promote the firm's economic success.	Managerial decisions must evince respect for persons and their basic rights, promote social well-being and development, support social harmony by their fairness, and promote the firm's economic success.
7. Order among responsibilities	The firm must first meet its legal and contractual obligations then its fiduciary duties to various stakeholders.	The firm must first meet the duties of strict (including legal) justice; it must next observe the priority of common goods over particular goods in a single genus; it must, finally, pursue solidarity with stakeholders according to their degree of association.
8. Resolving conflicts of interest	Management must balance the interests of all stakeholders impartially or under some other consistent, normative rule.	While observing the order among its responsibilities, management must respond to particular cases with practical wisdom.

Notes

1. See Thomas Donaldson and Lee E. Preston, "The Stakeholder Theory of the Corporation: Concepts, Evidence, and Implications," *Academy of Management Review* 20, no. 1 (1995): 65–91.

2. See. R. Edward Freeman, *Strategic Management: A Stakeholder Approach* (Boston: Pitman, 1984), 31ff., and A.F. Alkhafaji, *A Stakeholder Approach to Corporate Governance: Managing in a Dynamic Environment* (New York: Quorum Books, 1989), 104ff.

3. The stakeholder approach has been used as a theory of the firm: cf. J.C. y B. Hosseini and Steven N. Brenner, "The Stakeholder Theory of the Firm: A Methodology to Generate Value Matrix Weights," *Business Ethics Quarterly* 2, no. 2 (1992): 99–119; C.W.L. Hill and T.M. Jones, "Stakeholder-Agency Theory," *Journal of Management Studies* 29 (1992): 131–54; and T.M. Jones, "Instrumental Stakeholder Theory: A Synthesis of Ethics and Economics," *Academy of Management Review* 20 (1995): 404–37. It has been used to explicate corporate social responsibilities: cf. A.B. Carroll, *Business and Society: Ethics and Stakeholder Management* (Cincinnati: Southwestern, 1989); J.W. Anderson, Jr., *Corporate Social Responsibility* (New York: Quorum Books, 1989); R. Edward Freeman and J. Leidtka, "Corporate Social Responsibility: A Critical Approach," *Business Horizons* 34 (1991): 92–98; M.B.E. Clarkson, "A Stakeholder Framework for Analyzing and Evaluating Corporate Social Performance," *Academy of Management Review* 20 (1995): 105–8; and J.M. Logsdon and Kristi Yuthas, "Corporate Social Performance, Stakeholder Orientation and Organizational Moral Development," *Journal of Business Ethics* 16 (1997): 1213–26. It has also been used, among other subjects, as a guide to corporate strategy: cf. R. Edward Freeman and D.R. Gilbert, *Corporate Strategy and the Search for Ethics* (Englewood Cliffs, N.J.: Prentice Hall, 1998) and to corporate governance: Alkhafaji, *A Stakeholder Approach,* and R. Edward Freeman and W.M. Evan, "Corporate Governance: A Stakeholder Interpretation," *The Journal of Behavioral Economics* 19 (1990): 337–59.

4. See M. Starik, "The Toronto Conference," *Business and Society* 33 (1994): 89–95; T. Rowley, "Moving beyond Dyadic Ties: A Network Theory of Stakeholder Influences," *Academy of Management Review* 22 (1997): 887–910; J.J. Brummer, *Corporate Responsibility and Legitimacy: An Interdisciplinary Analysis* (New York: Greenwood Press, 1991); and M.B.E. Clarkson, *The Corporation and Its Stakeholders: Classic and Contemporary Readings* (Toronto: University of Toronto Press, 1998).

5. See William M. Evan and R. Edward Freeman, "A Stakeholder Theory of the Modern Corporation: Kantian Capitalism," in *Ethical Theory and Busi-*

ness, 3d ed., ed. Tom L. Beauchamp and Norman E. Bowie (Englewood Cliffs, N.J.: Prentice Hall, 1998); R. Edward Freeman and D.R. Gilbert, "Business Ethics and Society: A Critical Agenda," *Business and Society* 31 (1994): 9–17; R. Edward Freeman, "The Politics of Stakeholder Theory: Some Future Directions," *Business Ethics Quarterly* 4, no. 4 (1994): 409–21; and R. Edward Freeman, "Business Ethics in the New Milennium" *Business Ethics Quarterly* 10, no. 1 (2000): 169–80.

6. Donaldson and Preston, "Stakeholder Theory."

7. Thomas Donaldson and T. Dunfee, *Ties That Bind: A Social Contracts Approach to Business Ethics* (Cambridge: Harvard University Press, 1999).

8. See, among others, I. Maitland, "The Morality of the Corporation: An Empirical or Normative Disagreement?" *Business Ethics Quarterly* 4, no. 4 (1994): 445–58; J. Argenti, "Stakeholders: The Case Against," *Long Range Planning* 30 (1997): 442–45; J. Hasnas, "The Normative Theories of Business Ethics: A Guide for the Perplexed," *Business Ethics Quarterly* 8, no. 1 (1998): 19–42; and J. Dobson, "Defending the Stockholder Model: A Comment on Hasnas, and on Dunfee's MOM," *Business Ethics Quarterly* 9, no. 2 (1999): 337–45.

9. Although stakeholder theory in its normative version posits the intrinsic worth of all stakeholder interests (see Donaldson and Preston, "Stakeholder Theory," 67), its roots are still in the "logic of interests."

10. See Domènec Melé, "La empresa en el desarollo," in *Estudios sobre la encíclica "Sollicitudo rei socialis,"* ed. F. Fernández (Madrid: Unión Editorial, 1990), 513–19, and "Orientaciones éticas para la empresa," in *Estudios sobre la encíclica "Centesimus annus,"* ed. F. Fernández (Madrid: Unión Editorial, 1992), 561–80.

11. John Paul II, *Centesimus annus* (London: Catholic Truth Society, 1991), 43.1.

12. See United States Catholic Conference, *Catechism of the Catholic Church* (Washington, D.C.: United States Catholic Conference, and Rome: Libreria Editrice Vaticana, 1994), 1906–9.

13. John Paul II, *Christifideles laici* (London: Catholic Truth Society, 1988), 37.5.

14. As John Paul II goes on to state: "The dignity of the human person is manifested in all its radiance when the person's origin and destiny are considered: created by God in his image and likeness as well as redeemed by the most precious blood of Christ, the person is called to be 'child in the Son' and living temple of the Spirit, destined for eternal life of blessed communion with God" (ibid., 37.4).

15. Recognition of personal autonomy is very important, but autonomy is not—*pace* Kant—the supreme criterion of normative value: "The rightful autonomy of the practical reason means that man possesses in himself his own law, received from the Creator. Nevertheless, the autonomy of reason cannot create values and moral norms" (ibid.).

16. The human good is often excluded from consideration altogether, because it is deemed unknowable. However, common sense can recognize that there are certain basic human goods, and that there is such a thing as human flourishing—and such a thing as its opposite.

17. See John Paul II, *Sollicitudo rei socialis* (London: Catholic Truth Society, 1987), 4.

18. John Paul II, *Laborem exercens* (London: Catholic Truth Society, 1981), 20.

19. John Paul II, *Centesimus annus,* 32 (emphasis original).

20. See J.M. Elegido, "Intrinsic Limitations to Property Rights," *Journal of Business Ethics* 14 (1995): 411–16.

21. Donaldson and Preston, "Stakeholder Theory," 83 ff.

22. Donaldson and Preston's argumentation has been criticized by Hasnas ("Normative Theories," 28–29) on several counts: (1) some (notably Robert Nozick) would dispute the idea that property rights depend on underlying principles of distributive justice; (2) despite Donaldson and Preston's confident references to "the contemporary theory of property rights," property theory is much in dispute and the "contemporary theory" is not well-defined; (3) it is premature to claim (as Donaldson and Preston do) that all the critical characteristics incident to classical theories of distributive justice are present among stakeholders, since the criteria for identifying legitimate stakeholders remain a matter of serious dispute; (4) Donaldson and Preston rely on the purely academic opinion that pluralistic theories of distributive justice are "the trend" outside the ambit of their academic proponents. Hasnas concludes, then, that despite Donaldson and Preston's efforts, "the normative version of stakeholder theory is simply not well-grounded."

23. See, e.g., J. Messner, *Social Ethics: Natural Law in the Modern World* (London: Herder, 1948), 785–800.

24. According to traditional Catholic teaching, "the right to private property is subordinate to the right to common use, to the fact that goods are meant for everyone" (John Paul II, *Laborem exercens,* 14.2).

25. Freeman, *Strategic Management,* 46.

26. See R. Mitchell, B.R. Agle, and D.J. Wood, "Towards a Theory of Stakeholder Identification and Salience: Defining the Principle of Who and What Really Counts," *Academy of Management Review* 22 (1997): 860–62.

27. See S. A. Cortright, Ernest S. Pierucci, and Michael J. Naughton, "A Social Property Ethic for the Corporation in Light of Catholic Social Thought," *Logos* 2, no. 4 (1999): 138–54.

28. See John Finnis, *Natural Law and Natural Rights* (Oxford: Clarendon Press, 1980), chapter 7.

29. C. Llano, *El empressario ante la responsibilidad y la motivación* (Mexico City: McGraw Hill-Ipade, 1990), 70 ff.

30. Thomas Aquinas, *Summa Theologica* (Westminster, Md.: Christian Classics, 1981), I-II q. 18, a. 6.

31. John Paul II, *Veritatis splendor* (London: Catholic Truth Society, 1993), 78.

32. *Catechism of the Catholic Church*, 1737.

33. See Domènec Melé, *Ética en la dirección de empresas* (Barcelona: Folio, 1997), 122 ff.

34. John Paul II, *Centesimus annus*, 34.1 (emphasis original).

35. John Paul II, *Laborem exercens*, 12.6 (emphasis original).

36. See Thomas Aquinas, *Summa Theologica* I-II q. 113, a. 9, ad 2.

37. See Thomas Aquinas, *Summa Theologica* II-II q. 26.

38. Ibid., a. 8.

39. Llano, *El empressario*, 76 ff.

40. Robert Spaemann, *La responsibilitá personale ed it suo fundamento* (Rome: Ares-Cris, 1983), 15; cited in Llano, *El empressario*, 78–79.

41. Ibid., 78.

42. Freeman and Evan, "Corporate Governance."

43. See M. Meznar, J. J. Chrisman, and A. B. Carroll, "Social Responsibility and Strategic Management," *Business and Professional Ethics Journal* 10 (1991): 47–66.

44. See, B. K. Burton and Craig P. Dunn, "Feminist Ethics as Moral Grounding for Stakeholder Theory," *Business Ethics Quarterly* 6, no. 2 (1996): 133–47, and A. C. Wicks, D. R. Gilbert, Jr., and R. Edward Freeman, "A Feminist Reinterpretation of the Stakeholder Concept," *Business Ethics Quarterly* 4, no. 4 (1994): 475–97.

45. See, respectively, R. A. Phillips, "Stakeholder Theory and a Principle of Fairness," *Business Ethics Quarterly* 7, no. 1 (1997): 51–66, and E. Schlossberger, "A New Model of Business: Dual-Investor Theory," *Business Ethics Quarterly* 4, no. 4 (1994): 459–74.

46. Robert C. Solomon, "Corporate Roles, Personal Virtues: An Aristotelian Approach to Business Ethics," *Business Ethics Quarterly* 2, no. 3 (1992): 318.

47. Kenneth E. Goodpaster, "Business Ethics and Stakeholder Analysis," *Business Ethics Quarterly* 1, no. 1 (1991): 53–77, and Kenneth E. Goodpaster

and Thomas E. Holloran, "In Defense of a Paradox, " *Business Ethics Quarterly* 4, no. 4 (1994): 423–29.

48. Freeman, "Politics of Stakeholder Theory."

49. "Practical wisdom," in the words of Aristotle, "must be a reasoned and true state of capacity to act with regard to human goods" (*Nicomachean Ethics,* VI.5, 1140b20, trans. W. D. Ross, in *The Basic Works of Aristotle,* ed. R. McKeon [New York: Randon House, 1941]).

50. See John Paul II, *Veritatis splendor,* 60.

51. Ibid., 64.

52. See A. Argandoña, "The Stakeholder Theory and the Common Good," *Journal of Business Ethics* 17 (1998): 1093–1102.

53. See M. A. Gallo, *Responsabilidades sociales de la empresa* (Pamplona, Spain: Eunsa, 1980), 28 ff.

54. See Domènec Melé, "La actuación social de la empresa," in *La aportación de la empresa a la sociedad,* ed. A. Pastor, J. A. Pérez López, and Domènec Melé (Barcelona, Spain: Folio, 1997), 53–90.

55. See M. Velasquez, "International Business, Morality and the Common Good," *Business Ethics Quarterly* 2, no. 1 (1992): 27–40.

56. The author is grateful for comments on the preliminary manuscript by C. Llano, A. Argandoña, J. Fontrodona, E. M. Epstein, T. Ford, and Lee A. Tavis, and by various participants in the symposium, "The Nature and Purpose of the Business Organization within Catholic Social Thought," University of St. Thomas, St. Paul, Minnesota, August 13–16, 1998. Of course, the author in no way wishes to impute to these colleagues the defects of the present work.

10

Modern Contract Theory and the Purpose of the Firm

LEE A. TAVIS

This essay analyzes the two dominant theories of the firm and their relationship to Catholic social thought. The shareholder theory of finance and law focuses on the maximization of corporate wealth and its transmission to the shareholding owners. Stakeholder theory is more diverse. At its core, stakeholder theory can be expressed in terms of individual rights and of the fairness of contracts between the firm and its constituents. Each of these theories relates in a different way to Catholic social thought. Two principles from the Catholic tradition that apply to economic organizations—solidarity and subsidiarity—are selected for this comparison. A third principle, participation, is subsumed in the other two. Together, these principles have a great deal to contribute to the shareholder and stakeholder models in terms of morality and efficiency.

The analytical results differ substantially depending on whether the principle of solidarity or the principle of subsidiarity is the focus. Solidarity represents a radical point of departure for economic organizations. This communitarian principle stands to challenge the individualism of both shareholder and stakeholder theories. In contrast, subsidiarity is increasingly observable in corporate organizations. The locational component of decisions in business organizations is moving closer to those directly involved in and affected by those decisions—

215

the stakeholders. Thus, in terms of organizational decision-location, both the shareholder and the stakeholder models are supported by the principle of subsidiarity.

Still, for both models, the inclusion of stakeholders (including shareholders) in the decision-making process, as required by the principle of participation, remains a challenge.

This essay begins by comparing the shareholder and stakeholder theories of the firm on dual axes. The first axis is their shared focus on contracts. Both shareholder and stakeholder theories are based on the relationship among the firm's constituents expressed through explicit and implicit contracts. Shareholder and stakeholder theories, however, assign different priorities to various stakeholders' interests. On the second axis of comparison, contractual relationships and their prioritization will be considered in relation to the principles of solidarity and subsidiarity.

Contractual Relationships

The concept of the firm as a connected series of contracts—the contractual theory of the firm—is the basis of both the shareholder and the stakeholder models. R. H. Coase introduced the concept.[1] He was concerned with the question of why contracted relationships would be internalized in a firm rather than transacted in the marketplace. Coase concluded that the main reason was profitability. It is simply less costly to establish a firm using contracts within a firm rather than exercising contracted exchanges through the markets. There is a cost associated with negotiating a separate contract for each exchange transaction in the market. For Coase, the existence of the firm reduces the number of contracts and is far more efficient for contracts that are long-term in nature, where the purchasing party is unable to specify the supplier requirements over the full term of the contract.

Coase describes the contract as follows:

> The contract is one whereby the factor, for a certain remuneration (which may be fixed or fluctuating), agrees to obey the directions

of an entrepreneur within certain limits. The essence of the contract is that it should only state the limits to the powers of the entrepreneur. Within these limits, he can therefore direct the other factors of production.

He further states:

Now, owing to the difficulty of forecasting, the longer the period of the contract is for the supply of the commodity or service, the less possible, and indeed, the less desirable it is for the person purchasing to specify what the other contracting party is expected to do.

He defines the firm as follows:

A firm, therefore, consists of the system of relationships which comes into existence when the direction of resources is dependent on an entrepreneur.[2]

Coase's seminal definition of the firm as consisting of a set of contracts has become the core of the shareholder (often referred to as the "financial") theory of the firm. In this tradition, M. C. Jensen and W. H. Meckling define the firm as follows:

It is important to recognize that most organizations are simply *legal fictions which serve as a nexus for a set of contracting relationships among individuals.* This includes firms, non-profit institutions such as universities, hospitals and foundations, mutual organizations such as mutual savings banks and insurance companies and cooperatives, some private clubs, and even governmental bodies such as cities, states and the Federal government, government enterprises such as TVA, the Post Office, transit systems, etc.

The private corporation or firm is simply one form of *legal fiction which serves as a nexus for contracting relationships and which is also characterized by the existence of divisible residual claims on the assets and cash flows of the organizations which can generally be sold without permission of the other contracting individuals.*[3]

Stakeholder theorists also focus on contractual relationships among the firm's stakeholders—a commonality often obscured by the clash over the claim of financial theorists for shareholder primacy among the contracting parties.[4] Stakeholders are defined by their association with the firm: "A stakeholder in an organization is (by definition) any group or individual who can affect or is affected by the achievement of the organization's objectives."[5] These relationships between the stakeholder and the firm can be either implicit or explicit contracts. Some of these relationships meet the criteria of a legal contract, expressly approved by each party and covered by a particular body of law. Others are contracts only in the broadest sense of the term, encompassing explicit or implicit agreements or transactions. Product warranties, debt, or production contracts would meet the narrow, legal definition of explicit contracts. For workers, a contract could be a simple exchange of a day's work for a day's pay. Or, the same relationship could be covered by an explicit contract when the employee is a member of a union.[6] These stakeholder-defining relationships should be interpreted in their most inclusive sense. For example, communities would be defined as stakeholders in spite of the vague notion of that relationship.

Thus, relationships expressed in the form of implicit and explicit contracts form the contractual theory of the firm, which constitutes the core of both shareholder and stakeholder theory. The difference between these theories lies neither in their reliance on contracts nor in the relationship between principal and agent in the contracts, but in their prioritization of stakeholders.

Priorities among Contracts

Financial shareholder theory extends the contractual theory by arguing for a primacy of shareholders among the contracts that comprise the firm. This primacy leads to a measurable priority in allocating the resources of the firm. Stakeholder theorists deny this primacy and the resulting crispness of the firm's priorities. Stakeholder theory stresses stakeholder rights and the responsibilities of the firm, as represented by management, to each stakeholder.

Prioritization in the Shareholder Theory

In the shareholder theory of the firm, the argument for shareholder primacy is often assumed as part of the contractual theory. When specified, however, there are a number of arguments for shareholder primacy.[7] The oldest claim and the one that forms the basis of American corporate law is the right of private property. In this argument, shareholders provide their property in the form of capital to the firm and have a right to its earnings.

A second argument has to do with residual risk. The owner bears the residual risk of the firm and, thus, should have a priority claim to the residual earnings. This argument is based on the assumption that the providers of other inputs, such as labor or debt, prefer and are able to negotiate contracts for a fixed return for those assets they contribute to the firm, such as their labor or debt capital.

Other arguments have to do with the good of society. Society has allowed the creation of a fictitious person called the corporation with its legislated rights and responsibilities as a means of enhancing productivity. As Adam Smith noted, the combination of resources in a productive unit creates synergy. The optimal combination of these resources will lead to optimal productivity of each productive unit (business enterprise) over time, which, in an efficient equity market, will lead to the maximization of shareholder wealth. Hence, if one assumes that wealth is the shareholder goal, managerial accountability for wealth maximization will serve the productivity goals of society.

A closely related argument has to do with risk taking. It is important for the business enterprise as a productive unit to take risks if efficiency is to increase and the economy to expand. The returns to risk successfully undertaken will flow exclusively to the shareholders in this model. They should be motivated to force risk taking on the part of management.[8] The field of corporate finance is devoted to increasing and valuing the risk-adjusted residual returns to corporate resources allocated to specific uses. These wealth measures are an important component of shareholder theory.[9]

If the proper goal of the enterprise is to maximize shareholder wealth, how can the shareholders as principals in the contract ensure that managers as agents pursue these objectives? This issue absorbs

financial theorists as the need to minimize agency costs (see Alford/
Naughton, chapter 2). The contract between owner and manager fits
Coase's general description of contracts (cited earlier):

> The essence of the contract is that it should only state the limits to
> the powers of the entrepreneur. Within these limits, he can there-
> fore direct the other factors of the production. . . . Now, owing to
> the difficulty of forecasting, the longer the period of the contract
> is for the supply of the commodity or service, the less possible, and
> indeed, the less desirable it is for the person purchasing to specify
> what the other contracting party is expected to do.

To Coase, the contractual relationship is one of master and servant
or principal and agent. Using the legal terminology of the time, Coase
notes:

> (1) The servant must be under the duty of rendering personal ser-
> vices to the master or to others on behalf of the master, otherwise
> the contract is a contract for sale of goods or the like; (2) The mas-
> ter must have the right to control the servant's work, either per-
> sonally or by another servant or agent.[10]

Jensen and Meckling describe agency costs as consisting of the
costs of monitoring and controlling the manager; bonding costs such
as auditing, contractual limitations on managerial decision freedom, or
explicit bonding against maleficence; and the residual loss of noncon-
gruency in objectives on the part of the principal and the agent.[11] The
idea is to devise mechanisms that minimize the total of these three cost
components.

The shareholder theory of the firm, then, sets the objective for management as maximizing shareholder wealth and devotes substantial effort to minimizing the cost of ensuring that outcome. Managers would
then be constrained to serve the shareholder objective in their management of all other relationships within the nexus of contracts that comprise the firm.

The opportunities and constraints associated with the firm's nonshareholder contracts, and the principal-agent problems associated

with each, are vast. Some of these contracts are tightly binding on the manager; others are not. The freedom of action available to the manager within this nexus of contracts has been described as "the managerial area of discretion."[12] The implementation of the shareholder theory attempts to minimize this managerial area of discretion and to force managers to take advantage of any flexibility in other contracts as a means of enhancing wealth maximization. In contrast, stakeholder theory endorses the existence of the managerial area of discretion and considers how it should be used in the management of the complex of contracts, including but not exclusive to the shareholder contract.

Prioritization in Stakeholder Theory

In stakeholder theory, agency concerns are broader and are focused more on managerial responsibility. The notion of stakeholder rights is extended well beyond the property rights of the shareholder. The result of this more inclusive view is a loss in specificity.

The rich stakeholder literature analyzes virtually every determinant of managerial behavior in a broad range of theoretical structures. None of these stakeholder constructs, however, provides the kind of systemic, prescriptive, prioritizing guidance that is so crisply present in shareholder, wealth-maximization theory. At its core, a prioritizing theory must compare one stakeholder with another across the organizational network of the corporation. Under this systemic concept, trade-offs are analyzed as resources taken from one stakeholder group to be committed to another. Systems theory is the conceptual basis for the shadow price or economic cost of capital, which provides a useful wealth-maximization criterion rate.

In stakeholder theory, guidance for the establishment of priorities is available, however, through the combination of rights theory and the concept of fair negotiations. Rights theory provides a minimum threshold of resources to be allocated to each stakeholder. Beyond these minimums, fair negotiations can provide a process to guide the use of remaining resources within the business enterprise.

Each individual stakeholder has a set of fundamental human rights that should not be denied by those individuals or institutions with whom he or she is associated. Each institution, including the business enterprise, has the responsibility to ensure, to the extent possible, that the rights of its stakeholders are not violated through the actions of the institution. Thomas Donaldson outlines a specific set of fundamental rights for multinational corporate stakeholders and the associated minimum correlative duty of the multinational manager to help protect stakeholders from the deprivation of these rights.[13] However one might define specific rights within the limitations of conflicting rights and the problems of determining specific thresholds, the existence of individual rights dictates the core requirement for commitment of the firm's resources.

The concept of fair negotiations can define an upper bound on the allocation of resources to serve stakeholder interests. The concept is developed in ethics and in the legal requirement to negotiate a contract in good faith. Fair negotiations impose a moral responsibility beyond the legal minimum. Richard De George outlines the requirements for a fair agreement as a moral duty:

> All interested parties must be allowed to have a say. . . . Agreements in general are fair if both parties enter into them freely, both sides benefit from the arrangement, and both sides believe the terms fair.[14]

The notion of fairness is critical to the explicit and implicit contracts between the enterprise and its stakeholders. A fair process will lead to the "mutual and voluntary acceptability of bargains by all contracting stakeholders."[15]

Ensuring fair negotiations is a demanding ethical requirement. The negotiating process is essentially one of guaranteeing rights for each side. Each party decides whether to agree based on his perception of individual rights. If a stakeholder is being denied a fundamental right through the agreement, he will not perceive the agreement as fair. Alternatively, the process of fair negotiations is an efficient way of defining the limits on rights, claims, and duties in a specific context. While the right to subsistence, for example, has some relatively definable threshold, the boundaries of other rights such as access, education, and participation are not as readily determined. Thus, an agreement that is considered fair by both parties would define both the threshold and the upper limit on these rights.

The concept of fair negotiations is embedded in legal traditions of good faith, a principle that is central to the law of contracts:

> This prospect on the law of contracts, and on private law in general, has, ever since the heyday of Roman law, been symbolized by the notion of *bona fides* (good faith). . . . Therefore good faith is not so much a rule on the same level as other rules, but rather the principle on the basis of which the various elements enabling us to determine the contents of contractual obligations need to be integrated.[16]

James Gordley traces good faith in contract law as it is applied in judicial systems, including those of the United States, France, and Germany. He sees the principle as based on the notion of commutative justice as understood by St. Thomas Aquinas: "A contract of exchange is an act of voluntary commutative justice. Certainly each party obtains something of greater value to him personally than that which he gives in return." Although the courts do not use the term "commutative justice," Gordley concludes that the "principle explains most of the cases in which courts give relief. . . . We are talking about commutative justice whether we use that term or not."[17]

In its translation to rules, the principle of good faith is far from uniform. For example, there is a distinction between the duty to perform a contract in good faith and the duty to negotiate in good faith. There are a number of theories concerning the duty to perform a contract in good faith. As for negotiating contracts, however, Gordley notes, "No one is sure whether there is such a duty or not, though courts sometimes give relief when negotiations are broken off."[18]

Applying the principle of good faith is also an example of the recent divergence of English contract law from continental law. While applying the principle is well established on the Continent, in 1992 the British House of Lords "made it unequivocally clear that the introduction of good faith in English contract law would, and even could not happen."[19]

The source of the judgment as to what constitutes fairness and good faith differs between contractual law and ethics. For the ethicist, fairness is based on the judgment and utility of the parties to the negotiation.

For the courts, good faith is determined independently of the person: "In the first place, the court is not asking what intentions the parties actually had but rather, what intentions they would have had if they had been fair people, or if neither party had been able to exploit the other's ignorance or necessity."[20] In this way, the theory of rights and the concept of fair or good faith negotiations together provide a starting point for developing normative, prioritizing criteria.

Catholic Social Principles as Managerial Decision Criteria

The shareholder and stakeholder theories of the firm have evolved with little recognition of, or input from, Catholic social thought. The work of the John A. Ryan Institute for Catholic Social Thought is, to my knowledge, unique in this regard. There is an issue of the extent to which Catholic social thought should be integrated into these other theories, or whether it should develop its own managerial philosophy. This is a conceptual issue richly discussed in this volume (see Kennedy and McCann, chapters 3 and 8). A second issue is more empirical. Can we observe elements of Catholic social thought in modern corporate management?

In the following section, the conceptual issue will be addressed in the context of the individualism underlying the contractual theory of the firm (as applied to both shareholder and stakeholder theories), set against the communitarian emphasis of the principle of solidarity. The empirical question is whether we can observe the principle of subsidiarity in today's "globalizing" world.

Solidarity: The Community and the Individual

The principle of solidarity is a central component of Catholic social thought. Solidarity expresses the claim that the person is social in nature and can develop his potential only through interaction with other people.[21] As the Second Vatican Council put it, "By his innermost nature man is a social being, and unless he relates himself to others he can neither live nor develop his potential."[22]

The tension between the principle of solidarity and the individualism of shareholder and stakeholder theories as outlined above can be analyzed in three steps: (1) from the decision maker in the firm, conceptualized as an individual in shareholder theory; (2) to his humanity as reflected in the rights theory underlying the stakeholder model; (3) to the social human being of Catholic social thought.

The individualism of the shareholder and stakeholder models derives from the role of the market as envisioned by Adam Smith. The most often-repeated quotation from Smith is "It is not from the benevolence of the butcher, the brewer, or the baker that we expect our dinner, but from their regard to their own interests. We address ourselves not to their humanity but to their self-love."[23] This quotation is commonly used to support the idea that if we each pursue our own individual self-interest, we will all be better off. Smith spoke of the invisible hand of the marketplace that translates this pursuit of individual self-interest into the benefit of all.

The shareholder theory, which is based on Smith's market model, is not devoid of values. Trust is clearly a part of each contract among individuals—implicit and explicit. Indeed, trust is the core of implicit contracts—they do not exist without trust. Explicit contracts are also based on trust. As Coase noted, no contract can anticipate all contingencies.

As a moral philosopher, Smith recognized the importance of trust. Commenting on Smith, Amartya Sen notes:

> The concern of the different parties with their own interests certainly can adequately motivate all of them to take part in the exchange from which each benefits. But whether the exchange would operate well would depend also on organizational conditions. . . . [W]hat also must be considered now is the extent to which the economic institutions operate on the basis of common behavior patterns, shared trust, and a minimal confidence in the ethics of the different parties.[24]

Thus, the individual of the shareholder theory is not devoid of all virtue as is so often suggested by opponents of this viewpoint (see Gordley, chapter 4).

The stakeholder model moves beyond the idea of an individual—even an individual entering into contractual relationships based on trust—to the idea of a human being with dignity and rights. Stakeholder theory is founded on responsibilities of the manager as a corollary to the fundamental human rights of the stakeholder. Ensuring the rights of a stakeholder and the fairness of the bargaining process form the moral core of the prioritization process in stakeholder theory. Still, stakeholder theory concentrates on the relationships among individual stakeholders (and their representing institutions) in implicit or explicit contracts with the firm. That is, human rights, in the contractual stakeholder model, attach to the rights that are claimed for the individual.

By way of introducing Catholic social thought into this analysis, the historic tension between the concept of individual rights, as developed in the classic liberal philosophy that underlies the account of rights and responsibilities in stakeholder theory, and the communitarian notion of rights in Catholic social thought must be acknowledged. David Hollenbach addresses this tension:

> Catholic teaching on human rights today presupposes a reconstruction of the classic liberal understanding of what these rights are. The pivot on which this reconstruction turns is the traditional natural-law conviction that the human person is an essentially social being. Catholic thought and action in the human rights sphere, in other words, are rooted in the communitarian alternative to liberal human rights theory. Because of this stress on the communal rather than the individualist grounding of rights, contemporary Catholic discussions of constitutional democracy and free-market capitalism diverge in notable ways from the liberal theories of rights that are regnant today.[25]

Hollenbach analyzes the individual-communal tension on human rights in terms of rights as a negative immunity versus rights as a positive empowerment:

> In classical liberalism rights are identified with certain freedoms that are protected against coercion or interference by others. They are defenses against the intrusions that other persons or the government might try to make into the individual's zone of freedom. Freedom of religion, speech, association, and assembly are all viewed as analogous to the rights to private property. These rights are like the fenceposts that define the turf no one may enter without the owner's consent.[26]

This is the position of stakeholder theory, in which rights are conceptualized as a minimum threshold necessary to assure the dignity of the human person. The rights of the individual then require a corollary duty on the part of another not to violate those rights. The duty is initiated by the existence of the individual's rights.

Within Catholic social teaching, Hollenbach points to the pastoral letter of the United States Catholic Bishops, *Economic Justice for All,* as a document that effectively relates rights and community. He notes that in this document, "human rights have a social and relational meaning from the very start," and quotes paragraph 15 from the bishops' letter:

> Basic justice demands the establishment of minimum levels of participation in the life of the human community for all persons. The ultimate injustice is for a person or group to be treated actively or abandoned passively as if they were nonmembers of the human race.

Hollenbach continues:

> The Bible does not regard freedom as autonomous independence; rather liberation is from bondage into community. Such biblical perspectives are at the basis of the pastoral letter's insistence that "respect for human rights and a strong sense of both personal and community responsibility are linked, not opposed."[27]

In this communitarian understanding, rights are empowered by the community and are thus at one with the "responsibility of social living." In Hollenbach's view, "Human rights specify the minimum standards for what it means to treat people as members of this [human] community."[28] Empowerment, therefore, extends beyond political rights to economic rights:

> these economic rights call for enabling persons to express their agency through positive participation in the life of society. For example, the protection of rights to economic well-being is not simply a matter of assuring that all persons are minimally fed and housed. When individuals and societies have the resources to do this it is surely required. But respect for human agency demands more than this. It requires that people not only be maintained alive, but alive

as active agents of their own well-being through participation in social life, for example through being able to get a job with adequate pay and decent working conditions.[29]

Domènec Melé's essay in this volume (chapter 9) extends the distinction between rights as negative immunities and rights as positive empowerments to a prioritizing of responsibilities within the company as a community. Guided by the principle of solidarity, Melé defines the firm as a nexus of participants in a community, as opposed to the individuality of the contractual theory of the firm outlined above: "These nexuses may exist for the sake of interests (economic or otherwise) or psychological benefits (pleasant peers, work climate, culture, and so on)" or moral values such as "solidarity, the will to justice, loyalty, a spirit of service," and so forth. They reflect the fact of our interdependence with one another, which makes us responsible for each other and leads to the vision of the firm as a community. Melé's communitarian approach allows him to prioritize the responsibilities of management in three phases. In his scheme, responsibilities are ordered in priority according to their relationship to the contribution to the common good made by the firm through its specific activity: (1) *primary responsibilities* to the firm's stakeholders; (2) *secondary responsibilities* to social groups who are more indirectly affected by the firm; (3) *tertiary responsibilities* to improve society outside the firm's day-to-day activity.

In this way, Melé lays the foundation for a theory of management based on Catholic social tradition and addresses the critical issue of prioritization. His ordering of responsibilities is fundamentally different from the prioritizing prescribed by the shareholder or the stakeholder model. The shareholder model succinctly prioritizes the allocation of resources by their contribution to productivity and wealth. The stakeholder model allows a prioritization based on individual stakeholder rights as a minimum, and on stakeholder interests through fair negotiations.

While Melé's account of concentric responsibilities captures moral responsibility, including both the interaction of individuals in solidarity as a company, defined as a community, and the role of the company in the broader society, the resulting prioritized responsibilities can be seen as more general than either those resulting from the shareholder theory's principle of wealth maximization or from the stakeholder theory's reliance on human rights as a threshold and basis for fair negotiations. As the concept of the company as community, with its concentric circles of responsibility, is refined, the concept of solidarity will become more a part of managerial prioritization.

Subsidiarity: Location of Organizational
Decision Making and Participation

Subsidiarity is a central principle of Catholic social thought, with implications for both the shareholder and stakeholder models. As Whitmore states, "The principle articulates philosophically the insight that the best associations or institutions for addressing a particular situation are those that are most proximate to it."[30] Although in the Christian tradition the idea of subsidiarity appeared as early as the sixteenth century,[31] it has received its full development through the papal magisterium of the last seventy years. Dennis McCann's essay (chapter 8) provides a nuanced analysis of the evolution of this principle as a component of Catholic social thought. The principle, formulated in Pius XI's 1931 encyclical, *Quadragesimo anno*, states that "one should not withdraw from individuals and commit to the community what they can accomplish by their own enterprise and industry."[32] In its earlier development, the principle related only to the role of the state. Over time, it has been extended to all of the institutions in our society, including the business enterprise. As McCann notes in his essay: "the principle may be a remarkably concise way of symbolizing Catholic tradition's tacit ideal of the social order—any legitimate social order—to be discerned in any institutional setting, and used to evaluate that setting's ultimate organizational effectiveness" (p. 176).

The principle of subsidiarity serves a different role in Catholic social thought than others such as solidarity. Subsidiarity is a functional principle—a principle that is related to process. It provides guidance on how the other principles are brought to fruition in society. As reflected in papal encyclicals, there are two dimensions to the principle. The first is the natural right to associate and organize. The second, as Michael E. Allsapp notes, involves efficiency. "The principle also affirms that there is nothing done by a higher or larger organization that

cannot be done as well by a lower or smaller one; intervention, therefore, should occur only as a last resort to make up for deficiencies."[33]

Subsidiarity relates to the organization of the business enterprise—
first, to the location of decision making within the organization and,
second, to the specification of those who participate in organizational
decision making. The principle of subsidiarity is reflected differently
by the shareholder and stakeholder models, because each implies different forms of organization for the business enterprise.

The shareholder model implies a hierarchical organization. Hierarchical structures are typified by "unidirectionality and universality,"[34]
whereby tasks are grouped together and tightly monitored and controlled through bureaucratic organizations, and where critical resources
are centralized.[35] Proponents of the shareholder model focus on incentives and penalties to ensure that managers respond as agents to the
objectives of shareholders as principals. Shareholder theorists are generally silent about the organizational relationships among the managers
within the firm, implicitly assuming a command and control organizational framework.

The stakeholder model implies a heterarchical organization. Heterarchical organizations are distinguished from hierarchical structures by
three characteristics:

> First, resources, managerial capabilities, and decision making are
> dispersed throughout the organization rather than concentrated at
> the top. Control is achieved less through "calculative" mechanisms
> than through "normative" integration [managers imbued with or-
> ganizational culture and goals]. Second, lateral relationships exist
> between subsidiaries, in terms of product, people, and knowledge
> flows. . . . Third, activities are coordinated along multiple dimen-
> sions, typically geography, product, and function.[36]

Heterarchical structures diffuse decision making from the central core
to on-site managers in local business units (subsidiaries).[37]

Under the stakeholder model, it can be assumed that local managers are in the best position to judge the rights threshold for individual stakeholders and to ensure that negotiations are fair. In these
ways, the stakeholder model implies heterarchical organizations. Owing

to the competitiveness of today's corporate world—particularly for multi-national corporations spanning diverse cultural, economic, and political societies— heterarchical organizations and decision diffusion have become a necessity.

Paralleling the diffusion of decision making within corporations with heterarchical organizations, two external factors support the locational dimension of subsidiarity; the decentralization of governmental decisions and the growing importance of civil society are moving decisions in these sectors to the local level.

Governmental decentralization is occurring across the world, particularly in the developing countries of Latin America, Africa, and Asia, as well as in the transitional economies of Central and Eastern Europe. The causes, while varying with each country, include the inability of national governments to deliver development where it counts most—at the grassroots. A second moving force is the transition to democracy in these countries. As citizens become involved in the political process, the bureaucracy they can affect is the one closest to them. Although decentralization is a clear trend, it involves a slow and tenuous process.[38]

Closely associated, as both a cause and an effect, with governmental decentralization is the reemergence of civil society as a political and economic force. The key institutions of the civil sector are nongovernmental organizations (NGOs). They are a mixed lot, ranging from church-based organizations to temporary groups promoting their own, narrow self-interests. The surprising growth of indigenous NGOs across the developing world is clearly associated with the transition to democracy in those countries.

These observable trends—diffusion of corporate decision making, governmental decentralization, and the reemergence of civil society—reflect the locational component of subsidiarity. Subsidiarty's emergence in this form affects stakeholder priorities. The local manager's area of discretion is being enlarged by decision diffusion and the changes in government's regulatory function associated with decentralization. A mitigating factor that would impinge on the managerial area of discretion is the growth in the sophistication and power of indigenous NGOs. On balance, however, local stakeholder priorities are increasingly being determined by local managers.

Still, the principle of subsidiarity extends well beyond the location of a decision. At its core is the participation of those who will be impacted by the decision: stakeholders in the decision-making process. While the principle of participation is an integral component of both solidarity and subsidiarity, it is often articulated as a separate principle. In the document "Sharing Catholic Social Teaching: Challenges and Directions—Reflections of the U.S. Catholic Bishops," the principle is stated, "We believe people have a right and a duty to participate in society, seeking together the common good and well-being of all, especially the poor and vulnerable."[39] William J. Byron, a member of the "Reflections" drafting committee, expands on the definition:

> Without participation, the benefits available to an individual through any social institution cannot be realized. The human person has a right not to be shut out from participating in those institutions that are necessary for human fulfillment.[40]

Most organizations, including businesses, are not very good at including stakeholders in the decision-making process. It is a time-consuming, amorphous process. Still, the present trend—feeding on the locational dimension of subsidiarity—is toward stakeholders' greater participation in both governmental and business bureaucracies. Participation, the sufficient condition, is slow to join location, the necessary condition, but appears to be sure to follow: in development projects, national and multilateral institutional planners have finally come to realize that involvement of local groups from the very beginning is critical if the project is to succeed; in business, empowerment in heterarchical organizations is recognized as a technique for enhancing efficiency.[41]

Summary

Catholic social thought has an important contribution to make to the practice of management: it supports the rights-base of the stakeholder model through the principle of solidarity; it extends the liberal, philosophical concept of rights with the idea of the firm as a community, empowering stakeholders as members of that community. This reconceptualization mitigates the tension between rights as claims demanding corollary responsibilities and rights as integral features of community, involving individual and community responsibilities. The result should be a more satisfying work environment.

Subsidiarity also adds a functional principle to guide the process of diffusing corporate decision making and of decentralizing governmental regulation, as well as to channel the explosive growth of indigenous NGOs. Subsidiarity complements the observable, ongoing locational shift in decision making by introducing to it the importance of wide participation.

Notes

1. Ronald H. Coase, "The Nature of the Firm," *Economica,* n.s. 4, no. 16 (November 1937): 386–405.

2. Ibid., 391, 393. Coase did not distinguish between the owner and the manager; he concentrated on the owner-manager entrepreneur, whom he defined as "the person or persons who, in a competitive system, take the place of the price mechanism in the direction of resources" (ibid., 338 n.2). Moreover, he concluded with an interesting distinction between initiative and management: "Initiative means forecasting and operates through the price mechanism by the making of new contracts. Management properly merely reacts to price changes, rearranging the factors of production under its control. That the business man normally combines both functions is an obvious result of the marketing costs which were discussed above" (ibid., 405).

3. M.C. Jensen and W.H. Meckling, "Theory of the Firm: Managerial Behavior, Agency Costs, and Ownership Structure," *Journal of Financial Economics* 3, no. 4 (1976): 310–11.

4. Cf. R. Edward Freeman and W.M. Evan, "Corporate Governance: Stakeholder Interpretation," *The Journal of Behavioral Economics* 19, no. 4 (1990): 337–59.

5. R. Edward Freeman, *Strategic Management: A Stakeholder Approach* (Boston: Pitman Press, 1984), 46.

6. Cf. Scott E. Masten, "A Legal Basis for the Firm," in *The Nature of the Firm,* ed. Oliver E. Williamson and Sidney G. Winter (New York: Oxford University Press, 1991), 198.

7. For a nuanced discussion of these arguments, see John Boatright, *Ethics in Finance* (Oxford: Blackwell Publishers, 1999), chapter 6.

8. After his careful analysis of these reasons for shareholder primacy, Boatright finds them wanting: "In whose interest ought the corporation to be run? No definitive answer is forthcoming in this chapter because the debate over the question is still in progress" (ibid.).

9. Cf. Georges Enderle and Lee A. Tavis, "A Balanced Concept of the Firm and the Measurement of Its Long-Term Planning and Performance," *Journal of Business Ethics* 17 (August 1988): 1129–44.

10. Coase, "Nature of the Firm," 404. While, as noted earlier, Coase did not distinguish between owner and manager, his general description of the contract fits well with the owner-manager relationship understood as one of principal and agent.

11. Jensen and Meckling, "Theory of the Firm."

12. Lee A. Tavis, *Power and Responsibility: Multinational Managers and Developing Country Concerns* (Notre Dame, Ind.: University of Notre Dame Press, 1997), 96.

13. Cf. Thomas Donaldson, *The Ethics of International Business* (New York: Oxford University Press, 1989).

14. Richard T. De George, *Competing with Integrity in International Business* (New York: Oxford University Press, 1989), 34, 40.

15. Thomas Donaldson and Lee E. Preston, "The Stakeholder Theory of the Corporation: Concepts, Evidence, and Implications," *The Academy of Management Review* 20, no. 1 (January 1995): 80.

16. Mattias E. Storme, "The Validity and the Content of Contracts," in *Towards a European Civil Code,* ed. A.S. Hartkamp, M.W. Hesselink, E.H. Hondius, C.E. du Perron, and J.B.M. Vranked (Dordrecht, The Netherlands: Martinus Nijhoff Publishers, 1994), 183.

17. James Gordley, "Good Faith in Contract Law: The Problem of Profit Maximization" (paper presented at the Second International Symposium on Catholic Social Thought and Management Education, Antwerp, Belgium, July 27, 1998), 3, 19. See http://www.stthomas.edu/cathstudies/cstm/antwerp/, accessed November 2001.

18. James Gordley, personal correspondence, August 28, 1997.

19. Sjef van Erp, "The Formation of Contracts," in *Towards a European Civil Code,* ed. A.S. Hartkamp et al., 128.

20. Gordley, "Good Faith in Contract Law," 14.

21. See William J. Byron, S.J., "Ten Building Blocks of Catholic Social Thought," *America* 179, no. 13 (October 31, 1998): 11.

22. The Second Vatican Council, as quoted by Todd Whitmore, "Practicing the Common Good: The Pedagogical Implications of Catholic Social Teaching," in *Teaching Theology and Religion* (forthcoming), 24.

23. Adam Smith, *The Wealth of Nations,* cited in Amartya Sen, "Does Business Ethics Make Economic Sense?" in *Ethical Issues in Business,* 5th ed., ed. Thomas Donaldson and Patricia H. Werhane (Upper Saddle River, N.J.: Prentice Hall, 1996), 13.

24. Ibid., 15. Francis Fukuyama discusses trust in terms of a drive whereby "every human being seeks to have his or her dignity recognized (i.e., evaluated at its proper worth by other human beings). Indeed, this drive is so deep and fundamental that it is one of the chief motors of the entire human historical process" (*Trust: The Social Virtues and the Creation of Prosperity* [New York: Free Press, 1996], 6–7). Fukuyama then relates the level of trust to the economic success of various societies, noting "one of the most important lessons we can learn from an examination of economic life is that a nation's well-being, as well as its ability to compete, is conditioned by a single, pervasive cultural characteristic: the level of trust inherent in the society" (ibid., 7).

25. David Hollenbach, S.J., "A Communitarian Reconstruction of Human Rights: Contributions from Catholic Tradition," chapter 5 in *Catholicism and Liberalism: Contributions to American Public Philosophy,* ed. R. Bruce and David Hollenbach (New York: Cambridge University Press, 1994), 128.

26. Ibid., 141.

27. Ibid., 139, 141.

28. Ibid., 140.

29. Ibid., 146.

30. Whitmore, "Practicing the Common Good," 32.

31. Transnational Corporations and Management Division, United Nations' Department of Economic and Social Development, *World Investment Report 1994: Transnational Corporations, Employment, and the Workplace* (New York: United Nations, 1994), 315.

32. Pius XI, *Quadragesimo anno,* 79.

33. Michael E. Allsopp, s.v. "Subsidiarity," *The New Dictionary of Catholic Social Thought,* ed. Judith A. Dwyer (Collegeville, Minn.: Liturgical Press, 1994), 927–29.

34. Julian M. Birkenshaw and Allen J. Morrison, "Configurations of Strategy and Structure in Subsidiaries of Multinational Corporations," *Journal of International Business Studies* 26, no. 4 (1995): 735.

35. Cf. Tavis, *Power and Responsibility,* 430.

36. Birkenshaw and Morrison, "Configurations of Strategy," 737.

37. In Catholic social thought, there has been a gradual shift over a century from an emphasis on hierarchical structure to egalitarianism. For an analysis of the change from the writings of Leo XIII to John XXIII and John

Paul II, see Whitmore, "Practicing the Common Good"; cf. Tavis, *Power and Responsibility*, 353–54.

38. For an extended discussion of these trends and their implications for corporate responsibility, see Lee A. Tavis, "The Globalization Phenomenon and Multinational Corporate Developmental Responsibility," chapter 2 in *Global Codes of Conduct: An Idea Whose Time Has Come* (Notre Dame, Ind.: University of Notre Dame Press, 2000).

39. Cited in Byron, "Ten Building Blocks of Catholic Social Thought," 10.

40. Ibid.

41. For an extended discussion of empowerment and its distinct expressions in Anglo-American and social market capitalism, cf. Tavis, *Power and Responsiblity*.

11

Business as a Mediating Institution

TIMOTHY L. FORT

In the early 1980s, neoconservativism—advocating militant anti-communism, capitalist economics, a minimal welfare state, the rule of traditional elites, and a return to traditional moral values[1]—significantly influenced public affairs. This essay is not concerned with the revitalization or sustenance of the neoconservative movement. Rather, it is concerned with several largely discrete elements championed by neoconservatives, whose integration would be a healthy corrective for contemporary business ethics. In short, this essay argues that the emphasis placed on mediating institutions by neoconservatives, who drew on Catholic social thought, can be applied to business. This argument has been made elsewhere,[2] but the present essay makes explicit both the consistency of the neoconservatives' conception of business as a mediating institution, and the power of that conception to weld disparate sources into a communal understanding of corporate life. In a very real sense, this essay is a rhetorical attempt to prescribe the medicine offered by neoconservatives—namely, the need for small, mediating institutions to form moral identity—to business itself. In other writings I rely explicitly on anthropological evidence to demonstrate this need, but for purposes of this essay, I simply wish to extend the neoconservative logic, a logic derived from Catholic social thought, to business ethics.

Although neoconservatives have been accused of being "obsequious toward big business,"[3] capitalism itself is not necessarily a problem for moral behavior. A capitalism that respects the most fundamental of "mediating institutions" gains the pope's endorsement, and in this type of capitalism, the central virtue is solidarity. This virtue is one cultivated by family and "apart from family, other intermediate communities exercise primary functions and give life to specific networks of solidarity."[4]

The mediating institutions of which Pope John Paul II speaks are central to the neoconservatives' theory and are particularly important to those neoconservatives who take a strong religious line. These scholars have stressed that identity, moral responsibility, and public affections are formed in such institutions. The question for this essay is the extent to which business organizations are prime candidates for being mediating institutions, and what structures foster the solidarity necessary to engender business morality.

While the notion of mediating institutions has a long history, their reemergence in contemporary social thought can be traced in large part to the work of Peter Berger and Richard John Neuhaus, who defined them as "those institutions standing between the individual in his private life and the large institutions of public life."[5] Berger and Neuhaus clearly identified the state as the key "large institution" liable to prove alienating, but they left open the possibility that other large organizations, multinational corporations and labor unions, could also act as alienating megastructures. I do not claim that corporations are now mediating institutions, but instead that they can be and should be.

The legitimacy of infusing business responsibility with religious belief is a topic for another time, but religion assumes a significant role in the neoconservative account of mediating institutions and must therefore be addressed. Rather than ask whether religion ought to play a significant role in constructing ethical standards for business, let us ask why religious neoconservatives think religion is important. There are two answers.

First, neoconservatives contend that religion must play a role in public life generally. In political terms, neoconservatives wish to avoid a "naked public square" by assuring that the separation of church and state does not entail banishing religious values as such from public life and discourse.[6] Driving the neoconservatives' concern is the conviction that to sever religion from public life will make it impossible to develop or sustain an American public ethic, because American values are, sociologically speaking, deeply rooted in religion.[7]

Second, as noted in section 2, religious identification cannot be excluded from business affairs. As Neuhaus writes: "It is spiritually eviscerating that what millions of men and women do fifty or seventy hours of most every week is bracketed off from their understanding of their faith."[8] This point is even more strongly argued by Pope John Paul II, whose thinking is both a source and a critique of American neoconservative economics. In fact, in keeping Neuhaus's admonition that "the first obligation [of Catholics] is not to think like the Pope, but to think with the Pope,"[9] I (though a non-Catholic) suggest that, by thinking with the pope, we can, within the neoconservatives' own framework, conceive of corporations in a way that optimally fosters their social responsibility.

Indeed, this volume reflects an effort to think with the pope and with the richness of Catholic social thought. In that light, my notion of business as mediating institution is one that seeks to name a metaphor and sketch a structure for the contemporary business organization that may foster the commitment to solidarity and the common good as advanced in this volume's chapters by Helen Alford and Michael Naughton (chapter 2) as well as by Robert Kennedy (chapter 3). A mediating business organization operates according to the virtues described by James Gordley (chapter 4) and with a fairness implicit in Charles Clark's contribution (chapter 5) by allowing human beings to relate to one another as human beings rather than as labor inputs. The internally focused attention of "Business as a Mediating Institution" thus attempts to show how business can be a communal organization rather than a nexus of autonomously made contracts. The importance of this communal dimension finds support from the telling critique offered by S. A. Cortright and Ernest Pierucci (chapter 7). The emphasis on enhanced duties to internal constituents dovetails with Domènic Melé's notion (chapter 9) of concentric circles and Dennis McCann's notion of subsidiarity (chapter 8). In short, "Business as a Mediating Institution" attempts to portray an overarching concept for what a business organization would look like if it took seriously the insightful essays of this book.

Corporations and the Neoconservative Ambiguity

Neoconservatives' Classical Understanding of the Corporation

Berger and Neuhaus propose their notion of mediating structures in order to address a "double crisis" in meaning. That is, they see that the "megastructures" of society are alienating in that they do not offer "meaning and identity for individual existence." Those individuals who handle this crisis of meaning successfully, they argue, have access to institutions that mediate between individual, private life and the public life carried on in megastructures.[10] Mediating structures — neighborhood, family, church, and voluntary associations — have a private, personal dimension in which individuals forge an identity and a public dimension: they breathe meaning and value into the otherwise impersonal megastructures of society. The central role of such structures, according to Berger and Neuhaus, is empowering individuals to have an impact on the actions that affect them. Such empowerment fosters responsibility as well, since — owing to the personal scale of mediating institutions — individuals directly witness the consequences of their actions on others.

Berger and Neuhaus explicitly leave room for other structures which might be called "mediating" by analogy to family, church, and the rest. Therein lies the ambiguity. Are business corporations mediating institutions? Family businesses aside, corporations are not familial; they typically resemble neither neighborhoods nor religious institutions. They might be treated as institutions on the order of voluntary associations, but Berger and Neuhaus write:

> For our present purposes, a voluntary association is a body of people who have voluntarily organized themselves in pursuit of particular goals. (Following common usage, we exclude business corporations and other primarily economic associations.)[11]

Nevertheless, at least two other authors extend the notion of mediating institutions to corporations. The difficulty is that in doing so, they empty the concept of the mediating institution of its normative content. Richard Madden provides a classic description of the corporation and weds that description to the mediating analogy, when he writes:

> The corporation, as it originally evolved, meets the definition of a mediating structure. For the owners, the corporation is a means of seeking mutual financial benefits, while limiting the individual risks they might otherwise incur. A large, healthy corporation also provides security for numerous employees. As their numbers grow, it gives them the further opportunity to pool their resources in group insurance, pensions, credit unions, and even more unusual benefits—day nurseries, for example. In addition, the corporation provides alternatives for suppliers, customers, and investors in the communities in which it operates. Finally, the resources of a corporation can be used to support other mediating structures that improve the social climate in which the corporation exists and from which it must attract the kind of people it needs to excel. This might mean helping financially with the creation or maintenance of a senior citizens' center, a school for retarded children, or a center for the performing arts.[12]

According to Madden's description, the corporation "mediates" the relationship between the individual and the amorphous uncertainty of life by providing the resources necessary to make effective choices—and not only for individuals, but for what are (on Berger and Neuhaus's showing) recognizable mediating institutions as well. Above all, the corporation provides opportunities for monetary return, so that individuals can have financial security, owners can realize profit, and charities can be funded. Concern for the forging of individual identity has subsided, except perhaps as this identity might be expressed in individuals' choices over how to use this monetary return.

There is nothing inherently objectionable in Madden's description of the corporation's profit-making prowess, but it does stretch the notion of mediating institution beyond any recognizable form. Like Michael Novak, who also calls the corporation a mediating institution—and "perhaps (after the family), the crucial institution of civil society"[13]—Madden is clear that ethical virtues are necessary for the proper functioning of business, but he also argues that size "has relatively little to do with whether or not an organization can serve as a mediating structure."[14] To the extent one thinks that mediating structures' role is to provide individual opportunity, Madden's analysis is correct. But if Berger and Neuhaus are correct in describing these structures as "the people-sized, face-to-face institutions where we work day by day at our felicities and our fears,"[15] then the large corporation is not necessarily—if, indeed, it can be at all called—a mediating institution. For the large, bureaucratic corporation hides the consequences of individual action, so that a person acts without immediate knowledge of, or concern for, how actions affect others.

Berger and Neuhaus, in fact, are very much aware of the difference between what a mediating institution fosters and what working life often elicits. For the purpose of contrasting megastructures with meaning-laden institutions of private life, they invite us to: "Compare, for example, the social realities of employment with those of marriage."[16] Implicit in the comparison is that the effects wrought on individuals by their working lives are often quite different than the mediating empowerment fostered by institutions such as family.

Missing from the neoconservatives' description of the corporation is the communal element necessary to foster meaning and identity—an element which, as many of the contributions to this volume demonstrate, is an essential aspect of Catholic social thought's approach to the corporation. Now, capitalist economic activity of itself neither inevitably promotes nor obstructs such communal goods. But choice exercised in a bureaucratic rather than in a mediating setting provides no reason for a person to embrace moral responsibilities, unless there is a tangible connection between taking responsibility and enhancing self-interest. Given their commitment to individual freedom and economic choice, the neoconservatives cannot quite determine whether they ought to embrace a communal notion of the corporation. This is why an analyst of neoconservativism, Gary Dorrien, writes:

> When Novak and his American Enterprise Institute (AEI) colleagues organized a symposium on the policy implications of Berger and Neuhaus's book, they expanded the definition of mediating structures to include business and financial corporations and (to even the score) trade unions. The AEI's conference on "Democracy and

Mediating Structures" treated such "human-scale" enterprises as General Motors and Exxon as mediating institutions. . . . The conference's outcome was foreordained. The communitarian character of the mediating structures idea was sacrificed to protect corporate capitalism from criticism. The only megastructure worth worrying about, it turned out, was the state.[17]

Of course, the corporation, even as a megastructure, can very well foster the common good by satisfying customers, making a return for investors, creating new wealth and jobs, generating upward mobility, promoting invention and ingenuity, promoting progress in arts and sciences, and diversifying the interests of the republic.[18] But such goods are not goods of creating meaning and identity. Nor are such institutions necessarily communities that foster virtue. Thus, although there is a sense in which some may wish to characterize businesses as mediating institutions, they do not necessarily facilitate those elements that define a mediating institution. Saying that they are not necessarily mediating institutions does not mean, however, that they cannot become so.

Business Virtues and Business Community

The compelling critique of the capitalist corporation came from the (religious) neoconservatives' guide, Pope John Paul II. In his 1991 encyclical, *Centesimus annus,* John Paul dwelt on the importance of work to human identity, stressing the personal dimension of meaning and its connection to the common good:

> Work thus belongs to the vocation of every person; indeed, man expresses and fulfills himself by working. At the same time work has a "social" dimension through its intimate relationship not only to the family, but also to the common good.[19]

Of course, human beings work for their own material needs too, but in doing so they are involved in a "progressively expanding chain of solidarity."[20] Novak, however, had previously warned that solidarity was a "more proper term for the hive, the herd, or for the flock, than for the democratic community," a concept more Marxist than American.[21] Nevertheless, the pope had also endorsed a "market economy" that did embrace solidarity with the poor and within the workplace, though in both connections solidarity would require a wider conception of business than the classical notion could accommodate.

The difference between these two capitalisms—and they are both versions of the free market—is that the classical version views identity as an individual achievement apart from the material production of goods, whereas the spiritual alternative recognizes working as inherently moral, educational, and social. The worker's identification with the product of work and with those with whom she has collaborated in producing something, teaches her responsibilities to those around her. Again, the classical view practically identifies "self" with "individual" and knows no reason to be ethical (or the reverse) beyond individual choice. By contrast, the spiritual version proposes that we recognize our "self" in others, so that moral obligations are not to be conceived as the objects of choices but as responses to our social nature.

Novak addressed the moral, social dimension of business activity, in part, by concentrating on the notion of business as a vocation. He also—not unlike the contributors to this volume—rightly understood that to be a vocation in which an individual practiced certain virtues, business must also involve community. For Novak, businesspeople are always building community, because business success depends upon high levels of creativity, teamwork, and morale. Apart from ethical or legal requirements imposed on business activity from outside, business requires internal moral integrity. Thus, an important element of community belongs intrinsically to business organizations.[22]

Of course, business *can* involve the kind of community Novak describes: it can be an organization in which cooperation, trust, honesty, and commitment flourish. It *can* also support an atmosphere in which bureaucracy overwhelms individual identity and responsibility no less thoroughly than in certain political contexts (see Kennedy's essay, chapter 3). In his arresting book *Moral Mazes,* Robert Jackall describes interviews he conducted with managers for whom success was determined by luck, fealty to "the king," milking a division, and leaving before long-term realities caught up; by such factors as appearance, self-control, perception as a team player, style, and patron power. Very important to success, he found, was adeptness at inconsistency. Thus, "what matters in the bureaucratic world is not what a person is but how closely his many personae mesh with the organizational ideal; not his willingness to stand by his actions, but his agility in avoiding blame."[23]

Decentralization is thus necessary to assure that decisions are made as close to the problem as possible. "Decentralization" corresponds, in theological terms, to the principle of subsidiarity (see McCann's essay, chapter 8), a principle the neoconservatives have used to criticize the federal government. In business terms, Novak correctly writes:

> A successful corporation is frequently based on the principle of subsidiarity. According to this principle, concrete decisions must be made on the level closest to the concrete reality. Managers and workers need to trust the skills of their colleagues. A corporate strategy which overlooks this principle—and many do—falls prey to all the vices of a command economy, in which all orders come from above.[24]

It is important to note, as Berger and Neuhaus have, that "the management mindset of the megastructure—whether of HEW, Sears Roebuck, or the AFL-CIO—is biased toward the unitary solution."[25] In political terms, the danger in the absence of mediated responsibility and mediating decision making is that

> the political order becomes detached from the values and realities of individual life. Deprived of its moral foundation, the political order is "delegitimated." When that happens, the political order must be secured by coercion rather than by consent. And when that happens, democracy disappears.[26]

This is not to argue that corporations ought to be understood on the analogy of democratic republics. It is rather to argue that the conditions which make for human flourishing at the level of political organization hold also at other levels of human organization, including the economic level. The unitary solution—or order, or "plan"—imposed from above is no less stultifying when it emanates from a remote corporate headquarters than when it emanates from the Kremlin; business

organizations, too, can suffer a form of "delegitimazation." Neuhaus
seems to be relying on the notion that "democratic forms"—that is,
subsidiary modes of organization that promote individual initiative
and responsibility—should permeate all levels of social organization.
He argues for making "democratic capitalism more genuinely democratic . . . [since a] person deprived of freedom cannot do work that is
truly his, nor can he enjoy the benefits of that work."[27]

Meeting this challenge would thus require, in the neoconservatives' own terms, at least three elements. First, employees must have the
opportunity to exercise their creativity (this is a central concern for
John Paul II in *Centesimus annus*). Second, standards of performance
within the corporate community ought to be negotiated rather than
imposed (doing so freely has not only improved the quality of products, but is a corrective to the Jackall problem of managers who adopt
the style of bureaucratic functionaries). And third, decisions ought to be
made at the level closest to the problem (the notion of decentralization-
as-subsidiarity).

It is important to stress that this "democratic" approach hardly
threatens damage to corporations' economic efficiency. In canvassing
business executives during 1996, *Wall Street Journal* columnist Thomas
Petzinger, Jr., found that the strongest trend in business strategies is
"self-organization," by which employees are encouraged to take more
control over their work product without central planning or control:

> For 300 years leaders have built their organizations on the seem-
> ingly unassailable principles of Newton's mechanics, as if people
> were the gears of a timepiece. And it worked—until the speed
> and complexity of modern life began to overwhelm even the
> grandest control structures, from the Soviet Union to the main-
> frame computer.

The new model for organizations is the biological world, where un-
controlled actions produce stunningly efficient and robust results, all
through adaptation and self-organization.[28]

Political megastructures are not unique in their power to undermine meaning, personal identity, and individual responsibility. Economic megastructures' influence may be greater, given the amount of

time so many of us spend in such organizations. If we permit them to teach lessons of intrigue, deception, and self-interest—rather than the virtues of cooperation, honesty, and solidarity—we will have raised the bar for individuals interested in republican well-being, whatever the public setting of their interest.

Businesses that congratulate themselves for fostering individual choice or for promoting material prosperity alone are not mediating institutions; they are alienating institutions, because they set aside the spiritual-psychological solidarity upon which moral affections and practices are based. To be sure, fostering individual choice and material gain is no disservice, if it occurs in a context of extra- and intraorganizational solidarity; nevertheless, neither gain nor choice is the ethical end of business activity.

Alienating, self-interested, and self-centered business organizations draw the attacks of contemporary business ethicists, who hold corporations accountable for their treatment of employees, their contributions to environmental degradation, their communal irresponsibility, and their manipulative advertising. But there is danger in this unremittingly critical stance: the danger of asking corporations to do so much that they become economically untenable. In the next section, the notion of mediating institutions is offered, not as a corrective for business organizations and activities, but as a corrective for much of contemporary thought on business ethics.

Asking Corporations to Do Too Much

Probably, today's most influential approach to business ethics is stakeholder theory, which identifies corporate duties toward employees, suppliers, and the surrounding community (and perhaps others).[29] The theory thus paints a broad understanding of corporate responsibility, and its very broadness is intuitively appealing to anyone committed to "an expanding chain of solidarity."

However expansive, the chain of solidarity must find a limit, if mediating institutions are to be its vehicle. Typically, mediating institutions are concerned with the affairs of a limited membership. Family members are concerned (variously) with the well-being and well-doing of parents, children, and siblings; religious institutions are concerned with parishioners and congregates; neighborhoods are concerned with neighbors; and voluntary associations with members. Paradoxically, perhaps, mediating institutions' socializing influence seems to depend upon their limiting, intramural bent. The intimate size of natural or spontaneous mediating institutions suggests that their mediating function precludes extension to as many members as we may please.[30] Stakeholder theory seems to suppose, nevertheless, that business organizations are capable of taking what amounts to a personal or "inside" view of manifold, discrete interests.

I leave aside the philosophical question of whether stakeholder theory is conceptually coherent and commend the reader to the philosophical analysis offered in this volume by S.A. Cortright and Ernest Pierucci (chapter 7). The practical difficulty with stakeholder theory generally is that it requires corporations to do more—indeed, to accept a quasi-fiduciary duty to do more—than they are likely to be capable of doing, short of wholesale bureaucratization. More specifically, there are three major difficulties with stakeholder theory.

First, if a corporation must take into equal account *all* of the various constituents who are affected by its actions (which is the charge laid on it by R. Edward Freeman), it serves too many masters. Two negative consequences thus result. Rather than managing for the common good of all of the firm's constituents, managers may be tempted instead to play constituencies off against one another, thereby enhancing their own discretion.[31] A good-faith attempt by managers to consult the interests of manifold constituencies could create gridlock, thereby paralyzing the corporation.[32] Of course, managers regularly take into account a variety of constituents, such as creditors and shareholders,[33] but their adeptness is not unlimited: attempting to manage for everyone may well lead to gridlock or overreaching.

If we regard the firm as a mediating institution, rather than as a locus of (indefinitely complex) interests, we may broaden the interests represented in managerial decision making while avoiding too many masters. A business operating as a mediating institution would take into account (I leave the specific manner in which that accounting would be done open, at least for now), above all, the internal members of the organization. Essentially, it would recognize a pattern of concentric responsibilities not unlike that proposed in Melé's essay (chapter 9). Internal members would include those within the corporate "borders," such as shareholders and employees. Giving employees a voice not only makes the corporation into more of a community, but it does so in a workable manner. Taking into account the entire range of stakeholders would prove a tremendously complex undertaking, but taking into account employee and shareholder concerns is—no pun intended—manageable. Moreover, since employees are usually members of the geographic community in which the corporation is located, they may figure as proxies for other stakeholders.

A second problem is that a standard of fairness is far too ambiguous to serve as a guide for corporate managers. Corporations are not designed to determine what is just or fair; they are designed to satisfy market demands by carrying out distinctly utilitarian means-ends calculations.[34] Corporations require specific standards and constraints within which their inherently utilitarian rationality can be permitted to operate. Specific legal standards, such as *ultra vires,* support—even as they constrain—managerial decision making, since they can take a place among the reasonably well-defined factors that corporate decision makers must take into account. The broad notion of fairness, by contrast, resists being resolved into specific criteria for evaluating particular corporate actions.

Here again, treating business as a mediating institution preserves the best of stakeholder theory without its detriments. Determining what is fair to the entire range of corporate constituents would be difficult and cumbersome, whether managers approached it by becoming good-faith brokers or by orchestrating direct negotiations among the interested parties. But adding employees' interests to shareholders' as factors in decision making should prove manageable. Indeed, some have argued that "enlightened" boards of directors already take that range of interests into account.[35] If so, their practice should stand as a model to be replicated. The concept of business as a mediating institution does precisely that.

Third, stakeholder theory does not prioritize various constituents' interests, so it provides little concrete guidance for managers.[36] Should employees' interests take precedence over suppliers'? Should a down-wind population outweigh shareholders' interests in smokestack industries?

Here, business as mediating institution has a major advantage. Since primary duties are internal, the corporation's primary obligations are to employees and shareholders. Those duties can be described as follows:

> Business corporations are, in fact, voluntary communities unified by certain tasks to be performed and mutual duties to be met. Most of all, they are unified by the mutual respect that one human being owes another. . . . They . . . depend on a certain moral ethos, embodied, and practiced, by those who participate in them and deal with them. They can be frustrated by systematic moral failure in their own ranks.[37]

One can damage corporations by asking them to do too much. Structuring businesses as mediating institutions, however, does not fall prey to this problem. Instead, it limits the responsibilities of corporations to those they can perform, and does so in a way which recognizes and enhances the corporations' communal nature.

Problems for Business as Mediating Institution

The notion of business as a mediating institution remains relatively new. There is much more work to be done to tie down loose ends. To begin that work, one should ask, What are the moral, economic, and political challenges to the theory?

Since the religious neoconservatives argue from a Judeo-Christian perspective, it is fair to ask how a mediating institutions theory squares with what is probably the defining statement of Christian moral responsibility: the parable of the Good Samaritan (Luke 10:25–37). The point of that biblical parable is that anyone and everyone is the neighbor whom we are to love and for whom we are responsible, an approach which seems, prima facie, correlative to stakeholder theory.

In an important way, the theory of business as a mediating institution does not square with the parable, because the responsibilities it specifies do not compel business to be responsible for every person lying, so to speak, on the side of the road. According to the theory, businesses' duties are primarily internal.

At the same time, however, the theory can be squared with a Christian sense of moral responsibility, because business can address the concerns of its noninternal constituents. The theory directs businesses' obligations primarily, but not exclusively, to their internal members. Nothing in the biblical account indicates that the Samaritan ignored his obligations to other Samaritans. Similarly, businesses are not prevented from acting for the welfare of external stakeholders. Moreover, people do not belong to just one community, and in capacities beyond their business capacity they can act for the person on the side of the road. A manager who cannot direct corporate checks to a homeless shelter can volunteer there herself. Finally, nothing in the theory prevents an internal constituent from using her voice to present concerns of external constituents. Thus, the same manager could raise her concerns about the homeless in the corporation's area, and the corporate community could decide whether it would address that problem corporately. In a corporation organized deliberately as a mediating institution, the likelihood that such concerns will find a voice is probably higher than in the corporation driven solely by profit maximization.

The story of the Good Samaritan is, of course, not the only moral standard against which the theory could be measured, but it is an important one. It suggests that the theory may be flexible and strong enough to meet concerns growing out of other normative theories, such as stakeholder analysis, in a way that may be practicable.

The second question is economic. How does this structure ensure against a corporation's becoming noncompetitive, particularly if not everyone adopts the approach? One response is that the theory invites loss of competitiveness, because integrating more responsibilities may well burden businesses with problems that detract from their economic efficiency. It is fair to note that every normative theory of business is liable to this sort of objection, and it is fair as well to note that this sort of objection tells against normative theories only if we get down to actual managerial practice.

At that level, however, it does not appear that implementing the theory of businesses as mediating institutions will necessarily compromise competitiveness. Management experience has shown how an integration of normative with technical practices can offer competitive advantages. Among the lessons of quality management, for instance, is that decentralizing decision making in the workplace does not add burdens but fosters pride, responsibility, quality, and competitiveness.[38] In fact, it has been argued that the notion of solidarity is exactly the attitude required to promote the authentic, communal commitment to quality that leads to competitiveness.[39]

Further, leadership and hard work create new futures. Applying Novak's virtues of creativity and hard work to the notion of business as a mediating institution may well tap the potential of the human capital in a firm. That corporations do not currently tap their human resources as they should is no reason to suppose that by doing so they would make themselves noncompetitive.

Finally, what are the political implications of this approach? In particular, how will society restrain the power of corporate mediating institutions? For in one sense, making corporations into mediating institutions would expand civil society and would nourish public virtues that should strengthen democratic institutions. By the same token, however, it would be to cede to corporations a new dimension of influence over civil-social—that is to say, political—life, and such influence would be liable to abuse.

At one level, this is a telling concern, because small communities of shared values can be intolerant and bigoted. As Berger and Neuhaus write: "Of course, some critics will decry our proposal [to foster the proliferation of mediating institutions in society] as 'balkanization,' 'retribalizaton,' 'parochialization,' and such."[40]

We can frame a response in Madisonian terms: diverse institutions correct one another. Moreover, the multiplicity of organizations becomes in itself a corrective for those who would otherwise be trapped in standard organizational frameworks which irk or oppress them, and to which—because they are standard—there are few alternatives. Berger and Neuhaus, again, write: "The relevance of the Balkan areas aside, we want frankly to assert that tribe and parochial are not terms of derision. . . . *Liberation is not escape from particularity but discovery of the particularity that fits.*"[41] Businesses organized as mediating institutions are likely to be diverse, and their diversity will enhance the individual's ability to find the community in which she is most at home.

As to the potential for abuse, our shrinking world intrudes on the kinds of borders that oppressive institutions erect to maintain their evil. With cameras, televisions, fax machines, telephones, and the Internet lurking around every corner, exposure of wrongdoing cannot be discounted. Thus, the opportunities for erecting and maintaining oppressive communities are not as rich, nor the threats as significant, as they might have been in an earlier time.

A New Company Man?

Anthony Sampson has written of the increasing alienation and ambiguity suffered by employees in the modern corporation. His essential point is that corporations are no longer communities:

> Things have come a long way since the word "company" meant, as its etymology suggests, a community of interest, a mutually beneficial partnership of employers, employees, and investors. Gone is the *espirit de corps* implicit in incorporation; companies are now merely cash-flow machines, subject to the cruelest elements of stock-market speculation.[42]

The decline of the "company man" dimension of working life is not all loss. If the company man was a drab, nondescript gray suit with no idea except to follow the company line, his demise is not to be mourned. But aspects of his former life may still be missed. These include commitment to what can be called a mediating institution.

The hallmark of a mediating institution is the notion of community. It is a relatively small place in which we meet others face-to-face and thereby learn the direct consequences of our actions on them. We form our identities, develop our affections, and internalize our responsibilities. In short, we acquire the anchor for that expanding chain of solidarity of which the pope speaks when we collaborate in communal, shared tasks.

To learn business responsibilities and to form a moral identity requires a corporate mediating institution, not a megastructure. The neoconservatives are exactly right to champion the necessary element of such institutions in a democratic society. Business ethicists are right to call upon corporations to exercise social responsibility. The concept of corporations that can "mediate" the concerns of these two groups is the concept of the corporation as a mediating institution.

Notes

1. Gary Dorrien, *The Neoconservative Mind: Politics, Culture, and the War of Ideology* (Philadelphia: Temple University Press, 1993), 8.

2. See Timothy L. Fort, "Business as Mediating Institution," *Business Ethics Quarterly* 6, no. 2 (1996): 149–63; and "The Corporation as a Mediating Institution: An Efficacious Model for Stakeholder Theory and Corporate Constituency Statutes," *Notre Dame Law Review* 73 (1997): 173–202.

3. Dorrien, *The Neoconservative Mind*, 396.

4. John Paul II, *Centesimus annus*, in *Origins* 21, no. 1, May 16, 1991 (Washington, D.C.: Catholic News Service): 49.

5. Peter Berger and Richard John Neuhaus, *To Empower People: The Role of Mediating Institutions* (Washington, D.C.: American Enterprise Institute, 1977), 2.

6. See Richard John Neuhaus, *The Naked Public Square: Religion and Democracy in America* (Grand Rapids, Mich.: Wm. B. Eerdmans Publishing Co., 1984).

7. Ibid., 21.

8. Richard John Neuhaus, *Doing Well and Doing Good: The Challenge to the Christian Capitalist* (New York: Doubleday, 1992), 62.

9. Ibid., 91.

10. Berger and Neuhaus, *To Empower People*, 2–3.

11. Ibid., 34.

12. Richard B. Madden, "The Large Business Corporation as a Mediating Structure," in *Democracy and Mediating Structures: A Theological Inquiry*, ed. Michael Novak (Washington, D.C.: American Enterprise Institute, 1980), 112.

13. Michael Novak, *Business as a Calling: Work and the Examined Life* (New York: Free Press, 1996), 136.

14. Madden, "The Large Business Corporation, as a Mediating Structure," 110–11.

15. Berger and Neuhaus, *To Empower People*, 28.

16. Ibid., 2.

17. Dorrien, *The Neoconservative Mind*, 311.

18. See Novak, *Business as a Calling*, 139–45.

19. John Paul II, *Centesimus annus*, 6.

20. Ibid., 43.

21. Quoted in Dorrien, *The Neoconservative Mind,* 252.

22. Novak, *Business as a Calling,* 126.

23. Robert Jackall, *Moral Mazes: The World of Corporate Managers* (New York: Oxford University Press, 1988), 193.

24. Michael Novak, *The Spirit of Democratic Capitalism* (Lanham, Md.: Madison Books, 1991), 132.

25. Berger and Neuhaus, *To Empower People,* 41.

26. Ibid., 3.

27. Neuhaus, *Doing Well and Doing Good,* 150–51.

28. Thomas Petzinger, Jr., "Self-Organization Will Free Employess to Act like Bosses," *Wall Street Journal,* January 3, 1997, B-1.

29. William M. Evan and R. Edward Freeman, "A Stakeholder Theory of the Modern Corporation: Kantian Capitalism," in *Ethical Theory and Business,* 3d ed., ed. Thomas L. Beauchamp and Norman E. Bowie (Englewood Cliffs, N.J.: Prentice Hall, 1988), 101–5.

30. There may be good scientific reasons for the limited scope of mediating institutions, given that they are constituted by webs of personal relationships. Recent research indicates humans' cognitive abilities are limited. While the particular number varies, those who study the brain argue that human beings are able, optimally, to process relationships with between thirty (Julian Jaynes, *The Origin of Consciousness in the Breakdown of the Bicameral Mind* [Boston: Houghton Mifflin Co., 1976]) and 150 other individuals (Robin Dunbar, *Grooming, Gossip and the Evolution of Language* [Cambridge: Harvard University Press, 1997]).

31. See Katherine Van Wezel Stone, "Employees as Stakeholders under State Nonshareholder Constituency Statutes," *Stetson Law Review* 21 (1991): 45–72.

32. See James J. Hanks, Jr., "Playing with Fire: Nonshareholder Constituency Statutes," *Stetson Law Review* 21(1991): 97–120.

33. See Jonathon Macey, "An Economic Analysis of the Various Rationales for Making Shareholders the Exclusive Beneficiaries of Corporate Fiduciary Duties," *Stetson Law Review* 21 (1991): 23–44.

34. See Joseph Biancala, "Defining the Proper Corporate Constituency: Asking the Wrong Question," *University of Cincinnati Law Review* 59 (1990): 425–65.

35. See William J. Carney, "Does Defining Constituencies Matter?" *University of Cincinnati Law Review* 59 (1990): 385–424.

36. See Thomas Donaldson and Thomas W. Dunfee, "Toward a Unified Conception of Business Ethics: Integrative Social Contracts Theory," *Academy of Management Review* (1994): 252–84.

37. Novak, *Business as a Calling,* 165.

38. See W. Edwards Deming, *Out of the Crisis* (Boston: MIT Press, 1982), 83–85.

39. See Timothy L. Fort, "The Spirituality of Solidarity and Total Quality Management," *Business and Professional Ethics Journal* 14 (1995): 3–21.

40. Berger and Neuhaus, *To Empower People,* 43.

41. Ibid. (emphasis original).

42. Anthony Sampson, *The Company Man: The Rise and Fall of Corporate Life* (New York: Random House, 1995), 185.

Section III

Managerial Practices Informed by Catholic Social Thought

Introduction

The apparently endless debates between proponents of the shareholder and stakeholder views of the corporation may well strike business-people as wearisome exercises in academic abstractions far removed from the real, pressing concerns of ordinary corporations. The foibles of academics aside, what is at stake in the debate over the nature and purpose of the firm is our power to inform business activity, policy, and strategy by moral and, ultimately, spiritual principles. In this last section of the book we address two organizational operations, owner-ship of the firm and job design, as they relate to a theory of the firm informed by the Catholic social tradition. For as John XXIII wrote in *Mater et magistra,* "A social doctrine has to be translated into reality and not just merely formulated. This is particularly true of the Chris-tian social doctrine whose light is Truth, its objective Justice and its driving force Love."[1]

Ownership and job design have been discussed throughout the modern Catholic social tradition, from the 1919 United States Bishops' Letter on Social Reconstruction, to John Paul II's recent social encycli-cals. Throughout, the discussion turns on the recognition that as work-ers became separated from the means of production, they were reduced to instruments of productive forces.

While the popes and bishops are uniformly concerned with these issues, they are reluctant to ally themselves categorically with particular economic programs and solutions. In reference to worker associations, for example, Leo XIII wrote in 1891:

> the precise character in all details which the aforementioned direction and organization of associations ought to have cannot be determined by fast and fixed rules, since this is a matter to be decided rather in the light of the temperament of each people, of experiment and practice, of the nature and character of the work, of the extent of trade and commerce, and of other circumstances of a material and temporal kind, all of which must be carefully considered.[2]

Every organization is subject to political, economic, social, and technological changes in a complex of variables that is too unwieldy to predict. It is simply not wise for the Church or its spokesmen to issue universal pronouncements which cannot be universalized.

The popes and bishops who have been responsible for articulating official Catholic social teaching do not see their contributions, then, in recommending specific, programmatic remedies. In 1931 Pius XI wrote that the Church's moral authority does not reside "in technical matters, for which she has neither the equipment nor the mission, but in all those [matters] that have a bearing on moral conduct."[3] Or as John Paul II has stated more recently:

> The church's social doctrine is not a "third way" between liberal capitalism and Marxist collectivism nor even a possible alternative to other solutions less radically opposed to one another. . . . The Church has no models to present; models that are real and truly effective can only arise within the framework of different historical situations, through the efforts of all those who responsibly confront concrete problems.[4]

In light of these considerations, it is important to make clear what we are *not* arguing in this section. We are not proposing that Catholic social teaching requires a so-called third way for business. Still less are we arguing that the practical programs advocated in these chapters—employee stock ownership and innovative job design programs—are as such entailed by Catholic social teaching. The history of Catholic social thought is, unfortunately, littered with "Catholic solutions"—liberation theology and Christian socialism, Catholic integralism and corporativism, and so forth—which have proved political and economic failures. We fail to serve society and the Church if we gratuitously identify Catholic social teaching with specific, historically or culturally conditioned solutions.

Nevertheless, if we shrink from the task of essaying how the tradition's principles and insights might be embodied in organizational reality, we become "moralizers" of the kind Jesus condemns in the Gospel: those who make heavy demands, but who never lift a finger in aid of others who must shoulder them. So too, although the Church is reluctant to propose "third ways" or to endorse concrete and technical solutions, it realizes that its social tradition must not shrink from the workaday world or from embodiment in particular solutions and programs. As John Paul II notes:

> As far as the church is concerned, the social message of the Gospel must not be considered a theory, but above all else a basis and a motivation for action. . . . Today more than ever, the church is aware that her social message will gain credibility more immediately from the witness of actions than as a result of its internal logic and consistency.[5]

For these reasons, the practitioners, scholars, and educators who cooperated to plan and execute these studies agreed from the outset that the exploration of the theory of the firm must be extended to a description of the ways in which principle might achieve organizational embodiment. What patterns of ownership and job design, for example, might best realize the principles of the common good, solidarity, subsidiarity, and so foster the subjective dimension of work? As we mentioned in the preface to this volume, it belongs to practitioners, scholars, and educators to advance Catholic social thought by working out the implications of a moral and spiritual vision for the realities of the business organization.

Unsurprisingly, perhaps, the more concrete the discussions of the working group became, the more intractable the disagreements among its members became. Thus, Jeff Gates's proposals on ownership solutions sparked a significant disagreement between Gates and others who argued that ownership should be the vehicle connecting particular firms, employees, and communities, and those who judged that employee stock ownership plans (ESOPs) put employees' retirement investment at unacceptable risk. At the working group's August 1998 seminar, Thomas Bausch, for example, argued that in most cases ESOPs are unworkable or poor policy because they deny two principles of sound investment: liquidity and diversification. By way of respecting these investment principles, Bausch argued, employees would be much better off having ownership in the system (via mutual funds, for example) than having ownership in the company in which they happen to work.

Also in the same seminar, when James Murphy and David Pyke argued for job enrichment and just-in-time programs, Ellen O'Connor responded skeptically:

> I would go so far as to say that in the cases I have observed in my own research, the results [of job enrichment, job enlargement, and just-in-time programs] are dismal. This leads to a reflection on what it is about formal workplace "programs" generally that tends to confound, if not corrupt, the spirit of human flourishing that could be kindled otherwise. Above all, is human flourishing really the intent or aim of the programs—or is it faddishness, or is it the competitive thrust (as in the Japanese QC movement of the '80s), or is it simply the idea of looking good, espousing the "right" rhetoric, etc.? My sense is that unless the aim really is human flourishing, then the execution will leave something to be desired.

The (continuing) disagreements notwithstanding, the approaches to ownership and job design offered in this volume raise and develop questions which must be faced by Catholic social thought: How is the social nature of property to be implemented in the ownership of business organizations? How does human dignity become operationalized in job design? These questions do not lend themselves to obvious answers and have, often, been avoided, particularly by Catholic business educators, for whom they ought to be most urgent. As a result, Catholic social thought presents two embarrassing lacunae. Our two concluding chapters, therefore, look to renew the struggle to fill them.

Notes

1. John XXIII, *Mater et magistra,* 226.
2. Leo XIII, *Rerum novarum,* 76.
3. Pius XI, *Quadragesimo anno,* 41.
4. John Paul II, *Sollicitudo rei socialis,* 41 and 43.
5. John Paul II, *Centesimus annus,* 57.

12

Reengineering Ownership for the Common Good

JEFF GATES

Humans are intrinsically social beings who best approach their self-expression and their self-realization through living and working in community with others. Their essential interdependence builds social solidarity and concern for the long term. For this reason I advocate a reengineering of the property component of free enterprise so that people experience in their daily lives an element of "shared capitalism"—by which I mean a system of private ownership in which people feel personally empowered by those institutional arrangements through which the laws of property gain force. It is on the basis of widely shared ownership that the social nature of our humanity can best manifest property's inherent social nature (see Cortright and Pierucci, chapter 7, for a philosophical discussion on this point).

Catholic social thought has long struggled with the appropriate role of property in the human community as well as with the obligations of the business organization (see Calvez and Naughton, chapter 1). In *Rerum novarum* (1891), Leo XIII argued that "the law ought to favor this right (of private property) and, so far as it can, see that the largest possible number among the masses of the population prefer to own property."[1] In terms more specific to my essay, John XXIII argued in *Mater et magistra* (1961):

Economic progress must be accompanied by a corresponding social progress, so that all classes of citizens can participate in the increased productivity. . . . From this it follows that the economic prosperity of a nation is not so much its total assets in terms of wealth and property, as the equitable division and distribution of this wealth. . . . Experience suggests many ways in which the demands of justice can be satisfied. Not to mention other ways, it is especially desirable today that workers gradually come to share in the ownership of their company, by ways and in the manner that seem most suitable.[2]

Present-day capitalism has failed to distribute corporate property among the masses. Instead, corporate ownership has become dangerously disconnected from the concerns of people, communities, and the environment as ownership has become concentrated either in the hands of a relatively few individuals or in the hands of remote institutional investors.

As documented in my books *The Ownership Solution* (1998) and *Democracy at Risk* (2000),[3] the top 1 percent of households in the United States presently holds financial wealth exceeding that of the bottom 95 percent.[4] While it is true that more American adults own stocks and stock mutual funds than at any time in history, 86 percent of stock market gains between 1989 and 1997 flowed to the top 10 percent of households while 42 percent went to the most well-to-do 1 percent.[5] While the number of households grew 3 percent from 1995 to 1998, those with a net worth of $10 million or more grew 44.7 percent. Worldwide, the United Nations Development Program (UNDP) reports that the world's two hundred richest people more than doubled their net worth in the four years to 1999, to more than $1 trillion—an average of $5 billion each.[6] Their combined wealth now equals the combined annual income of the world's poorest 2.5 billion people.[7]

The moral and political legitimacy of both markets and democracies is based on the premise that they operate as systems of widely distributed human control. However, with the steady concentration of financial capital in the hands of a few plus its steady shift to money managers ($17 trillion–plus in the United States alone), today's "disconnected capitalism" often forfeits the feedback, foresight, concern, and even the common sense that reside uniquely with individuals and within their communities. For a system grounded in the Adam Smith notion of "self design," the missing ingredient is now the "self." That insightful Scottish moral philosopher would be shocked and dismayed to see the deference, even dominance, now granted financial signals, when what he envisioned was a system design fashioned from the complexity of purpose, motivation, and aspiration that makes humans so uniquely human.

Instead, money has become the measure of the public good through the capital market maximization of financial returns in a system I call "disconnected capitalism" or "money on automatic," a system Smith would consider a freak of free enterprise. Indeed, it is partly due to the massive institutionalization of capital that modern-day life seems so accelerated and compressed as money managers (and the businesses they invest in) do the bidding of those with an eye on that very limited bandwidth of values implied in the "time value of money," "net present value," and similar time-based financial measures with their built-in preference for speeded-up returns and their unstated assumption that financial values are an appropriate proxy for the common good. If the nature and purpose of the business organization articulated in this volume is to have any practical reality, I argue that ownership patterns must be reengineered to broaden ownership in corporations. Otherwise the social nature of property, the common good, solidarity, subsidiarity, and other key principles in the Catholic social tradition become mere moralistic abstractions wed to the money-measured concerns of capital markets and divorced from those locally attuned "human sympathies" that Smith saw as the driving force of free enterprise.

The Global Reach of Financial Forces

For the first time in human history, a single economic system encircles the globe. Today, 5 billion people live in market economies, up from 1 billion just a decade ago. Yet World Bank President James Wolfensohn points out that 3 billion people now live on less than $2 per day (1.3 billion get by on less than $1 per day), while 2 billion are anemic. With the world's population expanding by 80 million each year, unless we address what he calls "the challenge of inclusion," thirty years hence more than 5 billion people could be living on $2 or less per day while 3.7 billion could be anemic.

During his January 1998 visit to Cuba, Pope John Paul II commented on the fast-growing dominance of free-market policies, cautioning against the resurgence of a philosophy that subordinates the human person to blind market forces and conditions human development on the operation of those forces. "In the international community," he observed, "we thus see a small number of countries growing exceedingly rich at the cost of the increasing impoverishment of a great number of other countries; as a result, the wealthy grow ever wealthier, while the poor grow ever poorer."[8]

This statement echoes earlier concerns from *Centesimus annus* (1991), cautioning against "a risk that a radical capitalistic ideology could spread" and suggesting that "[i]t is unacceptable to say that the defeat of so-called 'real socialism' leaves capitalism as the only model of economic organization." Citing there the "need for ever new movements of solidarity," he advocates initiatives that "can and should also aim at correcting—with a view to the common good of the whole of society—everything defective in the system of ownership of the means of production or in the way these are managed."[9]

Today's defective system of ownership is manifested in today's rapid, worldwide widening of disparities in wealth and income. The United Nations offers the most candid assessment, concluding that, if this rich-poor divide continues (as the World Bank predicts it will), it will produce a world "gargantuan in its excesses and grotesque in its human and economic inequalities."[10] In 1999 the UNDP documented that eighty countries have per capita incomes lower than they were a decade ago.[11] According to UNDP research, the poorest 20 percent of the world's people saw their share of global income decline from 2.3 percent to 1.4 percent over the past thirty years. While global GNP grew 40 percent between 1970 and 1985, suggesting widening global prosperity, the number of poor grew by 17 percent. Although 200 million people saw their incomes fall between 1965 and 1980, more than 1 billion people experienced a decline from 1980 to 1993, while the UNDP reported in 1999 that sixty countries have been growing steadily poorer since 1980.[12]

In sub-Saharan Africa, twenty countries remain below their per capita incomes of two decades ago. Among Latin American and Caribbean countries, eighteen are below their per capita incomes of ten years ago. Even within the developed countries, more than 100 million people live below national poverty standards, 55 million are anemic, and more than 5 million are homeless. These findings led United Nations development experts to conclude, "Development that perpetuates today's inequalities is neither sustainable *nor worth sustaining.*"[13]

Yet this pattern—pockets of prosperity alongside widespread deprivation—has become the worldwide norm both within and among nations. Over the past thirty years, those countries that are home to the richest 20 percent of the world's people increased their share of gross world product from 70 percent to 85 percent. In 1960 the income gap between the fifth of the world's people living in the richest countries and the fifth in the poorest was 30 to 1. By 1990 the gap had widened to 60 to 1. By 1998, it was 74 to 1. World Bank President Jim Wolfensohn confirmed in January 2000 that the gap continues to widen. The facilitation of cross-border capital flows and the World Bank's promotion of "emerging markets" further widens the gap. In Indonesia, 61.7 percent of the stock market's value is owned by the nation's fifteen richest families. The comparable figure for the Philippines is 55.1 percent and 53.3 percent for Thailand.[14]

Frances Moore Lappe, author of *Diet for a Small Planet,* documents the correlation between concentrated land ownership in agrarian economies and a high incidence of hunger, malnutrition, and infant mortality. In Latin America, for instance, large landowners often allow vast tracts of arable acreage to lie fallow while landless peasants eke out a hardscrabble existence or cut down endangered rainforest in order to feed their families for a season or two before moving on. A United Nations study of eighty-three nations found that 5 percent of rural landholders controlled three-quarters of the land.[15]

Turning to corporate ownership, Lappe challenges the laissez-faire argument that markets best serve freedom because they best respond to human choices, pointing out that "the market can only reflect human choices—and can therefore only serve human freedom—on one condition: that we all can make our choices felt in the market, and that requires a wide distribution of wealth and income. The concentration of wealth and income destroys the entire justification for the market." Further, she notes, markets don't respond to people and their rationale; they respond to people *with money.* Otherwise, she asks, "how can we explain a half billion people worldwide living in market economies and going hungry?"[16]

The global widening of economic disparity and economic disconnectedness creates an array of challenges for the business organization, the fundamental unit in which wealth is created and through which the bulk of wealth and income are dispersed worldwide. It is my premise that a worldwide effort directed at broadening the ownership of private enterprise is the most effective antidote to divisive forces that today are eroding human values, and it is a solution which is consistent with Catholic social principles.

Inequity in the United States

In the United States, the most obvious challenge is the ongoing deterioration of social cohesiveness and the erosion of civil society, made worse by the fast-growing economic disparity between the have-nots and have-everythings. Inflation-adjusted 1998 wages are 7 percent lower than in 1973.[17] The typical work year expanded by 184 hours over the past decade—that's another 4.5 weeks on the job for the same or less pay.[18] One in every four American preschoolers now live in poverty.[19] The current poverty rate remains above that for any year in the 1970s. In 1998 the top-earning 1 percent had as much income as the 100 million Americans with the lowest earnings.[20] This growing rift is also racial. The percentage of black households with zero or negative net worth (31.3 percent) is double that of whites. The modest net worth of white families is eight times that of African-Americans and twelve times that of Hispanics.[21]

This fast-widening gap has well-known social and political implications. Two-tiered, racially divided societies are not the fertile ground in which robust democracies thrive. Historians have long documented the threat posed to open political systems by extreme economic disparities, as the possession of great wealth by a few confers on their holders inordinate power, which they are tempted to use in ways that run counter to the general welfare. The wealth of the *Forbes 400* richest Americans grew by an average $940 million *each* from 1997 to 1999 while over a recent twelve-year period the modest net worth of the bottom 40 percent of households plummeted 80 percent.[22] For the well-to-do, that is an average increase in wealth of $1,287,671 *per day*.[23] If that run-up in riches were wages earned over a traditional forty-hour week, it would amount to $225,962 an hour or 43,876 times the $5.15 per hour minimum wage. Just 400 Americans now own wealth equivalent to one-eighth of the nation's GDP. Meanwhile, the middle quintile of income earners, if they lost their jobs, have enough savings to maintain their standard of living for just 1.2 months (36 days), down from 3.6 months in 1989,[24] while the after-tax income flowing to the middle 60 percent of households in 1999 was the lowest recorded since 1977.

This challenge must be met through the business organization because the corporation has proven itself one of the world's most prevalent and durable organizational forms, second only to the nation-state and the Church. As yet, however, the political forces that give shape to societal organizations remain strangely "agnostic" when it comes to the multidimensional impact of ownership patterns.

In 1999 the U.S. government paid out $841 billion in income support programs, including Social Security, Medicare, and other income security programs.[25] The bulk of these funds were paid to people who had accumulated insufficient assets to sustain themselves. Moreover, the 1999 figure reflects the fiscal situation well before the first of the nation's 76 million baby boomers begin to retire (over the next decade, someone will turn age fifty every seven seconds).

Income redistribution programs are the "third rail" of American politics: touch them only at the risk of your political life. Yet, absent a capitalism engineered to enable people to accumulate significant capital in a practical way, Americans will continue to turn to their political assets (their votes) to ensure some semblance of economic security. Given a more broadly self-reliant populace—which can only come from the commercial sector—much of the nation's fiscal capacity which now goes to income redistribution could instead be invested in infrastructure, education, training, research, health care, environmental restoration—or simply left in people's pockets.

In an increasingly globalized, information-age economy, the threat to national security and to business is no longer an opposing ideological system (capitalism vs. communism); it is rather the certain deterioration of the free enterprise system if we continue to neglect the need to provide proper education, training, and infrastructure—basic societal requirements that are fast being crowded out by the accelerating costs of income-support programs. By facilitating the concentration of ownership and income, the business organization undermines its own long-term success by ensuring a siphoning off of the fiscal resources required by government to promote the general welfare.

It comes as a surprise to most to find just how few "capitalists" American business has created in the world's mentor "capitalist" nation. The United States was founded by property owners who limited the vote to property owners (initially to white, male property owners). Yet, despite the crucial role that ownership has always played in the nation's development, we still lack a national ownership policy. Instead, our guiding economic policy remains enshrined in the half-century-old Employment Act of 1946, obliging policymakers to promote not ownership but jobs as the way to connect Americans to the business organization, to their economy, to their workplace, to their community, and to each other.

For a "capitalist" country, the irony of this "jobs myopic" policy environment runs even deeper. At present, America's hugely regressive Social Security tax (levied on a flat percentage of pay) is the largest single tax paid by most taxpayers, accounting for one-third of federal tax receipts. It is the largest tax paid by 90 percent of GenXers. For a majority of American workers in private industry, Social Security is their only old-age pension. Most revealing of all, the present value of those anticipated payments now represent the most significant "wealth" for a majority of U.S. households.

Thus, in the world's most avowedly "capitalist" economy, the most important "asset" for a majority of its citizens is an assurance that someone else will be taxed on their behalf. Adding insult to the injury, that tax is levied on employment, the sole link that most Americans have to their private property economy. Globalization exacerbates the problem by reducing the ability to tax highly mobile capital, ensuring that a growing share of the tax burden will be levied on labor (see

Koslowski, chapter 6). Free trade also expands the supply of labor while lowering its cost, ensuring that personal saving becomes a steadily less viable route to personal capital accumulation.

The Congress is now focused on how best to finance Social Security's very modest benefits, rather than on the obvious and more disturbing issue: why, sixty-five years after its inception, are so many Americans still so reliant on it? One key proposal recommends that budget surpluses equal to 2.3 percent of the national payroll be invested in a portfolio of equities. That translates into $100 billion-plus *each year* joining the torrid chase to bid up share prices further, at a time when the typical stock is already trading at record price-to-earnings multiples. It does not take a financial genius to realize that the well-to-do will fare best in that scenario.

While it is true that the only realistic alternative is an asset-accumulation strategy, it is obscene to invest payroll taxes in a way that is certain to exacerbate today's rich-get-richer phenomenon—particularly when a key reason we remain so dependent on Social Security is because the net worth of the top 1 percent of Americans already dwarfs that of those who most rely on Social Security. Perhaps most ominous of all, U.S.-trained economists are now advising almost one hundred countries worldwide that are in the throes of making the difficult transition from state to private ownership, spreading this highly suspect "ownership solution" to business organizations abroad.

The Hidden Forces of "Disconnectedness"

Today's epidemic of economic "disconnectedness" suggests that the business organization is not fulfilling a fundamental duty to the society in which it exists and on which it ultimately depends for its success. It is my contention that today's little-understood forces of finance fuel this trend and that business leaders have an obligation to transform those forces in a way that creates a more inclusive capitalism. Let me explain. The corporate sector finances itself within what can most aptly be described as a "closed system of finance" (see table) that is engineered not for inclusion but for exclusion. In order to fully grasp the challenge facing those who might prefer a more inclusive capitalism, it is essential to realize just how it is that "the rich get richer." Everyone knows that is the case; surprisingly few understand its remarkably simple mechanics. As the following chart indicates, companies fund themselves in a way that is designed not to create more owners but to finance more capital for existing owners:

Sources of Funds

Internal {	Undistributed profits—Reinvested for current owners
	Depreciation reserves—Reinvested for current owners
External {	Debt—Repaid on behalf of current owners
	Equity—Most affordable by current owners

The second practical reality that must be understood is the role played by personal versus business savings. As the following chart indicates, business savings (that is, internally generated funds) are the dominant form of national savings—and are rapidly becoming more so. Yet business savings fuel the rich-get-richer, closed system of finance.

One thing is abundantly clear: individual stock purchases alone are an inadequate point of entry to ownership. Expecting wage earners to buy their way into significant capital accumulation from already stretched paychecks is what I call "Marie Antoinette capitalism"—only instead of urging "Let them eat cake," the modern refrain is "Let them buy shares." After all, it's a free market. To date, the Church has taken the stance that, "property is first acquired through work and is to be used for work."[26] In truth, significant ownership is more often now acquired through financial sophistication. In addition, financial engineering is typically driven by cost concerns that minimize opportunities for work—not only through the use of labor-saving advances in production technology but also through corporate reengineering, downsizing, rightsizing, and so forth—because labor costs are often the most controllable of a firm's four key expenses (labor, capital, energy, and raw materials).

If ever we hope to experience the benefits of a property system that includes more than heirs, entrepreneurs, and the financially sophisticated,

Gross Savings: 1950–1990, Personal Savings versus Business Savings
(in billions)*

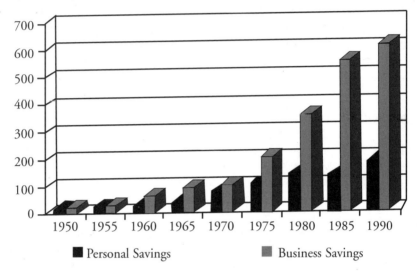

Source: Adapted from U.S. Department of Commerce, Bureau of Economic Analysis

we need not a financially abstract level playing field but a system engineered to ensure that more players have a reasonable chance of making it onto the field. In its current form, capitalism is not designed for inclusion. Nevertheless, the intelligent reengineering of conventional financing techniques can steadily broaden ownership, based on the same financial principles that have proven so successful in concentrating ownership.

Opening today's closed system of finance is not only feasible but desirable and, I submit, essential. One disturbing fiscal trend: as wealth disparities have steadily widened in developed countries, the ratio of public to private spending has grown, according to *The Economist,* on average, from 30 percent of GDP in 1960 to 46 percent in 1997, belying the notion that the worldwide expansion of laissez-faire economic prescriptions will necessarily reduce the size of government.

The conventional wisdom, reflected in the two "Job Summits" of the G-8 (group of industrialized democracies) suggests that government policy should focus on employment alone as the relevant form of economic "connectedness." Touting its own job-creation record, the United States regularly urges the major industrial countries to embrace a variety of employment-focused policies, including job-training programs and lifelong learning. However, despite the level of education and training that people receive, certain fundamentals are unlikely to change in the way people participate in the economy with their labor.

To provide a glimpse into this future, *Financial Times* columnist Samuel Brittan proposes a scenario comprised of a "single economy world" with freely mobile physical and financial capital. In that world, pay differentials among workers of comparable skill will tend to narrow as the owners of capital (seeking their highest return) gravitate toward those locales with the most favorable wage rates. Given this scenario, Brittan asks: "If the liberalization of the world economy is going to make northern countries richer, but make many industrial or clerical workers within them worse off, then who will gain the difference?" He concludes the obvious: those who own the capital. That is a key reason why I suggest that leaders in the business organization are obliged to make capitalism consistent with itself by reengineering free enterprise into a system that is systematically inclusive. In short, for capitalism to succeed, it must become widely populated with people who own capital. That will not happen absent a new policy environment.

Techniques for Advancing an Inclusive Capitalism

As currently engineered, capitalism is a certifiably poor creator of capitalists. Yet 1998 saw the United States finance over $2.5316 trillion— $931.6 billion in new capital expenditures (for plant, equipment, and nonresidential structures) plus another $1.6 trillion in mergers and acquisitions.[27] We know how to finance; we just don't choose to do that financing in an inclusive manner, even though there are numerous mechanisms adaptable to that purpose.

One of the best known inclusive financing mechanisms is the employee stock ownership plan (ESOP). For example, through an ESOP, founders gain a tax-favored way to sell their shares, companies gain a tax deduction for funding an employee benefit plan, and employees gain an ownership stake on a tax-deferred basis. In essence, employees gain access to today's "closed system of finance" to build a nest egg, often without having to lay out cash, because federal legislation championed by Senator Russell Long of Louisiana (retired) encourages ESOPs as a new ownership-broadening technique of corporate finance.

Some 11,000 American corporations have ESOPs and similar employee ownership plans, covering almost ten million employees. United Airlines is one of the more high-profile companies where employees turned to ESOP financing to acquire 55 percent of the company in a transaction valued at $5 billion. In most cases, employee ownership is far less dramatic. Ninety percent of ESOPs are in unlisted companies, most commonly used as an exit mechanism for a retiring shareholder or as a way for an entrepreneur to liquidate an investment without "going public." However, the number of ESOPs is growing quite slowly; ESOP transactions in 1999 totaled only $1.16 billion. To make employee ownership attractive, companies need additional encouragement, such as a preferred corporate income tax rate for maintaining a prescribed level of broad-based ownership.

Another possibility: more favorable depreciation rates could be granted to ownership-broadening firms. A tax deduction might also be allowed for, say, half the proceeds realized on an estate's sale of stock to an ESOP—encouraging today's well-to-do to ensure that part of their shares end up in the hands of the company's natural owners, the employees. Government contracts could be limited to ESOP companies. To make ownership a common experience requires a comprehensive policy environment in which ownership is viewed as an appropriate economic opportunity.

The ESOP notion could be expanded to include the *RESOP* (related enterprise stock ownership plan), creating an ownership stake for those employed by firms (including suppliers or distributors) related to an ESOP-sponsoring firm. RESOPs are now encouraged by law in Jamaica. Such employment-focused ownership initiatives are consistent with John Paul II's endorsement (in *Laborem exercens* [1981]) of "proposals for joint ownership of the means of production, sharing by workers in the management and/or profits of business, so-called shareholding by labour, etc." and with his recommendation for "associating labour with the ownership of capital, as far as possible." John Paul recognized the keen psychological benefits that can accompany this component of an ownership strategy, arguing that "every effort must be made to ensure that in this kind of system also the human person can preserve his awareness of working 'for himself.' If this is not done, incalculable damage is inevitably done throughout the economic process, not only economic damage but first and foremost damage to man."[28]

Where the Cash Flows, Ownership Grows

As a general guide to ownership-engineering, it is helpful to remember an investment banking adage: "where the cash flows, ownership grows." That guide can be used to make owners not only of employees but also of customers or even the general public (Pius XII likened money to "blood," suggesting its potential life-supporting properties). For example, CSOPs (customer stock ownership plans) could be implemented in investor-owned power companies, thus financially reengineered so that a portion of shares become owned by their customers (the utilities' sole source of revenues). As investment bankers know, practically any revenue stream can be used to "owner-ize" income-producing assets over time. The goal of the CSOP is to capture some of that resulting financial value for those whose (typically nonoptional) patronage maintains that value.

Similar "self-financing" techniques can be used to create personal ownership based on geography or citizenship through GSOCs (general stock ownership corporations) crafted to "owner-ize" natural resources such as mining deposits or drilling rights on public lands. A GSOC could, for instance, retain a royalty interest in an oil field, while a more traditional company, say with a combination ESOP-RESOP, is awarded extraction rights. Some shares (or warrants) could be allocated to fund local education or infrastructure. For example, since 1977 the Alaska Permanent Fund has maintained an interest in the state's oil fields for all Alaskan residents. More than $7 billion has since been paid on a principal now exceeding $26 billion. The 1999 dividend was $1,769.84. Families who have reinvested their money since the dividends began to flow in 1982 are now sitting on a nest egg of about $100,000.

However, as I document in *Democracy at Risk*, today's intensely concentrated ownership, when combined with future concentration certain to accompany the ongoing operations of today's closed system of finance, suggests that an element of wealth reallocation is the only feasible strategy for ensuring equitable and workable ownership patterns. For instance, a National Share Our Wealth Corporation could hold the wealth now in the hands of those whose accumulations are deemed excessive, with Congress determining how shares in the holding company are distributed among the populace. Because of the dynamics now in place in the financial realm, that approach offers the only feasible strategy for ensuring that production remains the province of private enterprise while distribution reflects the essential quality of social justice.

It should be noted that all of these ownership-sharing structures are focused on personal ownership, not on some neocollectivist model. Those familiar with Catholic social thought and management need only recall Pius XI's 1931 warning, "No one can be at the same time a good Catholic and a true socialist."[29] Yet, as John Paul II notes in *Centesimus annus* (1991), the defeat of so-called real socialism leaves behind a dangerous "risk that a radical capitalistic ideology could spread," blindly entrusting a world of growing inequity and poverty to "market forces."[30]

I subscribe to the Church's cautionary comments that neither the true socialist nor the radical capitalist model offers a sustainable alternative. John Paul II put well the challenge facing those struggling to discard an unworkable capitalist system in order to give birth to a new, more-equitable model:

> In the struggle against such a system, what is being proposed as an alternative is not the socialist system, which in fact turns out to be state capitalism, but rather a society of free work, of enterprise and of participation. Such a society is not directed against the market, but demands that the market be appropriately controlled by the forces of society and by the State, so as to guarantee that the basic needs of the whole of society are satisfied.[31]

Disconnected or Self-Designed—Which Shall It Be?

Both pricing and voting reflect a preference for "self-designed" systems based on personal preference. "The true case for the market mechanism," *Financial Times* columnist Sam Brittan argues in *Capitalism with a Human Face,* "is that it is a decentralized and non-dictatorial method of conveying information, reacting to change and fostering innovation."[32] Again, a genuinely person-based *self-design* is the moral foundation on which both markets and democracies are grounded.

However, it is clear that pricing alone—whether of products or of property (such as share prices)—is insufficient. For instance, when the environmental effects of commercial activity are taken into account, today's pricing systems offer, at best, the illusion of choice, because the environmental impact is often too remote in time or place to be registered by the pricing system. The same is true of impacts on numerous key domains—such as fiscal sustainability, social cohesion, and other crucial areas (cultural, political)—where pricing is out of place. Though pricing is essential, it is clearly insufficient as a signaling system for conveying the information needed "to guarantee that the basic needs of the whole of society are satisfied."

For that reason, I suggest that the business organization engineer into its capital structure a component of "up-close capitalism." It is clear, for example, that the employee-owners at United Airlines have something far more complex at stake than just the size of their paycheck. Their up-close ownership stake has changed the very context of their workaday lives; their focus is now much more holistic and long-term. Additionally, so long as a culture of ownership is fostered, they are empowered to act on their concerns, injecting more "self" into a system whose moral foundation rests on the assumption that it takes into account the full range of concerns implied in the phrase "self-design." From the perspective of organizational learning, an up-close ownership stake provides a means for generating more richly textured and robust feedback, so that the organization itself can better assess its impact on those many domains affected by its operations—fiscal, social, cultural, political, and environmental.

As presently structured, capitalism is not only disconnected and divisive, it is also badly "dumbed down." Today's combination of concentrated and institutional ownership not only discourages valuable feedback, it also denies to those affected by business activity (typically called stakeholders) any property-based mechanism for having their concerns heard. That is fundamentally bad systems design. Without genuinely robust feedback loops, the organization is guaranteed sub-optimal performance. Management guru Peter Drucker insists that "the role of management is to make knowledge productive."[33] That goal requires a network of relationships—both inside and outside the organization—motivated to gather information and empowered to act on that information.

Harvard Business School professor Michael Porter found in a 1992 report for the U.S. Council on Competitiveness that, in order to compete, companies must be capable of focusing on the long term. He argues that this focus requires that stakeholders be transformed into shareholders by making owners not only of a company's "insiders" (managers, directors, and employees) but also of others within its network of long-term relationships, including traditional "outsiders" such as customers and suppliers.[34] Kevin Kelly, editor of *Wired,* offers a network metaphor. To his systems-savvy way of thinking, the coordination of information is crucial. "The challenge is simply stated: extend the company's internal network outward to include all those with whom the company interacts in the marketplace. Spin a grand web to include employees, suppliers, regulators, and customers; they all become part of your company's collective being: they *are* the company."[35]

It is instructive to note that the root of the word *religion* means "to reconnect," suggesting that those teaching Christian social thought should consider how private property might be more productively dispersed and "reconnected" in order to tap into this potential human-based information and knowledge (this self-design), using an extended network of ownership to amplify both commercial and societal feedback.

As business organizations focus on fostering an element of community—through "connectedness" to those their operations affect (and whose actions can affect their operations)—the business purpose may well be broadened, and for the better. John Paul II implies something along these lines when, in *Centesimus annus* (1991), he suggests: "the purpose of the business firm is not simply to make a profit but is to be found in its very existence as a *community of persons* who in various ways are endeavoring to satisfy their basic needs, and who form a particular group at the service of the whole of society." The challenge, he suggests, is to focus on the "social ecology of work" and to create "more authentic forms of living in community" as an antidote to the alienation and the indignity that permeates both true socialist and radical capitalist societies.[36]

Who Should Own the Wealth of Nations?

Former Brookings Institute economist Margaret Blair notes in *Ownership and Control* that changes underway in the business organization (downsizing, rightsizing, outsourcing, reengineering, total quality management, learning organizations) tend "to push authority, responsibility, risk, and reward—that is, all the attributes we associate with 'ownership'—outward and downward to employees, subcontractors, and, in some cases, former employees who are now subcontractors."[37]

Because this constituency bears many of the risks of ownership, Blair argues that work should be restructured to provide for them a greater sense of "proprietorship," pointing to employee ownership as one way that can be encouraged. She proposes that the search for corporate flexibility, resilience, and responsiveness be combined with a movement to allocate ownership rights and responsibilities to those who control critical assets (such as suppliers and distributors) and to those who have made "firm-specific investments"—particularly employees who have invested in education and training useful to their employer. Blair's expansive view of ownership suggests that today's core of conventional shareholders (whether institutional or individual) should be expanded to *all* those who have put capital at risk, and not just financial capital. This approach to ownership, Blair insists, would also do a far better job of enhancing the nation's capacity for wealth creation.

In a 1993 survey of the various "cultures of capitalism," Charles Hampden-Turner wryly notes that workers are asked to agree that the company belongs to the shareholders, and that the workers' function is to earn a profit for those shareholders.[38] Not surprisingly, this is not a wildly popular idea among those who contribute their lives while shareholders contribute their money. Others suggest that, as human capital becomes the most valued asset in a business organization, it makes no sense to limit ownership to those who provide financial capital. Charles Handy, a British business futurist, takes that insight the next logical step: "When the assets of an enterprise are primarily its people, it is time to rethink what it means to say that those who finance the enterprise can in any sensible way 'own' those assets."[39]

Chronicling in *Liberation Management* the important role played by human relationships, author Tom Peters argues "relationships are all there is," a remarkably close re-rendering of Christian mystic Meister Eckhart's fourteenth-century insight, "Relation is the essence of everything that exists." In short, the business firm evolves through relationships: with financiers, with markets, with people—including people both inside and outside the organization—through people listening, learning, and constantly adapting. What I suggest here is that those firms informed by a broadly participatory capital structure will do a far better job not only of meeting conventional commercial expectations, but also of promoting human dignity, by enhancing both personal autonomy and community at work. Such property-empowered relationships could also help people "cope with the spiritual frustrations and yearnings generated in the vast anonymity of global society," as historian Arthur Schlesinger, Jr., phrases today's key psychological challenge.[40]

This theme of connectedness is both old and new. It is old in the sense that agrarian cultures had a definite sense of "place" to which their members were connected by common history, inhabitation, and relationships. That remains largely the case, particularly in lesser-developed countries. Worldwide, the dominant form of ownership is family- and community-oriented, centered on the land. Those bonds are often nurtured by cross-generational linkages based on a place-defined sense of belonging. In traditional cultures, the worst form of punishment is not jailing but banishment—the denial of a person's natural longing to be a part of the community. In that sense, what I propose is quite ancient.

However, this theme is also new in the sense that modern man (particularly in the more-developed countries) is increasingly uprooted and cut off from traditional means for weaving past and future into each day's activities. Organizational innovation is required to overcome this uniquely modern lack of place (a contributing factor to today's widespread sense of angst). Broad-based (and community-focused) ownership is one component of the remedy to this modern malady. While that alone is not a complete cure, it is also unlikely that a fully satisfactory solution can be devised without it.[41]

Toward a More Intentional Free Enterprise

Approaching this issue from a spiritual perspective, Buddhist monk Thich Nhat Hanh insists that the mindful living of communities is key to our survival. The goal, as I see it, is to cultivate a field of collective knowing in our various human communities, including the firm, in order to set the stage for the emergence of new organizational forms that better serve our long-term goals. That is why I envision ownership itself as a "field" of sorts, a collective agreement about the importance of private property as a powerful social tool for fostering human connectedness.

Where it works well, that personal stake not only summons mindfulness, it also evokes accountability; it aligns self-interest with the collective interest; it energizes individual and organizational learning; and it enhances the collective intelligence and the intergenerational foresight of the species. That is a very ambitious agenda, I admit, but one that we fail to pursue at our peril. Indeed, I suggest that much of today's violence—physical, psychological, and environmental—stems from a collective crisis of disconnectedness, a sense of being apart from everything rather than a part of anything.

Today's lack of connectivity is not some immutable law inscribed in the organizational DNA of capitalism and fixed for all time. Quite the contrary. Capitalism's current exclusiveness and disconnectedness is nothing more than a habit, a design feature that was steadily solidified from within by blind financial forces to become what John Paul II might call a "structure of sin."[42] Like any habit, it can be broken and replaced with behavior that is no longer dysfunctional. Over time, the economic system that we have allowed to become impersonal, divisive, disconnected, and dumbed-down can be reengineered to thrive on human connectivity, and so promote equity and community.

Ownership and the Renewal of Economic Purposes

Ownership provides a means for ensuring that decisions affecting peoples' lives are no longer left solely in the abstract domain of pricing or consigned to a detached financial and managerial elite. Inclusive ownership engineering also addresses how the commercial domain can better provide what we want without endangering what our descendants need. Effective environmental stewardship requires a signaling system composed of something more than monetary units of reckoning. It also calls for personalized and localized business relationships that afford those affected an opportunity to give voice to their full range of concerns. St. Thomas Aquinas recognized this in advancing his notion of "the dignity of causality." All people want to feel that they are, at least in some small part, co-creators. Again, self-design is the missing piece. In a property-based system, up-close ownership is the missing relationship.

While the demands of return-seeking capital have their place, those sometimes strident demands also must be kept in their place. And while the abstract notion of a level playing field has about it an alluring intellectual elegance, as does the concept of fair play via laissez-faire, it is time to recognize that we can no longer take cultural cohesion for granted. It is clear that there is no "invisible hand" busily fashioning equal opportunity. The bad news is that capitalism's current design concentrates capital ownership; the good news is that it need not, and that the tools are at hand to ensure that it will not.

John Paul II offers several key operating principles that should serve Christian business leaders well when crafting a vision statement or otherwise articulating the firm's broader, more interdependent purpose. In *Centesimus annus* (1991) he points to

> the reality of interdependence among peoples, as well as the fact that human work, by its nature, is meant to unite peoples, not divide them. Peace and prosperity, in fact, are goods which belong to the whole human race; it is not possible to enjoy them in a proper and lasting way if they are achieved and maintained at the cost of other people and nations, by violating their rights or excluding them from the sources of well-being.[43]

Through the conscious creation of a field of shared economic connectedness, a more intelligent and more just economic system can be evoked. We may even escape today's money-myopic version of national purpose and again recall that the nation's founders foresaw for it a transcendent purpose: to fashion, through a regime of human rights, one people out of many (*E pluribus unum*). Instead, today's obsession with financial returns, combined with an all-encompasing "agnosticism" about ownership patterns, has realized Abraham Lincoln's worst nightmare: we have become a nation divided, economically and socially, a condition dramatically at odds with the very rationale for the nation's founding.

In addition, our oftentimes mindless striving for steadily rising living standards has put an unsustainable burden on nature. Insight comes from not one but two volumes, from the written word *and* the world of nature. Stuck in a verbal and mental construct (capitalism even traces its roots to the Latin *capitalis* for "head"), we have become strangers to ourselves, wedded to a system that unwittingly divides the indivisible in a futile attempt to pretend that humanity can exist apart from nature, and that humanity can divide itself without damaging itself.

What the business organization can offer (and the Catholic business curriculum support) is new means for injecting vitality and human meaning into the seemingly mundane activity of everyday market exchange. Fundamentally, we need organizational structures enlivened with *spiritus* ("life-breath"). That requires commercial relationships that foster a sense of belonging while providing avenues for exercising personal responsibility according to a self-perceived sense of place, commitment, and community. That new context will, in turn, awaken people to their opportunities to serve (both inside and outside the firm) and provide them (through ownership) an institutionally empowered means for taking up those opportunities. My hope and expectation is that a renaissance in service would evoke in its turn a renaissance in commitment to the democratic process, as those who have gratitude for the opportunities accorded them will be eager to extend those opportunities to others.

This suggested reengineering of ownership for the common good, necessarily a step-by-step process, is meant primarily for the benefit of the next generation. What parents are to their children, a nation's institutional design is to future generations. The worldview adopted by our children (like the shareholder-value concept that now dominates policy making and the firm) cannot remain locked in so small a frame of reference that future generations have difficulty seeing the whole. We forget—though indigenous peoples, Christian mystics, and modern physicists strive to remind us—that the whole is as necessary to the understanding of the parts as the parts are necessary to the understanding of the whole.

The crafting of a successful response to our current social and ecological challenges requires, I submit, an awakening of our inherent capacities for common knowing, collective foresight, and combined action. That awakening, I suggest, requires the crafting of a more inclusive capitalism, marked by broad-based personal connectedness, as the antidote to today's dangerously divisive, disconnected, dumbed-down version of free enterprise. If both real socialism and radical capitalism are morally suspect and operationally deficient, an ownership solution offers a third way. I suggest that through engineering for societal connectedness Christian business leaders can advance the common good in ways consistent with the evolving nature and purpose of the business organization.

Notes

1. Pope Leo XIII, *Rerum novarum*, 35. Pius XII states something similar in his 1942 Christmas address: human dignity requires "the right to the use of the goods of the earth . . . [which] corresponds the fundamental obligation to grant private ownership of property, if possible, to all" in *The Major Addresses of Pope Pius XII*, ed. Vincent A. Yzermans, vol. 2 (St. Paul: The North Central Publishing Co., 1961), 58–59

2. John XXIII, *Mater et magistra*, 73–77. For a theological reflection on ownership and property, see Helen J. Alford and Michael J. Naughton, *Managing As If Faith Mattered: Christian Social Principles in the Modern Organization* (Notre Dame, Ind.: University of Notre Dame Press, 2001), chapter 6.

3. Jeff Gates, *The Ownership Solution* (Reading, Mass.: Addison Wesley, 1998); *Democracy at Risk* (Cambridge, Mass.: Perseus Books, 2000).

4. Edward N. Wolff, "Recent Trends in Wealth Ownership," paper presented at the conference "Benefits and Mechanisms for Spreading Asset Ownership in the United States," New York University, December 10–12, 1998.

5. Reported in David Wessel, "U.S. Stock Holdings Rose 20% in 1998," *Wall Street Journal*, March 15, 1999, A6.

6. *United Nations Human Development Report 1999* (New York: Oxford University Press, 1999). See also Kerry A. Dolan, "200 Global Billionaires," *Forbes*, July 5, 1999, 153.

7. *United Nations Human Development Report 1998* (New York: Oxford University Press, 1998), 30.

8. John Paul II, at a mass during his visit to Cuba, January 21–25, 1998, www.nando.net/nt/special/morecuba98.html, accessed November 2001.

9. John Paul II, *Centesimus annus,* 35 and 42.

10. *United Nations Human Development Report 1996* (New York: Oxford University Press, 1996).

11. *United Nations Human Development Report 1999,* 2.

12. Ibid., v.

13. *United Nations Human Development Report 1996,* 4 (emphasis added).

14. Stijn Claessens, Simeon Djankov, and Larry H. P. Lang, "Who Controls East Asian Corporations?" (Washington, D.C.: The World Bank, 1999).

15. Frances Moore Lappe, *Diet for a Small Planet* (New York: Ballentine Books, 1971).

16. Frances Moore Lappe, *Rediscovering American Values* (New York: Ballantine, 1989).

17. Median earnings based on Commerce Department's Bureau of Economic Analysis data reported in *State of Working America,* 1998–99, tables 3.2, 3.3, 3.6; labor's share of nonfarm business-sector income based on Bureau of Labor Statistics data reported in *Economic Report of the President* (Washington, D.C.: U.S. Government Printing Office, 1999), table B-49, 384.

18. Juliet B. Schor, *The Overworked American* (New York: Basic Books, 1991), indicating that the annual work year increased by 139 hours from 1969 to 1989. The Washington, D.C.-based Economic Policy Institute found that the annual hours worked expanded by forty-five hours from 1989 to 1994.

19. The national child poverty rate expanded 26 percent from 1970 to 1996. Laura Meckler, "Poverty Rising among U.S. kids," *Atlanta Journal-Constitution,* July 10, 1998, B1; Tamar Levin, "Study Finds That Youngest U.S. Children Are Poorest," *New York Times,* March 15, 1998, Y18. The U.S. child poverty rate is the second highest in the developed world (one-third of British children are living in poverty). Decca Aitkenhead, "Small Expectations," *Search* (published by the U.K.-based Joseph Rowntree Foundation) (Summer 1999): 12. According to Census Bureau data, poverty rates among all children fell a percentage point in 1998, to 18.9 percent. That level remains well above the rate in the 1970s, and higher than in Canada or Western Europe.

20. Congressional Budget Office Memorandum, "Estimates of Federal Tax Liabilities for Individuals and Families by Income Category and Family Type for 1995 and 1999," May 1998.

21. Wolff, "Recent Trends in Wealth Ownership."

22. Ibid. The period cited was from 1983 to 1995.

23. The *Forbes 400* wealth was $624 billion in 1997, $738 billion in 1998, and $1 trillion in 1999. See www.forbes.com, accessed November 2001.

24. Wolff, "Recent Trends in Wealth Ownership," 10.

25. *Economic Report of the President* (Washington, D.C.: U.S. Government Printing Office, 1999), 421.

26. John Paul II, *Laborem exercens,* 14.

27. *Economic Report of the President,* 348.

28. John Paul II, *Laborem exercens,* 14–15.

29. Pius XI, *Quadragesimo anno,* 120.

30. John Paul II, *Centesimus annus,* 42.

31. Ibid., 35.

32. Sam Brittan, *Capitalism with a Human Face* (London: Edward Algar, 1995).

33. Peter Drucker, "The Age of Social Transformation," *Atlantic Monthly,* September 1994.

34. Michael Porter, *Capital Choices: Changing the Way America Invests in Industry,* a research report presented to the Council on Competitiveness and cosponsored by the Harvard Business School (1992).

35. Kevin Kelly, *Out of Control* (Reading, Mass.: Addison-Wesley, 1994).

36. John Paul II, *Centesimus annus,* 35 and 38.

37. Margaret Blair, *Ownership and Control* (Washington, D.C.: The Brookings Institution, 1995), 287.

38. Charles Hampden-Turner and Alfons Trompenaars, *The Seven Cultures of Capitalism* (New York: Currency Doubleday, 1994).

39. Interview by Carla Rapaport, "Charles Handy Sees the Future," *Fortune* (October 31, 1994), 162.

40. Arthur Schlesinger, Jr., "Has Democracy a Future?" *Foreign Affairs* 76, no. 5 (September–October 1997): 2.

41. As Paul Kennedy notes: "The internationalization of manufacturing and finance erodes a people's capacity to control its own affairs. . . . The real logic of the borderless world is that nobody is in control—except, perhaps, the managers of multinational corporations, whose responsibility is to their shareholders, who, one might argue, have become the new sovereigns, investing in whatever company gives the highest returns. . . . The people of the earth seem to be discovering that their lives are ever more affected by forces which are, in the full meaning of the word, irresponsible" (*Preparing for the Twenty-First Century* [New York: Random House, 1993], 12).

42. John Paul II, *Sollicitudo rei socialis,* 36.

43. John Paul II, *Centesimus annus,* 27.

13

Humane Work and the Challenges of Job Design

JAMES B. MURPHY AND

DAVID F. PYKE

Chesterton said that when it comes to sex, we are all a little bit crazy. Well, work is also the occasion of a good deal of moral confusion. Our intuitions about the value of work—even the value of our own work—can shift dramatically from moment to moment, revealing a deep incoherence. Often we see work, if not as a necessary evil, then as a mere instrument for "making a living"; in this mood we may hope for emancipation from work, either as an individual, by (say) winning the lottery, or as a society, by some miracle of automation. At other times, however—perhaps as we contemplate our lives devoid of work—we realize that we might actually enjoy our work, that we value it even apart from the income, status, and power it might bring. As we recall the skills we have acquired at work and the pleasure of exercising them—the obstacles we have faced and surmounted, the projects accomplished, the services rendered—we realize that we find in work a unique source of human fulfillment, that work, along with friendship, religion, knowledge, play, and marriage, is a basic good of human life. Indeed, if we consider the amount of time many of us devote to our work (far beyond the need to earn our keep), and if we compare this to the amount of time we devote to our spouses, to our children, to our friends, to our church, to beauty, or to play, we might have to conclude that in practice we have made work not just one intrinsic good among others, but actually our *summum bonum.*

Our conflicting intuitions about work are indicative of a widespread moral confusion about the value of work: we live in a society in which work, like sex, is simultaneously overrated and undervalued. On the one hand, looking at the hours we spend at work, it is clear that many of us overrate work and make it an idol, on the altar of which we happily sacrifice the equally valuable goods of family, religion, beauty, play, and friendship; on the other hand, we also degrade work into a merely instrumental good, purely a means to money—even though work can be intrinsically valuable as an opportunity for self-realization through the acquisition and exercise of skills. What we wish to argue in this essay is that work ought to be seen as neither a mere necessary evil nor as the highest good; rather work is something in between: more than a mere instrumental good, but less than the highest good. Work affords a unique opportunity for human flourishing; as such, it is an intrinsic good on a par with play, beauty, friendship, marriage, knowledge, and religion.

Our focus, however, is not the appraisal of work in our society generally but, rather, the appraisal of work by managers, as manifested in the practices of job design. By both statutory labor law and collective bargaining agreements, job design in our society is virtually the sole prerogative of management. The design of jobs by managers, of course, is constrained by productive techniques and by competitive markets; still, within these broad constraints, managers make decisions about the hours of work and about the skill content of work that reflect their views of the value of work and the purpose of business. These decisions reflect the general tendency to both overrate and undervalue human labor and the business organization.[1]

The Problem: Overrated Work, Overworked Americans

That work has become seriously overrated in our society as a whole is evident in the trends documented by Juliet Schor in her book *The Overworked American.* While European workers have been gaining vacation time since the 1960s, American workers have been losing it.[2] For nonsupervisory workers, overtime is at record levels, while supervisors and professionals are working the longest hours since the Second World War. Schor's argument that individual workers in the aggregate are working longer hours than since the 1950s has been disputed, but no one denies that families are working more jobs and longer hours outside the home than we have seen since the war. We are now reaping the bitter harvest of families juggling two, three, or four full-time jobs: the deprivation of sleep, the marital stress, the neglect of children, the neglect of school by working teenagers, and the decline of civic association and volunteerism. According to economist Sylvia Hewlett, "child neglect has become endemic to our society," in large part because children are left to fend for themselves while their parents are at work. Another economist, Victor Fuchs, found that between 1960 and 1986, the time parents had available to be with children fell ten hours a week for whites and twelve for blacks.[3]

What is curious is that although productivity per capita has doubled since 1948, meaning that we could produce a 1948 standard of living by working half the hours we now work, virtually no one has proposed that we use our productivity growth to buy more time for family, friends, community, church, and play. Instead, while we are richer than ever we have less leisure than ever: all that money and no time to enjoy it. By contrast, from 1840 to 1940 rising productivity was translated into shorter working hours and more leisure on the sound theory that work and wealth ought to create time for the enjoyment of a range of human goods. Since the 1940s, however, work has increasingly crowded out those other goods. Why Americans, unlike many Europeans, have lost interest since the 1940s in translating growing productivity into a shorter work week is rather mysterious and may simply reflect the decline of the labor movement.[4]

How do managers in particular foster this overrating of work? By designing jobs with fixed, one-size-fits-all, and often very long, hours. The rigidity of work schedules combined with the sheer number of hours required or expected gives work undue dominance over all other human goods. Work, then, becomes the first priority, crowding out the pursuit of other equally valuable goods: family, friends, church, play, knowledge, and beauty are relegated to the interstices of work. The job alone is fixed. Everything else must conform to its demands—even church services. In a very poor society, where basic needs cannot be met, such a priority for work might be justified; in our society it is harder to justify the dominance of work.

Still, much contemporary overwork is voluntary, as can be seen in the rising labor force participation of teenagers and women as well as in the rise of moonlighting. For the majority of American workers whose real incomes have fallen since 1973, longer hours are, in part, a conscious or unconscious attempt to preserve an eroding standard of living. But longer hours also reflect a rising aspiration for consumer goods and the joys of shopping. Let's face it, many of us are caught in what Schor calls the "squirrel cage" of working and spending. Our consumer ambitions outpace our incomes: the more we earn the more we want. Our squirrel cage of working and spending was eloquently denounced by Monsignor John A. Ryan back in the 1930s:

> One of the most baneful assumptions of our materialistic indus-
> trial society is that all men should spend at least one-third of the
> twenty-four hour day in some productive occupation. . . . If men
> still have leisure [after needs are satisfied], new luxuries must be
> invented to keep them busy and new wants must be stimulated. . . .
> Of course, the true and rational doctrine is that when men have
> produced sufficient necessaries and reasonable comforts and con-
> veniences to supply all the population, they should spend what
> time is left in the cultivation of their intellects and wills, in the
> pursuit of the higher life.[5]

A Solution: Creating a Market in Leisure Time

The problems of the overworked American cannot be solved unilater-
ally by managers: government, unions, political parties, and business leaders must all play a role in redressing the balance between work and the other goods of human life. As the essays throughout this volume have argued, dealing with issues such as the purpose of business or the problem of overwork requires us to have the right end in mind and to

employ effective techniques toward bringing about this end. As is the case with all our activities within the framework of the Catholic social tradition, the goal is to create work structures that promote human development, both individually and communally. It is always worth reminding ourselves of this goal, even if, as is the case here, the technical problems may need more creative imagination and thought. Since these latter problems are more challenging and interesting technically, we can all too easily get tied up in them and forget the goal for which we are working. We do not want leisure just for the sake of consumption, or just for the sake of leisure itself. We want to create more leisure time so that people have the chance to more fully develop, in the context of the promotion of the common good.

A challenge is how to provide mechanisms that enable us as individuals and as a society to translate economic growth into the growth of leisure. After all, from the point of view of optimal economic performance, it is a matter of indifference whether productivity growth is distributed as higher incomes or more free time. Yet we have good reason to believe that our existing market institutions will not spontaneously turn rising productivity into more free time. Interestingly, in the 1950s and 1960s, rapid economic growth led many social scientists and commentators to announce, in somewhat ominous tones, the arrival of the new "leisure society"; fears were expressed in many quarters that average people (them, not us) would not know what to do with the vast amounts of free time soon to be on their hands. Of course, all this sounds quite silly now, as families find it increasingly difficult to find any free time at all amidst the growing demands of work. We now see that these false prophecies rested on the naive assumption that productivity growth in a market economy inevitably translates into shorter working hours. Unfortunately, we know from history that widespread reductions in working hours have come mainly through legislative interventions, such as the Ten-Hours Act and the Fair Labor Standards Act.

One key reason why existing market institutions do not translate productivity gains into more free time is that we have not yet developed a market for free time, meaning that the supply and the demand for free time are unlikely to find a spontaneous equilibrium. The challenge is to design jobs with enough flexibility so that employees can trade off income gains for a shorter workday or an occasional sabbatical. The first step in creating a true market in free time is to enable prospective workers to make a trade-off between income and leisure in the choice of jobs. Schor suggests that firms be required to standardize the hours of their salaried employees; they can set the standard at any level, but then work beyond that standard would have to be paid for.[6] This standardization, by giving prospective employees more information about the job, would facilitate a better equilibrium across firms between the demand and the supply of free time.

Consulting firms provide an interesting example. Many graduates of MBA programs are hired by consulting firms at extremely high salaries and with generous signing bonuses, but the job requires an enormous amount of travel and very long hours. The graduates often make an explicit choice to sacrifice free time and family life in exchange for the consulting experience and financial rewards. Our observation is that most move to other jobs within a few years because the travel schedule takes its toll on young families. No one is surprised by the demands of consulting, and graduates can make thoughtful choices if they are so inclined. The demands of jobs at other firms are not always so clearly communicated. It would be a great service to prospective employees if the information were available so they could make the trade-offs we are advocating.

The second step in creating a market in free time would be to design jobs so employees within a firm can make trade-offs between income and leisure. Here managers must take the lead role in designing mechanisms to facilitate these trade-offs. One small software firm uses an interesting approach with new employees. Each new software engineer is offered the going salary for her level. The president of the company then offers to lower the salary in exchange for a larger year-end bonus. This bonus is based on the firm's financial performance and the employee's contribution to it. Employees therefore can choose, to some extent, the level of their contribution and the level of risk they are willing to take on.

Many companies are recognizing the need for flexible working hours, particularly at a time when management talent is in such short supply. A manager at the consulting firm of Deloitte and Touche arranged a schedule with 15 percent fewer working hours so that she could spend more time with her children. The same firm arranged a lighter workload for another employee, even though he does not have children. These firms may require intense commitment at times, particularly when projects are nearing completion. However, there appears to be a new willingness to arrange flexible hours so employees will remain happy and not move to another firm.[7] As part of a survey of 238 companies, *Fortune* magazine called dozens of employees to find out why they were staying in their current jobs rather than moving. Answers included flexible hours without inhibiting opportunities for advancement, opportunities for promotion from within the firm, and exciting overseas assignments. Interestingly, not one person mentioned money.[8]

Some additional examples may be helpful to managers and business students. Moog, an aerospace company near Buffalo, has no time clocks or strict work rules and gives employees an additional thirty-five days of paid vacation on the tenth year of service and every five years thereafter. In a similar vein, Corning gives employees ten extra days of vacation every five years. Ohio National Financial near Cincinnati uses flexible schedules, profit sharing, an on-site fitness center, and other perks to keep employees enthusiastic about their work. About 8 percent of employees at USAA, an auto and life insurance firm in San Antonio, work a four-day week. John Deere of Moline, Illinois, has superb relations with its unionized workforce. In fact, Deere managers say that their workforce is their primary competitive advantage in the marketplace. Deere has a no-layoff policy, on-site medical clinics, and a good pay and benefits package. These firms have discovered that such initiatives are important to employee retention, productivity, and general enthusiasm for work.[9]

We have observed an interesting pattern in these examples. Firms in which workers' functions are tightly linked to one another tend to be less flexible than firms in which individuals can work on their own. The former tend to use profit sharing, additional vacation or sabbatical time, on-site child care, and other incentives, while the latter can allow employees to have much more flexible work hours. Notice that Deere does not use flexible hours. Today's manufacturing firms are often required to reduce inventory drastically if they want to maintain parity with foreign competitors. Work-in-process inventory is a buffer between stages of production, and these buffers must increase in the presence of variability or uncertainty. Poor quality and variable process times, for instance, generate variability in production, leading to higher levels of inventory. Imagine trying to operate a tightly linked assembly line if some workers choose to work 9:00 A.M. to 6:00 P.M. while others work 7:00 A.M. to 4:00 P.M. Inventory would need to increase, or the factory would slow down for hours at a time. Deere has no choice but to provide incentives and benefits that do not create a scheduling and inventory nightmare on the assembly line. Like Corning, Deere can provide extended vacations because these are easier to accommodate than daily disruptions and variability. USAA, on the other hand, can be much more flexible in scheduling employees. As long as there are enough people to answer phones each hour, it is not necessary that an entire department be on-site at the same time.

In general, managers may be constrained in their ability to provide flexible hours, regardless of their desire to do so. Common constraints include production scheduling, workforce scheduling, and the necessity for teamwork and communication. These depend in turn on the type of production process, the products produced, and the industry in which the firm competes. Complex assembly processes, for instance, often require more teamwork and communication among stages of production than simple modular assembly. The new Volkswagen plant in Resende, Brazil, provides an interesting case. In this truck assembly plant, suppliers of seven major components actually perform the assembly operations on the Volkswagen assembly line. Although we do not have information about flexible work hours, this type of modular assembly can certainly accommodate them. Volkswagen claims that this innovation cannot be employed at its engine assembly plant because of the complex interactions among engine components. Communication and teamwork are more important in the engine plant than in the modular truck assembly operations. In our view, managers should examine the possibilities for employees trading off work and leisure in light of how tightly coupled the work is. Even if work is tightly coupled, however, there are many options for allowing employees to choose among the basic goods of human life.

Of course many workers, especially in times of stagnant real wages, will resist opportunities to shorten their working hours by reducing their incomes. The first thing to be said about this is that shortened hours need not always require reduced pay. Many managers who have experimented with shorter workdays and weeks have found that the increased productivity makes up for the lost time. Shorter hours mean fewer breaks and less fatigue, better morale and lower absenteeism. So some reductions in working hours, say from forty to perhaps thirty-five, can be had with little loss of income or rise in unit labor costs. Since workers are much more willing to trade off future earnings for leisure than current earnings, Juliet Schor recommends that every firm be required to offer each employee a choice about how to share the productivity dividend: either more money or more leisure. Every year, each employee could then choose whether to take, for example, a 5 percent raise or a 5 percent reduction in working hours.[10] Over time, many workers would realize that they are better off keeping their income constant, in real terms, and watching their free time grow. As it stands now, most of us have little or no choice over how much of our lives to give to work; rather, we take the demands of our work as a given, and we reduce our commitments to family, friends, church, beauty, and play accordingly. Such constrained choices reflect the ways in which we overrate the value of work compared with the other basic goods.

The Problem: Underrated Work, Degraded Workers

If pervasive overwork in our society reflects in part the way in which we overrate work, so the ubiquity of repetitive and stultifying work reflects the way in which we undervalue work. Work is valuable not just because of what it produces but also because of its intrinsic potential for the self-realization and well-being of the worker. For most people, work is the primary arena for the transformation of aptitudes into skills; thus, the character of work has a profound effect on the character of workers.

We often do not value things properly until they are threatened, and it is noteworthy that the first profound insights into the intrinsic value of work came only when many highly skilled trades had been fragmented into degrading routines during the industrial revolution. Observing how the degradation of labor caused a stultification of the laborers, Adam Ferguson and Adam Smith came to realize the unique value of skilled work in perfecting the character and intellect of workers. Although Adam Smith is best known for his celebration of the role of the division of labor in promoting the productivity of firms and, hence, the wealth of nations, he also believed that this same division of labor would take a terrible toll on the intellect and character of individual workers:

> the understandings of the greater part of men are necessarily formed by their ordinary employments. The man whose whole life is spent in performing a few simple operations, of which the effects, too, are, perhaps, always the same, or very nearly the same, has no occasion to exert his understanding, or to exercise his invention in finding out expedients for removing difficulties which never occur. He naturally loses, therefore, the habit of such exertion and generally becomes as stupid and ignorant as it is possible for a human creature to become.[11]

What Smith is saying is that work affords a unique opportunity for self-actualization, but one that can be squandered or corrupted. Work that challenges us to exercise our capacity for invention, that develops mental and manual skills, will greatly contribute to our well-being, just as work that never poses challenges, that requires no real skills, will cause our minds to atrophy.

Smith applies Aristotle's argument that human beings flourish by actualizing their potential in the development of complex skills. As John Rawls describes this Aristotelian principle: "Other things being equal, human beings enjoy the exercise of their realized capacities (their innate or trained abilities), and this enjoyment increases the more the capacity is realized, or the greater the complexity."[12] Or in the words of John Paul II, since "the (primary) purpose of any kind of work that man does is always man himself," so that "man does not serve work, but work serves man,"[13] humanly sound job design implies an insistence on the primacy of the person throughout the work process, so that at no point is human activity reduced to a mere instrument for economic gain. This principle has been stressed repeatedly throughout this volume, but it becomes concretely manifest when we look at the way jobs are designed. Work must be an activity in which the person is seen and felt to be the "subject," that is, the active agent who both transitively accomplishes a task through working on "objects" and reflexively accomplishes her own development by deploying and developing specifically human powers.

In a landmark series of studies, Melvin Kohn and Carmi Schooler have clearly demonstrated the profound role of work in promoting or stunting intellectual growth. By carefully testing the intellectual capacities of a group of men in 1964 and then again in 1974, and by measuring the complexity of their job tasks, Kohn and Schooler found that the cognitive capacities of men with simple and repetitive jobs deteriorated.[14] Adam Smith's supposition that a worker "whose whole life is spent in performing a few simple operations . . . generally becomes as stupid and ignorant as it is possible for a human creature to become" has now been given empirical support. In short, we now have a great deal of evidence not just that people value challenging work, but also that such work is objectively valuable to them.

Work has dignity to the extent that the worker shares in both the conception and the execution of his tasks. Managers undervalue work by designing jobs that require many workers to execute mindless tasks conceptualized by others. Many studies have shown how fragmented, monotonous, and repetitive work causes the deterioration of the cognitive and moral capacities of workers. A detailed manpower survey by the New York State Department of Labor, for example, found that "approximately two-thirds of all the jobs in existence in that state involve such simple skills that they can be — and are — learned in a few days, weeks, or at most months of on-the-job training."[15] Jeremy Rifkin estimates that about 75 percent of the workers in most industrial nations engage in work that is little more than simple repetitive tasks.[16] With so many jobs requiring so few skills, it is perhaps not surprising that only one-quarter of American jobholders say that they are working at full potential.[17] As a Case Western business consultant put it: "We have created too many dumb jobs for the number of dumb people to fill them."[18] The great tragedy in all this, as Pius XI observed in 1931, is that "dead matter leaves the factory ennobled and transformed, where men are corrupted and degraded."[19]

A Solution: Job Enrichment

Instead of our existing practice of habituating workers to the degrading tedium of their jobs, jobs too small for the human spirit, we must rather explore the possibilities of redesigning jobs to serve the human quest for self-realization. One reason for the ubiquity of degraded jobs is the widespread assumption, from Adam Smith to Frederick Taylor and beyond, that the technical division of a labor process into discrete tasks requires that workers be limited to one or a few such tasks. Yet, as we shall see, although efficiency does require that labor processes be analyzed into discrete tasks, it does not follow that workers must be limited to one or even a few such tasks. Let us consider Adam Smith's famous description of the division of labor in a pin factory: "One man draws out the wire, another straightens it, a third cuts it, a fourth points it, a fifth grinds it at the top for receiving the head."[20] Although readers for two centuries have accepted this as a simple and unambiguous description of the division of labor, Smith is actually describing two very different operations. The first is the analysis and separation of a process into distinct steps; the second is the assignment of these steps to distinct workers. What is misleading about Smith's description is his assumption that there must be a one-to-one correspondence between the division of the work and the division of the workers.

There is no doubt that the analysis and separation of a productive process into its constitutive parts greatly enhances the efficiency of labor. A single worker, however, can often realize this efficiency: he would draw wire for, say, a thousand pins, then straighten them all, cut them all, point them all, grind them all, and so forth. This division of labor is known as batch production. Since each step in many productive processes requires setup and cleanup, batch production can greatly reduce the time spent moving from one operation to another. The size of the batch depends directly on the time it takes to set up and clean up an operation. One of the innovations of just-in-time manufacturing is setup time reduction, allowing the batch size to decrease in some cases to one unit. We will have more to say about this below. The first and essential conclusion is that efficiency does require a detailed technical division of tasks, but it does not require an equally detailed division of workers. There are, of course, constraints upon the number of tasks that can be performed efficiently by a single worker; at some point, the division of tasks requires the division of workers. Nonetheless, there is considerable flexibility in the efficient distribution of specific tasks to specific workers.

In craft production, a single worker can make an entire product from start to finish or he can make component parts in batches, which are later assembled. In other words, in craft production, a single worker performs a variety of tasks: the workers are not divided but the work is divided into distinct tasks. Craft production remains an efficient mode of production for certain products and industries. Let us illustrate with several examples. At Beretta, an Italian small arms manufacturer, the nature of work remained unchanged for several centuries, from 1500 to about 1800. [21] A craftsman would make an entire product or component alone or with the help of a master. Each product was unique because the craftsman forged, filed, and fit it together before it was hardened. Thus, fabrication and assembly were closely intertwined, and the worker performed both. A craftsman would work most of his life to become a master, and then he would train his apprentices as well as perform his tasks. Craft production is evident today in a number of industries and firms, including building cruise ships and Rolls-Royce automobiles, and some software development. Workers in craft production often are required to blend intellectual and manual work, and frequently the ideal of shared conception and execution is realized.

For some firms, a possible solution to the degradation of labor is for managers to organize their operations using craft production. Volvo's heralded experiment with a team-built car at its Uddevalla plant is an example. Unfortunately, craft production is simply not competitive in many industries. High volume, repetitive manufacturing is not efficient using this method. Rolls-Royce, for instance, has lost money for years on automobile production, and that business has now been sold; and Rolls-Royce is not even a high volume manufacturer. Likewise, Volvo's Uddevalla plant ended in failure.[22] It should be noted that Volvo is reopening the Uddevalla plant for production of low-volume, niche-market vehicles. It remains to be seen whether Volvo can successfully operate a team-build plant in the auto industry, but it is clear that this method is not feasible when production volumes are high.

The more common forms of production in the automotive industry are "scientific management" and "just-in-time" production. The scientific management movement started around 1900 with the work of Frederick Taylor. Taylor determined that humans could be analyzed with the same methods and precision as machines. Time study, a stopwatch, piecework, and other financial incentives became the industrial engineer's tools for increasing productivity. Managers controlled line workers by measuring them against a standard. There was "one best way" to do any given job. Managers and industrial engineers performed all the intellectual work, while line workers performed repetitive menial tasks. For the first time in history, the study of the procedure of manufacture was independent of the process of manufacture. Scientific management is evident today in high-volume automobile assembly, as well as in many other industries, including apparel, shoes, and other discrete parts assembly operations. As scientific management gained acceptance in the automotive industry, most notably at Ford, craft manufacture rapidly died out, except in a handful of low-volume producers.

Toyota and other Japanese automotive and consumer electronics firms pioneered the development of just-in-time (JIT) manufacturing. JIT is a multifaceted system that fundamentally addresses waste in the production system.[23] Inventory is wasteful, for example, and JIT attempts to reduce it as much as possible by, among other things, improving quality and reducing the batch size. One of the innovations of just-in-time manufacturing is setup time reduction, allowing the batch size to decrease in some cases to one unit. In pursuit of waste reduction, JIT relies on line workers to suggest and implement improvements to the production process. Workers are required to meet in teams to brainstorm ways to streamline production, improve quality, lower costs, and so on. Thus, JIT gives workers more responsibility and more opportunities for using their creative capabilities. In fact, managers often seek input from line workers when developing the assembly line for a new product, enabling workers to share in the conception and execution of tasks. JIT is employed at Toyota, Nissan, and other Japanese automotive assemblers, many U.S. and European automotive assemblers, and a host of other discrete parts manufacturing facilities. In fact, because of the clear superiority of JIT over scientific management, most automotive firms are striving to implement it.

This leads us to a second possible solution to the problem of the degradation of labor: instead of reverting to craft production, managers in factories employing scientific management could move to JIT manufacturing. The benefits for workers seem obvious, and the evidence suggests that JIT is more competitive. Once again, however, there are pitfalls. For instance, JIT often creates a highly stressful environment. Many researchers argue that the outcome of workers' improvement efforts is simply that they work faster. A significant amount of the debate about Volvo's Uddevalla plant has centered on the stress levels of JIT, or lean, manufacturing. Our discussions with managers at several successful JIT factories in the United States, Europe, and Japan suggest that workers actually perform intellectual activity quite rarely. The content of the jobs is almost entirely menial unless a new product is being introduced or a problem arises in assembly. In fact, all managers said that the workers, while appreciating the fact that managers value their input and ideas, do not like their jobs. Most were surprised that we would even raise the question. We should emphasize, however, that the attitude of management toward workers is dramatically different in scientific management and JIT; and workers know the difference. Nevertheless, the bulk of the workday in both systems is spent on mind-numbing activities.

From this discussion emerges the difference between two fundamental strategies that have been proposed for the problem of the degradation of human labor: job enlargement and job enrichment. Job enlargement gives more activities to each worker. For instance, instead of one person setting up the machine and another running the batch, one person can do both activities. This highlights our point above that there need not be a one-to-one correspondence between the division of the work and the division of the workers. Workers in factories utilizing any type of manufacturing can benefit from this insight, but the primary application is in scientific management because of its reliance on mind-numbing work. Recent research on apparel manufacturing, for instance, describes U-shaped lines in which workers share tasks. Each worker performs several operations and often helps other workers if needed.[24] The U-shape facilitates communication among workstations. Some apparel firms, and many firms in other industries, have implemented similar methods.

If, as we have said, work has dignity to the extent that a worker participates in the conception as well as in the execution of tasks, then job enlargement cannot do much to enhance the dignity of work. Job enlargement means a greater variety of tasks to execute, but no greater responsibility in the conceptualization of those tasks. For example, apparel workers on U-shaped lines perform multiple jobs using one set of skills; this is enlargement. Job enrichment, on the other hand, involves giving workers a greater role in the planning of work tasks. Workers at JIT plants who help with a new product introduction perform tedious tasks for part of the day and then use their creativity to help conceptualize the layout and sequence of operations for the new product. They even make suggestions for how to improve the product design so that it will be easier to assemble. At a sweat suit factory in North Carolina, managers encouraged teams of workers to determine the sequence of jobs and the division of work. Managers provided incentives and goals, but the workers made all other decisions regarding the tasks. In these cases, the distinction between intellectual and manual work, between line and staff, is blurred, and workers share in both the conception and the execution of their tasks.

Job enrichment is found today at Beretta, the Italian small arms manufacturer. Beretta had implemented both scientific management and JIT, as they became popular. The advent of numerically controlled (NC) machine tools, however, propelled Beretta into an entirely new world, that of computer integrated manufacturing (CIM). In CIM factories, workers hardly ever touch the product because numerically controlled machines perform the work according to numerically coded instructions. The worker is no longer the source of any variability in the product because the machine will repeat the same instructions perfectly every time. In some cases these machines can operate untended for up to eight hours. Workers often write the programs for the machines and thus focus their attention on how a *procedure* behaves rather than how the *process* behaves. Workers using NC equipment must integrate knowledge of the process with knowledge of the product. NC equipment is used in metal cutting, plastic injection molding, robotic painting and welding, and so on.[25] CIM links multiple NC machines with automated material handling equipment to create an automated factory. In some cases, the factory is connected to computer-aided design equipment as well. Workers in a CIM factory have to understand procedures, their own stage of the production process, and how their stage links to other operations in the factory. In other words, they must have knowledge of the entire system.

It is tempting to suggest that all firms pursue CIM because jobs are clearly more interesting and challenging than in JIT, or even in craft production. Unfortunately, in some industries CIM is prohibitively expensive. For example, sewing operations are very difficult to automate; manual human labor is still required. Most industries seem to fit naturally with a particular type of manufacturing: sewing with scientific management, automotive assembly with JIT, metal cutting with CIM. Certain shifts are possible and indeed can provide competitive advantage, such as when, in the automotive industry, scientific management displaced craft production, and later JIT displaced scientific management. In the meantime, however, managers should seek to mitigate the onerous dimensions of each type of manufacture.

We have a final recommendation for managers in these factories. When work reverts to the daily tedium, managers should encourage workers to use their creativity to devise ways to make the jobs more interesting and intellectually stimulating. Instead of spending a half hour in team meetings each day discussing improvements to quality and ways to lower costs, workers could devote that time one day a week to generating new ideas for using their creativity. These employees may discover interesting new challenges. Some firms, for instance, encourage workers to participate in hiring, in training to become team leaders, or in visiting suppliers and customers.

Conclusion: Job Design and the Nature
and Purpose of the Business

Work derives its dignity from the challenge of conceiving a task and then executing it; we best grow in knowledge and skill through the process of carrying out our own ideas. Where workers are challenged to execute not just the plans of managers and engineers, but also, in part, their own plans, they are far more likely to flourish at work. Work, as a fundamental opportunity for human flourishing, must be designed in such a way that it respects the worker's capacity for self-direction and for self-development.

Hence, it is quite fitting that this book on the nature and purpose of the business organization conclude with an essay on job design. As John XXIII put it, "if the whole structure and organization of an economic system is such as to compromise human dignity, to lessen a man's sense of responsibility or rob him of an opportunity for exercising personal initiative, then such a system, . . . is altogether unjust—no matter how much wealth it produces, or how justly and equitably such wealth is distributed."[26] While the firm ought to distribute justly the fruits of those who labor in the enterprise, as Jess Gates's essay proposes, if jobs that promote the development and preserve the humanity of those who do them are lacking, no other "good deed" of the organization can make up for that deficiency. Job design, then, is the acid test of the organization's pursuit of the principles and virtues that have been the focus of this book: justice, solidarity, subsidiarity, the common good, and, central to all of these, human development.

As the Catholic social tradition reiterates constantly, the basic principle on which any business enterprise should be built is that the organization of human work must reflect the nature and dignity of the human beings who do it. Apart from this informing purpose, there is a good chance that the job design programs we have mentioned will succumb to the "economistic" logic of managers who see employees as just one more factor of production. It will also confirm in employees one more time that "to manage" is merely "to use."

The reorganization of work along lines conducive to human development is dauntingly, achingly difficult. Business leaders who unite unrivaled business acumen with deep practical wisdom will have to show the way out of the poorly designed work which dominates the practice of our organizations, colors the thinking of management and labor alike, and cramps our expectations of working life. Only with real commitment to a purpose of business that drives us toward the growth of others, can we hope to rethink and rehumanize our workplaces.

Notes

1. For a more Thomistic and philosophical treatment of this issue, see James Murphy, "The Quest for a Balanced Appraisal of Work in Catholic

Social Thought," in *Labor, Solidarity, and the Common Good,* ed. S.A. Cortright (Durham, N.C.: Carolina Academic Press, 2001).

2. See Juliet B. Schor, *The Overworked American* (New York: Basic Books, 1991), 32.

3. For Schor's data on aggregate working hours, and for evidence from Hewlett and Fuchs, see *The Overworked American,* 29 and 12–13.

4. Of course, one may ask, "If people choose to put in longer and longer hours, why not let them?" To begin with, many people do not always choose longer hours. Individual workers often have little say about the hours of work; many jobs do not come in a variety of hours. So long as there are more workers chasing jobs than jobs chasing workers (let us recall that this is the normal condition of capitalism), the hours of work will be set unilaterally by managers, giving workers a take-it-or-leave-it option. As Paul Samuelson noted: "In contrast with freedom in the spending of the money we earn, the modern industrial regime denies us a similar freedom in choosing the work routine by which we earn those dollars "(Samuelson, as cited in Schor, *The Overworked American,* 128). This has changed recently, especially in high-tech industries, where skilled workers are increasingly dictating conditions of employment.

5. John A. Ryan, as cited in ibid., 121.

6. For suggestions on how this market in free time might be created, see Schor, *The Overworked American,* 3 and 143.

7. See A. Fisher, R. Levering, and M. Moskowitz, "The 100 Best Companies to Work for in America," *Fortune,* January 12, 1998, 69–70.

8. Ibid., 69, 84–95.

9. See ibid. for these examples and many more.

10. See Schor, *The Overworked American,* 146–48.

11. Adam Smith, *The Wealth of Nations* (New York: Random House, 1937), 5.1. Smith goes on to contrast this grim portrait with the varied and more challenging occupations of men in simpler societies which "oblige every man to exert his capacity, and to invent expedients for removing difficulties which are continually occurring. . . . Every man has a considerable degree of knowledge, ingenuity, and invention."

12. John Rawls, *A Theory of Justice* (Cambridge: Belknap Press of Harvard University Press, 1971), 426.

13. John Paul II, *Laborem exercens,* 6. The translation is unfortunate: the word rendered "man" here is, of course, *homo*—"human being"—in the Latin original.

14. See Melvin Kohn, Carmi Schooler, et al., *Work and Personality* (Norwood, N.J.: Ablex Publishing, 1982), 304. As Kohn states, "Exercising

self-direction in work—doing work that is substantively complex, not being closely supervised, not working at routine tasks—is conducive to favorable evaluations of self, an open and flexible orientation to others, and effective intellectual functioning. . . . People thrive in meeting occupational challenges" (Melvin Kohn, "Unresolved Issues in the Relationship between Work and Personality," in *The Nature of Work,* ed. Kai Erikson [New Haven: Yale University Press, 1990], 42).

15. For details of this survey, see Harry Braverman, *Labor and Monopoly Capital* (New York: Monthly Review Press, 1974), 433n.

16. Jeremy Rifkin, *The End of Work* (New York: Putnam's, 1995), 5.

17. This is according to a 1982 survey by Daniel Yankelovich and John Immerwahr, cited in Robert Lane, *The Market Experience* (Cambridge: Cambridge University Press, 1991), 239–40.

18. Cited in Braverman, *Labor and Monopoly Capital,* 35.

19. Pius XI, *Quadragesimo anno,* 135.

20. Smith, *The Wealth of Nations,* 1.1. In this section we draw freely from James B. Murphy, *The Moral Economy of Labor: Aristotelian Themes in Economic Theory* (New Haven: Yale University Press, 1993), chapter 1.

21. See R. Jaikumar, "From Filing and Fitting to Flexible Manufacturing: A Study in the Evolution of Process Control," Division of Research, Harvard Business School, 1988.

22. There is enormous debate about whether Uddevalla would have succeeded if Volvo had continued operations for a few more years. See, for example, P.S. Adler, and R.E. Cole, "Designed for Learning: A Tale of Two Auto Plants," *Sloan Management Review* (Spring 1993): 85–94; J.P. Womack, D.T. Jones, and D. Roos, *The Machine That Changed the World: The Story of Lean Production* (New York: Harper Perennial, 1991); M. Maccoby, "Is There a Best Way to Build a Car?" *Harvard Business Review,* November–December 1997, 161–171; R. Milkman, *Farewell to the Factory: Auto Workers in the Late Twentieth Century* (Berkeley: University of California Press, 1997); and J. Rinehart, C. Huxley, and D. Robertson, *Just Another Car Factory? Lean Production and Its Discontents* (Ithaca, N.Y.: Cornell University Press, 1997).

23. See chapter 16 of E.A. Silver, D.F. Pyke, and R. Peterson, *Inventory Management and Production Planning and Scheduling,* 3d ed. (New York: John Wiley and Sons, 1998) for more on JIT.

24. See for example E. Zavadlav, J.O. McClain, and L.J. Thomas, "Self-Buffering, Self-Balancing, Self-Flushing Production Lines," *Management Science* 42, no. 8 (1996): 1151–64; and J.J. Bartholdi, L.A. Bunimovich, and D.D. Eisenstein, "Dynamics of 2- and 3-Worker 'Bucket Brigade' Production Lines," University of Chicago Working Paper, 1995.

25. This type of manufacture closely parallels cellular manufacturing as described in Helen J. Alford and Michael J. Naughton's chapter, "Job Design: Prudence and Subsidiarity in Operations," in *Managing As If Faith Mattered* (Notre Dame, Ind.: University of Notre Dame Press, 2001). Cellular manufacturing, however, can be implemented without high-technology NC machines.

26. John XXIII, *Mater et magistra*, 83.

Afterword

In conclusion, we return to the question of this volume. Dennis Mc-Cann put it most directly: "whether Catholic social thought contains, at least implicitly, a distinctive, substantive view of the modern business economy and the management of business corporations," or whether Catholic social thought "can and must restrict itself to defining and promoting a merely ethical agenda within the accepted limits of conventional theories of business corporations and the modern business economy." McCann's initial reaction to this challenge was to see the contribution of Catholic social thought as merely a so-called ethical agenda. Yet, from the conversations and debates of the first two years of the International Symposium on Catholic Social Thought and Management Education, from which the volume developed, he believes that we should take the following question far more seriously: "Does Catholic social thought contain its own paradigm for understanding business corporations, and however latent at present, does this paradigm offer superior potential as a theoretical model for understanding business management and for teaching business ethics?" While not everyone in this volume will answer this question in the same way, we believe that Catholic social thought offers a substantive critique of current business thinking and practice. We also believe that its first principles concerning the person, work, property, and community provide a rich theological and philosophical framework within which to consider the purpose of business.

The critique from Catholic social thought of the shareholder and stakeholder models does not deny the many important insights they generate, particularly those into techniques and analyses. Rather, the critique challenges the philosophical and theological presuppositions found within these models of purpose. The shareholder model provides rich financial techniques but a poor understanding of the human person. The stakeholder model provides a powerful form of analysis of the various constituents in decision making, but a weak vision of a community of work. In other words, the shareholder and stakeholder models fail to give us a good social philosophy and theology in which to grow and find meaning in an activity that for many people occupies a third to a half of their waking hours. These models simply do not have an explanatory power adequate to the fullness of the human person, largely because they are grounded in notions of person and property that fail to take seriously the social nature of either.

In terms of the *person,* both the shareholder and stakeholder models see human beings as agents of preference: this is the *logos* attached to human beings, the key to understanding their lives as doers. It is a slippery key, however. "Preference" signifies an inherent indefiniteness in the "whys" of human action, such that among individual humans and within single individuals the rule is heteronomy.

It is difficult, therefore, to say that we know what preference amounts to, except that it leaves us in the philosophically uncomfortable position of beginning explanations from a denial. For what we know (not in an empirical, but in a philosophical vein) about preference as the "rule" of human action is that it rules out a kind of understanding. Preference means that there is finally no such thing as a shared human end or good: there is nothing really common, nothing to which the coeval activities of many or the serial activities of one stand in identical relation. Hence, there is no intrinsic measure of actions; we can only sort them into empirical baskets.

In terms of *property,* the shareholder and stakeholder theories can extend only to possession; there can be no normative theory of use. This result is a reflection on anthropology: if there can be no intrinsic measure of actions, there can be no intrinsic measure of use. Property therefore consists in individuals' holding things for, and even as, the satisfaction of preference. Nevertheless, we may observe that inseparable from its very notion is that possession be either conditional or unconditional, subject in some way to the preferences of others or not. Reflection on anthropology will move a person toward one or the other side of this dichotomy, yielding distinct accounts of property relations among individuals and, in turn, implying distinct accounts of community.

As complicated as the integuments get, they clothe—and may tend to obscure—a fundamental set of relations: philosophical (or theological) anthropology drives conceptions of property relations; conceptions of property relations drive normative management theory. The immediate implication is one we wish to underscore: management theorists and teachers of management, if they choose to address normative questions, can find no stopping place short of ultimate questions. It is on precisely these questions that the shareholder and stakeholder models come up short. But management theorists and teachers of management can avoid addressing normative questions only at the cost of obfuscation, for management is an inherently social and ethical enterprise.

An Alternative

The essays of this volume, however, are not only critiques of the prevailing theories of the firm. They also address basic principles of Catholic social thought that form parameters within which the purpose of a firm can be worked out. We certainly do not suppose an exhaustive definition of the purpose of business. This volume stands, we hope, at the beginning of a much greater work. As we mentioned at the outset, there has simply not been enough engagement between Catholic social thought and management theory and practice to come to any definitive conclusions. Yet, this volume gives a form and direction that allows us to make some tentative claims concerning the controlling purposes of the business organization.

Let us imagine what an alternative to living with the irresolvable shareholder-stakeholder conversation would look like. If we are correct in our assessment of the nexus between anthropology, property theory, and normative management theory, an alternative will have to take us from a theory of the human agent to a theory of property and its role in community and further to a theory of the social role of corporate management. It will offer a total alternative to liberalism as a form of practical rationality.

We will know that the alternative is total if it opposes to the denial that there is a common measure of human action the affirmation that there *is* such a measure; if it opposes to the denial that there is a normative account of the uses of property the affirmation that there *is* a normative account; if it opposes to the denial that the managerial function—right down to its most technical details—is a social, because ethical, undertaking, the affirmation that management *is* at once a social and an ethical undertaking.

We may imagine, too, the forms some of these affirmations might take. Thus, with respect to the measure of human action, it might be affirmed:

> The morality of acts is defined by the relationship of man's freedom with the authentic good. . . . Action is morally good when the choices of freedom are in conformity with man's true good and thus express the voluntary ordering of the person towards his ultimate end: God himself.[1]

Or, with respect to the uses of property, it might be affirmed:

> the right to private property is subordinated to the right to common use, to the fact that goods are meant for everyone.[2]

The affirmation might be explained thus:

> It follows from the two-fold character of ownership, . . . individual and social, that men must take into account in this matter not only their own advantage, but the common good.[3]

Or again, and with respect to the managerial function, it might be affirmed that

> all the institutions of public and social life must be imbued with . . . justice, and this justice must above all be truly operative, . . . able to pervade all economic activity,[4]

Thus corporate managers might prove to be "distributors of justice."[5]

Here, perhaps, we may cease imagining. To connect the operative terms of these affirmations—the person and the human good, property and the universal destination of goods, and management and justice—would be to elaborate an alternative form of practical rationality which already exists in the tradition of Catholic social thought. Consistent, proximate principles of a normative theory of the corporation and of corporate management may be found, too, among the conceptual resources of that tradition. If, as we have argued, shareholder and stakeholder theories alike cannot erect a consistent, normative theory for the corporation, the ground is open to theorists and practitioners of Catholic social thought to demonstrate the possibility of a successful alternative and to elaborate it. This of course is no easy project, but its difficulty cannot excuse us from trying.

Notes

1. John Paul II, *Veritatis splendor* (Washington, D.C.: United States Catholic Conference, 1993), 72 (emphasis added).

2. John Paul II, *Laborem exercens* (Boston: St. Paul Editions, 1984), 14 (emphasis original).

3. Pius XI, *Quadragesimo anno* (Washington, D.C.: National Catholic Welfare Conference, 1936), 17.

4. Ibid., 29.

5. Cf. Michael J. Naughton, "Managers as Distributors of Justice," in *Labor, Solidarity and the Common Good,* ed. S. A. Cortright (Durham, N.C.: Carolina Academic Press, 2001).

Contributors

Helen Alford is Dean of the Faculty of Social Sciences at the Pontifical University of Saint Thomas (the "Angelicum"), Rome. Her most recent book is *Managing As If Faith Mattered: Christian Social Principles in the Modern Organization* (Notre Dame, Ind.: University of Notre Dame Press, 2001, coauthored with Michael J. Naughton). She has served as a research assistant and lecturer in the Engineering Department, University of Cambridge, where she received her Masters in Engineering and Ph.D. in Management and Engineering. Her dissertation employed central elements of the Catholic social tradition to assess and evaluate the system known as "cellular manufacturing" and the development of "human-centered" technology. At present, she is carrying out studies among small, high-technology industries in central and northeastern Italy.

Jean-Yves Calvez, S.J., is a philosopher and theologian who teaches at the Centres Sèvres of philosophical and theological studies and the Institut d'Etudes Politiques in Paris. He was Provincial Superior of the French Jesuits (1967–71), and served as director of CERAS (Center for Social Research and Action) (1989–95) and as editor in chief of the monthly journal *Etudes* (1989–95). He was a member of the Pontifical Council for Justice and Peace (1990–95) and of the Pontifical Council for Non-Believers. He is currently chairman of the Study Group on Religion and Politics of the International Association of Political Science. Calvez is the author of numerous works in the areas of Catholic social thought, most notably the coauthor of *The Church* *and Social Justice: The Social Teachings of the Popes from Leo XIII to Pius XII* (1959).

Charles M.A. Clark is Professor of Economics at St. John's University, New York, where he works closely with the Vincentian Center for Church and Society on projects relating to poverty and Catholic social thought. His past positions include Visiting Professor, University College Cork, Ireland. Clark earned his Ph.D. at the New School for Social Research, writing his thesis under Robert Heilbroner's supervision. His most recent book is *Basic Income: Economic Security for All Canadians* (1999; with Sally Lerner). He recently completed a research project on basic income for the Irish government and is currently working on designing basic income proposals for Ireland, Canada, and the United Kingdom. His current research includes a book on Catholic social thought and economic theory and another on the equality and efficiency trade-off.

S.A. Cortright is Associate Professor of Philosophy and the Integral Curriculum of Liberal Arts at Saint Mary's College of California. He serves as chair of the St. Mary's department of philosophy and as the founding director of the college's John F. Henning Institute, which is dedicated to the study of the philosophical and theological principles of Catholic social thought.

Timothy L. Fort is Associate Professor of Business Law and Business Ethics at the University of Michigan. He holds his J.D. and Ph.D. (in theology and business) from Northwestern University and his M.A. and B.A. from the University of Notre Dame. In 1998 he received the Academy of Legal Studies in Business's Junior Faculty Award of Excellence, which is given to an outstanding untenured professor in the United States. His work has appeared in *Business Ethics Quarterly, Notre Dame Law Review,* and the *Journal of Corporation Law.*

Jeff Gates served as counsel to the U.S. Senate Committee on Finance (1980–87), where he crafted federal law on pensions and employee stock ownership plans. He has since advised more than twenty-five governments on various components of "ownership engineering." He is president of the Atlanta- and Cambridge-based Shared Capitalism Institute. His two most recent books are *The Ownership Solution* and *Democracy at Risk* (2000), both published by Addison-Wesley Longman.

James Gordley is Shannon Cecil Turner Professor of Jurisprudence at the School of Law of the University of California at Berkeley. He received a J.D. from Harvard Law School and an M.B.A and B.A. from the University of Chicago. He is a fellow of the American Academy of Arts and Sciences and has been a Guggenheim Fellow, a Fulbright Fellow, a Fellow of the Consiglio Nazionale delle Ricerche, a Senior NATO Fellow, and a Fellow of the *Deutscheforschungsgemeinschaft*. He is the author of *The Philosophical Origins of Modern Contract Doctrine* (Clarendon Law Series, Oxford University Press, 1991) and *The Civil Law System: An Introduction to the Comparative Study of Law* (Boston: Little, Brown and Co., 1977; with Arthur von Mehren).

Robert G. Kennedy is Associate Professor in the Department of Management and Catholic Studies at the University of St. Thomas (St. Paul, Minnesota). He received his Ph.D. in medieval studies (with a concentration in philosophy and theology) from the University of Notre Dame, and holds master's degrees in both biblical criticism and business administration. At St. Thomas, Kennedy was the Founding Director of the Institute for Christian Social Thought and Management, which aims to bring the principles and insights of Christian social thought to bear in constructive ways on business and professional issues. A regular contributor to Catholic publications, he is currently working on a book on business ethics and on a second book on business and the Catholic social tradition.

Peter Koslowski is Founding Director of the Forschungsinstitut für Philosophie Hannover, Hannover, Germany, and Founding Director of its Centrum für Ethische Ökonomie und Wirtschaftskultur. He earned an M.A. in philosophy, a Dr. phil., and an M.A. in economics at Munich University, where he taught as Assistant Professor from 1979 to 1985. From 1985 to 1987 he was Full Professor at the University of Witten/Herdecke. His most recent book is *Ethik der Banken und der Börse* (Tübingen: Mohr Siebeck, 1998).

Dennis P. McCann is the Wallace M. Alston Professor of Bible and Religion at Agnes Scott College in Atlanta and Decatur, Georgia, and former Executive Director of the Society of Christian Ethics. McCann received his STL in theology from Gregorian University in Rome in 1971 and a Ph.D. in theology from the University of Chicago Divinity School in 1976. With Max Stackhouse and Shirley Roels, he edited an anthology of materials for teaching business ethics within an ecumenically Christian perspective, *On Moral Business: Classical and Contemporary Resources for Ethics and Economics* (Grand Rapids, Mich.: Eerdmans Publishing Co., 1995). McCann has had extensive academic experience in Hong Kong, China, and other countries in East Asia. In 1998 McCann was the Au Yeung King Fong University Fellow at the Centre for Applied Ethics at Hong Kong Baptist University, where he did research on East Asian business ethics within the framework of comparative religious ethics.

Domènec Melé is Professor and Chairman of the Business Ethics Department at IESE (International Graduate School of Management), University of Navarra, Spain. He has a doctorate in industrial engineering and another in theology. He is the author of *Ética en dirección de empresa* (1997), *Ética en la empresa familiar* (coauthored with M.A. Gallo, 1998), and *Cristianos en la sociedad* (1999). In addition, he has edited eight books on business ethics issues, such as market economy, work and unemployment, business and family life, business policy, finance, marketing and advertisement, family business, and leadership, apart from numerous articles and contributions to books.

James B. Murphy is Associate Professor of Government at Dartmouth College. His Ph.D. in philosophy and political science is from Yale University, where he received the Theron Rockwell Field Prize for his doctoral dissertation in 1990. He has published numerous articles on the ethics of work, jurisprudence, rational choice theory, and semiotics. His first book, *The Moral Economy of Labor: Aristotelian Themes in Economic Theory*, was published by Yale University Press in 1993. His new book, *The Normative Force of the Actual: The Morality of Positive Law*, also from Yale University Press, is forthcoming. In addition to finishing his book on positive law, he has begun a project on the ethics of self-perfection. He teaches courses in political theory, jurisprudence, and ethics.

Michael J. Naughton is Associate Professor at the University of St. Thomas, where he teaches in the Theology and Catholic Studies Departments and the College of Business. He is the director of the John A. Ryan Institute for Catholic Social Thought, which examines Catholic social thought in relationship to business, Catholic education, and urban issues. He has organized international conferences in the United States, Europe, Asia, and Latin America on the theme of Catholic social thought and management. His most recent book is *Managing As If Faith Mattered: Christian Social Principles in the Modern Organization* (Notre Dame, Ind.: University of Notre Dame Press, 2001, coauthored with Helen Alford). He received a Ph.D. in theology and society from Marquette University and an M.B.A. from the University of St. Thomas.

Ernest S. Pierucci practices corporate law in San Francisco, California. He is a member of the Steering Committee of the John F. Henning Institute at St. Mary's College of California and a member of the Board of Visitors of the Columbus School of Law of the Catholic University of America. Pierucci has taught business law, philosophy of law, and the collegiate seminar (Great Books Program) at St. Mary's College.

David F. Pyke is Associate Professor of Operations Management at the Amos Tuck School of Business Administration at Dartmouth College. He obtained his M.A. and Ph.D. from the Wharton School of the University of Pennsylvania in 1987. Since 1987 he has taught at the International University of Japan, the Helsinki School of Economics, the WHU-Otto-Beisheim-Hochschule, Vallendar, Germany, and the Wharton School. His research interests include supply-chain management, inventory systems, logistics, assembly systems, manufacturing in China, and manufacturing strategy. His book *Inventory Management and Production Planning and Scheduling,* coauthored with E. A. Silver and R. Peterson, was published in 1998 by John Wiley and Sons.

Lee A. Tavis is C. R. Smith Professor of Business Administration and the founding director of the Program on Multinational Management, as well as a fellow of the Helen Kellogg Institute for International Studies and the Joan B. Kroc Institute for International Peace Studies. His most recent book, *Power and Responsibility: Multinational Managers and Developing Country Concerns* (Notre Dame, Ind.: University of Notre Dame Press, 1997), addresses the appropriate role of multinational corporations in the emerging global, economic, political, and cultural system.

Index

The use of *f* indicates a figure or table found in the text.